Pricing for Profit

The Manager's Guide to Market Oriented Pricing

Hans Peter Zell

To order additional copies of this book, contact:
Xlibris LLC
1-888-795-4274
www.Xlibris.com
Orders@Xlibris.com
552540

CONTENTS

The single most important decision in evaluating a business is pricing power. If you've got the power to raise prices without losing business to a competitor you've got a very good business. And if you have to have a prayer session before raising the price by 10 per cent, then you've got a terrible business.

Warren E. Buffett[1]

Preface

Price too high and you lose the sale! Price too low and you can't make money! [2]

Around the clock and around the world thousands upon thousands of sales transactions are continuously being consummated between sellers and buyers. For each of the many diverse products and services offered, the seller must first set a price and state the terms of sale to which the buyer must agree before a sales transaction can take place. Setting the price which will be profitable to the seller and acceptable to the buyer is the topic of the present volume.

With so many books on pricing on the market already why another one? The answer is that *Pricing for Profit: The Manager's Guide to Market Oriented Pricing* is unique in both content and presentation. There is nothing comparable on the market today. In fact, the author has set himself the ambitious task of writing the most innovative and useful pricing book to be found anywhere. Only the reader can judge whether he succeeded. The general theme in this work is that a sell price should not be based on the seller's costs but on the customer's value perception of the product or service. *Pricing for Profit* goes much beyond this now commonly accepted concept by offering many new insights, based on detailed analyses, on how this may be achieved most profitably.

Pricing for Profit was written with three primary audiences in mind. First among these are business and corporate managers with direct pricing responsibilities including general managers, marketing, product, and brand managers, regional and national sales managers, and individuals specifically charged with setting prices for their firms' products and services. The second group includes business students with a concentration in Marketing or Finance and especially those studying for their MBA degrees. For them *Pricing for Profit* could serve as an economical substitute for a more costly pricing book or as a supplement to a standard marketing text such as Kotler and Keller's *Marketing Management*. Finally, corporate managers and executives who would like to learn how proactive, market oriented pricing can favorably impact their firms' bottom lines will find this book a rich source for new ideas.

What distinguishes *Pricing for Profit* from other pricing books is a practical, problem-solving approach that heavily relies on mathematics, graphs, and diagrams to arrive at answers. Many marketers will be put off by this approach and the book is therefore not for everyone. Conventional pricing books tend to deliberately avoid using quantitative techniques and to rely more on a conversational, non-mathematical approach. There are at least two reasons for this. For one, many marketers have a liberal arts background and a phobia of anything mathematical or analytical. Yet it is also a fact that pricing involves the manipulation of numbers because a sell price is a number that cannot simply be pulled out of thin air. One must therefore ask whether someone who is uncomfortable with mathematics should be pricing in the first place.

The second reason for the dearth in math and formulas in conventional pricing books is the belief that pricing cannot be done by formula. That is a valid argument. "Cost-plus," the most popular pricing method, is a formula approach that has been consistently decried by pricing theorists for this very reason. The formulas presented in *Pricing for Profit* are of an entirely different kind. They make use of a marketing metric known as the price elasticity of demand which lets a marketer determine an optimal sell price that balances two needs and aspirations—a company's to sell its products or services at prices that will be profitable and a customer's to buy these products or services at prices that seems fair and equitable. Thus, the formulas developed and presented are entirely market-based and customer oriented. Since *Pricing for Profit* is not intended as a mathematics text, these formulas are not only very useful but easily understood and applied presupposing not much greater knowledge of mathematics than Algebra 101. Most derivations have been relegated to the Appendix where the interested reader may peruse them.

The emphasis on this analytical approach should result in a deeper understanding of pricing and allow this work to offer many insights and pricing guidelines not found elsewhere. In fact, much of what appears in *Pricing for Profit* is entirely new to the pricing literature. Thus, the book presents thirty pricing propositions, pricing rules, and rules of thumb which the marketer can use over and over again as a guide to arriving at sound pricing decisions. A special feature of the book is three chapters devoted to price optimization. This is a topic of great importance to marketers but not adequately covered in the standard pricing and marketing texts. Here the pricing practitioner will not only learn what the required and well-known optimization conditions for sales revenue or profit maximization are but also by how much existing sell prices must be adjusted, if necessary, to arrive at the optimum prices for all of their products and services.

Because this book is not about pricing theory but pricing practice, many practical examples are included throughout the main text while two hypothetical case studies on sales revenue and profit maximization appear in the Appendix. These examples are to teach the pricer how to use the formulas, graphs, and pricing rules and apply them to solve his or her own pricing problems. Furthermore, to reduce the marketer's dependence on these formulas and minimize the necessary calculations, several tables are included that list the computed values for the most important of these formulas. These tabulations should make this book not only a useful tutorial but a valuable pricing reference as well.

On a personal note, I came to appreciate the importance of proactive, market oriented product pricing after a disastrous experience in my first marketing position after obtaining the MBA degree. When I joined a Pittsburgh-based conglomerate for work at their Chicago facilities, this division had seen a continuous erosion of sales, market share, and profits for a number of years. While the company had a stellar reputation for its quality products that were much in demand by electric utility companies nationwide, upper management adhered to a very rigid pricing scheme based on production and overhead costs. With declining sales and mounting losses, the Chicago division had to be shuttered resulting in job terminations for most of its many talented and devoted employees.

The debacle in Chicago sparked my interest in pricing and, after my transfer to another division of the company, I started to devote many off-hours to find an alternative to so-called "cost-plus" pricing as it was practiced at the Chicago division. After reading the relevant pricing literature and finding little in the way of practical rules and guidelines but many unproved and questionable assertions instead, I decided to use my engineering background to solve some price optimization problems mathematically. The outcome was two papers which I mailed off to well-known experts in the field of pricing for their comments.[3] When I left this company to work for a small, start-up in their marketing and sales department, I was fortunate in that the owners were not professional managers and very open to new management and marketing ideas.

To assist with their company's pricing problems, the owners and managers brought in Daniel A. Nimer, a well-known pioneer in value-based pricing techniques, for a two-day seminar.[4] Mr. Nimer told participants, among other things, that "price determines cost and not vice versa," "a product that is unique requires a unique price," and "a company should establish prices based on what the market will bear." His concept was revolutionary at a time when "cost plus" was still the model of choice at most firms. After this seminar, I felt vindicated in my belief that cost-plus pricing was obsolete as a model for profitable pricing and that a more flexible approach was needed.

I subsequently decided to write a book on a new approach that would apply mathematical analysis to market oriented pricing.

Because of my corporate work assignments, that included several extended stays overseas, I was able to make only sporadic progress on the manuscript for such a book and decided to leave that work to my retirement years. When that time came, I returned to *Pricing for Profit* only to be temporarily sidetracked by two other books I had intended to write.[5] With those out of the way, I was able to complete writing and publishing the work you have before you.

Product and services pricing is a complex but extremely important exercise that draws on many academic disciplines including accounting, economics (macro and micro), finance, jurisprudence, marketing, mathematics, psychology, and sociology. Clearly, it is an interdisciplinary and exciting field of study to which people in many fields have made important contributions. Yet despite the importance and seriousness of the topic, one also speaks of the *pricing game*. This would suggest that there is some measure of fun and enjoyment attached to pricing. This I can confirm from my corporate marketing career and reconfirm now. It was certainly a pleasure working on this book and I hope that my readers will enjoy reading and using it at least as much as I enjoyed writing it.

Notes

1. Warren E. Buffett is the CEO of Berkshire Hathaway Inc. and reportedly one of the world's three or four wealthiest people. Buffet made the quoted remark before the Financial Crisis Inquiry Commission (FCIC) during a hearing in 2010. The comment was reported by Bloomberg News at www.bloomberg.com on February 17, 2011 under the heading "Buffett Says Pricing Power More Important Than Good Management."

2. Benson P. Shapiro, "Precision Pricing for Profit in the New World Order," *Harvard Business School Note 9-999-003*, 7 Dec. 1998, 1.

3. The author's early work on pricing was summarized in two unpublished papers, namely, *Price Optimization for Industrial Products* dated March 6, 1979 and *Pricing for Maximum Profits* of October 25, 1982. Among the professors he contacted between 1979 and 1983 for an evaluation of his work were: Philip Kotler of the Graduate School of Management, Northwestern University; Thomas T. Nagle of the Graduate School of Business, University of Chicago; Alfred R. Oxenfeldt of the Graduate School of Business, Columbia University; and Benson P. Shapiro of the Graduate School of Business Management, Harvard University. All professors responded and the author is indebted to them for their helpful comments that ranged from a cautiously supportive "...clearly you are developing interesting theory" to a dismissive "It is really not new knowledge. Rather it is a clever and able manipulation using existing knowledge and generally known techniques."

4. The Nimer in-house seminar on pricing techniques and strategies was sponsored by Emily Jonas Hill and Roger Gettys Hill and their firm Gettys Manufacturing Company, makers of servomotors and drives for the machine tool industry. It was held at the Racine Motor Inn in Racine, Wisconsin on April 29 and 30, 1980.

5. The author's previous non-technical publications include *A Poetical Offering with Commentaries* written under an assumed name and published by Xlibris in December 2006, and *Just Passing Through: A German-American Family Saga* published by Xlibris in March 2011.

1

The Art and Science of Pricing

Pricing is at once a science and an art.... Scientific, artful pricing can provide the firm with the maximum profits obtainable during any specific state of economic weather.[1]

This chapter presents a brief introduction to price and the pricing of goods and services. Topics covered include the role of price at the micro- and macro-economic levels, the relationship between price and the other marketing mix strategy variables, the uniqueness of the price variable, pricing objectives, and the two major approaches to pricing in use today.

1.1 The Role of Price in the Economy

How a business firm's products and services are priced is crucial to its success and viability. Prices set too high may throttle demand and require the product's eventual withdrawal from the market. If prices are set too low, the firm may experience large but unprofitable sales. Thus, price can determine what can be sold and in what quantities and, perhaps more importantly, whether or not a business will be profitable. A business enterprise cannot consistently sustain losses without being in jeopardy of becoming extinct.

At the macroeconomic level, the price system in a free-market economy, as our own, ensures the proper allocation of scarce resources both human and non-human. Such resources include labor, raw materials, machinery, buildings, and land. Where such a system is inoperative, as was the case in the former socialist (Marxist) economies of Eastern Europe (the Soviet Union, the German Democratic Republic, Poland, Czechoslovakia etc.), scarce resources are employed for the production of goods and services for which there may be no or little demand while products and services needed and wanted by consumers are regularly in short supply or often not available at all.

In such economies, instead of letting the market determine price and production levels, state central planners typically mandated production levels for all goods together with the prices to be charged. These state-controlled economies collapsed around the year 1990 and mutated into free-market economies. Once freed from the shackles of Marxist economic dogma, these countries began to flourish resulting in strong and politically engaged middle classes. The pricing of goods and services was an integral part of this process as prices based on supply and demand replaced state-mandated ones.

According to economists, present-day Western economies are not purely private enterprise nor socialist economies but a "mixture of socialism and private enterprise."[2] Some of an economy's output is produced in the private sector which is predominantly profit-oriented. A second part relates to the public sector, often termed socialist, which is generally not profit-oriented, such as public transportation, while a third output category is in the not-for-profit sector that includes schools, hospitals, and charitable organizations. In *Pricing for Profit*, we are mainly concerned with private sector pricing.

1.2 Price as a Marketing Strategy Variables

The major marketing strategy variables have been identified as Product, Price, Advertising and Promotion, and Distribution and are often referred to as the *four Ps* (Product, Price, Promotion, and Place).[3] Price, therefore, is just one element available to the marketer for reaching the firm's marketing objectives. All four variables should be viewed as co-equal in importance to the marketing effort and therefore never be treated in isolation but rather be made part of a comprehensive marketing strategy.

The greatest product or service ever dreamed up will not sell at any price if there is no demand for it. Likewise, the most desirable product will not sell well if it is priced wrong for the intended product-market. Furthermore, potential customers must know about the existence of the product or service which may not be the case if it has not been properly advertised and promoted. Finally, if there is no convenient place for potential customers to acquire the product or service, sales are likely to suffer or may not materialize at all.

Clearly then, all marketing activities, including pricing, must be coordinated and goal oriented for optimum results. Specifically, the individual strategy variable goals, including those for pricing the product or service, must be consistent with each other and support the overall objectives for the intended target market or markets.

1.3 The Uniqueness of Price

Among the mix of four marketing strategy variables, price has some very unique properties. One of these, and perhaps the most important, is its direct and strong impact on profits. In fact, as McKinsey and Company's Michael Marn and Robert Rosiello have pointed out, a small percentage improvement in the sell price has a far greater impact on profitability than do similar improvements in variable cost, fixed cost, and sales volume.[4] "The fastest and most effective way for a company to realize its maximum profit is to get its pricing right," these pricing consultants noted. This notion was echoed by pricing authors Robert Dolan and Hermann Simon who wrote that "Price drives profit like no other factor."[5]

Another unique feature of the price variable is that it is the only one of the four that does not generate significant costs. All the others—product development and manufacture, advertising and sales promotion, and distribution—involve money outlays. That is not to say that a price is never without costs. If it is the wrong price for the product or service, it can be very costly. Finally, price is the only strategy variable which generates revenue by which the company's investments and costs can be recouped and a profit earned. The need to price *proactively* rather than to simply respond to competitor price changes or let market forces dictate changes is clearly apparent.

1.4 Pricing as Art and Science

Pricing is both an art and a science. A sell price is a number and pricing involves the manipulation of numbers by means of simple or more complex mathematical formulas. Furthermore, the results of price changes are measurable in terms of sales revenue, market shares, and profits or losses. Quantifiable parameters and measurable results are the hallmark of scientific inquiry. Pricing, therefore, may properly be classified as a science much like biology, economics, or physics are. The analytical tools developed and used in *Pricing for Profit* are meant as another step in that direction.

At the same time, pricing is an art because not every pricer is equally proficient in applying pricing principles and techniques to actual pricing situations. Pricing is, of course, much more than merely using computed values to establish the price of a new product or adjust the price of an established one. That is why some marketers and pricers are eminently successful while others are not. Considering that the information available to the pricer is always imperfect and incomplete and the behavior of customers and competitors is never entirely predictable, much skill and intuition is still required for successful pricing moves, both in size and timing. Clearly, the quality of management's pricing decisions has a profound impact on a company's fortunes.

1.5 Pricing Objectives

Depending on the industry they are in and the markets they serve, firms usually establish marketing objectives to be achieved. Pricing goals typically differ among the firm's product-markets and may be for either the short or long term. Also, a company may have multiple goals for the same product-market because the goals are not necessarily exclusive. Among the most common pricing objectives are these:

* Profits
* Return on capital
* Sales revenue
* Market share
* Price leadership
* Image
* Meeting competition

Empirical studies have shown profit maximization to be the most common goal found in practice.[6] In fact, among publicly held companies, profit-oriented pricing goals predominate. Within these mostly equity-financed firms there is a strong incentive and expectation for quarterly increases in earnings, dividend payouts, share prices, and market capitalization. Furthermore, a good and uninterrupted earnings stream is desirable to pay down debt, fund research and new product development, and finance future expansion.

Market share, i. e., the percentage of industry sales of a particular product or product class the company accounts for, is the second-most popular pricing objective. This goal may be expressed either in terms of sales revenue or, as is common in the automobile industry, in terms of sales volume. Market share is a measure of the company's market power, dominance, and viability and is often made the pricing goal as it has been shown that firms with a dominant position in the industry tend also be the most profitable.

Price leadership goals are especially prevalent in industries and markets with few competitors. The price leader gets to set the prices which will ensure that it is and remains the most profitable in its industry. Another pricing goal is image which is especially important in the luxury goods industries. Products are usually premium-priced and purchased on account of the aura of exclusivity they convey. Some companies have goals that simply seek to meet competition. This is not a pro-active but passive and safe approach to the market.

Among other, more altruistic pricing goals, are those in furtherance of some worthwhile cause such as preserving a clean and healthy environment, combating hunger and diseases, or ensuring employment for disadvantaged people. However, even with these socially engaged firms, profits can never be far from consideration. As noted British pricing author André Gabor has written: "It is undeniable that profit maximization is seldom, if ever the sole aim of a firm, but it seems that most, if not all, the other legitimate aims of businessmen are either means toward furthering profitability or can be pursued in the long run only if the firm is working profitably."[7] Clearly, profits are highly important to the viability of a business regardless of any stated business goal.

While these objectives are useful for giving the marketing and pricing effort the needed direction, they are insufficient to make a plan actionable. Management must, in addition, develop more detailed strategy goals to include specific performance levels and deadlines that are measurable. Examples of such specific product pricing goals are:

* Increase sales revenue by 10% by (date)
* Maintain market share at 20% through at least (date)
* Achieve break-even sales by (date)
* Improve profits by 5% by (date)

These goals must obviously be realistic and in line with the other marketing strategy variables for the particular product-market.

!. 6 Pricing Methods

One can distinguish between two major approaches to pricing. Both are in common use world-wide but differ radically in their focus and the results achieved. Professor Peter Drucker, the management guru, has described the two methods as "cost-led pricing" and "price-led costing."[8] The cost-based approach to pricing focuses on the company's costs and is generally known as "cost-plus" the "plus" referring to the markup that is added to product costs to arrive at a sell price. It is by far the older of the two pricing methods. *Cost-plus* pricing may be described by this simplified flow diagram:

$$Product \longrightarrow Cost \longrightarrow Price \longrightarrow Customer$$

In this method, the product is developed after which its costs are determined. A total cost for manufacturing and marketing the product is then computed to which a suitable profit margin is added to obtain the sell price. This package of product, price, and terms of sale is offered to the customer who is then free to chose between it and other competing product offerings on the market.

The more modern approach to pricing is customer and market rather than seller oriented and is usually referred to as *market oriented* or *value oriented* pricing. In this approach, the focus has shifted away from the seller to the customer and prices are based on the product's perceived value to the customer and the product-market segment being served. The approach is the reverse of the above as illustrated by this new event sequence:

$$\textit{Customer} \longrightarrow \textit{Price} \longrightarrow \textit{Cost} \longrightarrow \textit{Product}$$

The marketing process begins with customers and their wants and needs in a product or service and the value it represents to this product-market segment of potential customers, i. e., its *perceived value*. The price is the one these potential customers are able and willing to pay for the product or service offered. This information tells the company what the costs must be to cover its manufacturing, marketing, and overhead costs and make an acceptable profit. Product development to meet the product and price specifications is the final link in the marketing chain.

Pricing for Profit is devoted to the market oriented approach to pricing. However, because of the continuing popularity of cost-plus pricing, the following chapter will review this pricing method discussing some of its advantages but also its severe limitations for pricing profitably.

Notes

1. Spencer Tucker, *Pricing for Higher Profit*, 5.

2. Ross Eckert and Richard Leftwich, *The Price System and Resource Allocation*, 18.

3. The four Ps were popularized by Professor E. Jerome McCarthy of Michigan State University in his *Basic Marketing: A Managerial Approach* first published in 1960.

4. Michael Marn and Robert Rosiello, "Managing Price, Gaining Profit," *Harvard Business Review on Pricing*, 46-49.

5. Robert Dolan and Hermann Simon, *Power Pricing*, 24.

6. Robert Dolan and Hermann Simon, supra at 32.

7. André Gabor, *Pricing*, 32.

8. Peter F. Drucker, "The Information Executives Truly Need," *Harvard Business Review*, January-February 1995, 58.

2

Cost-Plus Pricing

Cost-plus pricing is, historically, the most common pricing procedure because it carries an aura of financial prudence.[1]

Products and services have traditionally been priced by a cost-based method which carries the generic term of *cost-plus* and is also known as full-cost, absorption cost, markup, or formula pricing. While it is not possible to quote statistics, one may safely assume that cost-plus is, in some form or another, still the most popular method world-wide despite its many severe deficiencies. While many marketing texts no longer discuss cost-plus or do so in passing only, every marketer should have at least some familiarity with it even though its use cannot be recommended. In fact, this chapter could be subtitled *How not to price your products or services*.

In this chapter the concept of cost-plus pricing is introduced together with a list of the benefits the method promises. A basic technique required using this method, called overhead allocation, is discussed next. An example of pricing by overhead allocation is presented followed by an actual case study. The chapter concludes with a summary of both the promised benefits and actual shortcomings of cost-plus as a pricing method.

2.1 The Method

While it is generally true that a firm must eventually recover all of its costs before it can generate a profit regardless of which pricing method is used, be it cost-plus or market oriented pricing, in cost-plus pricing the firm seeks to recover the product's full cost, including a portion of company overhead, on each and every sale. In other words, each unit sold must bear its share of company overhead costs with the assumption being that if these costs are covered by the sell prices, a full recovery of all overhead costs will be achieved and the firm will always be profitable.

Overhead may be defined as that portion of a company's costs that cannot be objectively traced to the manufacture or marketing of any of its products such as direct labor and material costs. From a practical standpoint this means that the company's total overhead costs, i.e., costs that it incurs regardless of the level of output, must be distributed among its products in a process known as *overhead allocation*.

For a one-product firm, the product's sell price could be computed using this simple formula:

$$P = (VC + F/Q) \times (1 + m) \qquad \text{Eq. (2.1)}$$

where,

P = Sell price ($)
VC = Unit variable cost ($)
F = Total fixed (overhead) cost ($)
Q = Sales volume (units)
m = Profit markup (%)

In the above expression, VC, the unit variable cost, is the cost directly associated with the production of this particular product. The total fixed cost, F, is the company's overhead cost. This cost must be divided by the product's sales volume to arrive at an overhead cost per unit. The profit factor, m, is a percentage profit markup expressed as a decimal.

Example

Alpha Company's Product X costs $20 to produce and the firm's yearly overhead cost is $100,000. If total forecasted sales for the year are 10,000 units, the unit overhead cost charged to this product is $10 ($100,000 / 10,000). Suppose that a profit of 20% is to be made on each sale. By Equation (2.1), the product's sell price would be:

$$P = (\$20 + \$10) \times 1.2 = \$36$$

Depending on the competitive situation, the markup percentage and thus the price could be raised or lowered. This is, in fact, the only manner in which some flexibility could be added to this pricing scheme.

2.2 Overhead Allocation

Since a company typically produces and markets more than one product, its total overhead cost must be *allocated* among these different products. There are any number of allocation formulas a firm may choose from but, to make the method work, it must consistently apply the same one to all its products. We shall illustrate use of three typical allocation formulas and compute sell prices in a three-product company. These formulas for the overhead rate are:

$$\text{Rate} = \frac{\text{Overhead}}{\text{Direct labor cost}} \qquad (I)$$

$$\text{Rate} = \frac{\text{Overhead}}{\text{Direct material cost}} \qquad (II)$$

$$\text{Rate} = \frac{\text{Overhead}}{\text{Direct labor} + \text{material costs}} \qquad (III)$$

These and many other allocation formulas may be found in the pricing and cost accounting literature.[2]

2.3 Application

The following example will illustrate the method in the case of a manufacturing company with three products.

Illustrative Example: Sun Valley Products Co.

Sun Valley Products manufactures and markets three products with the following manufacturing costs:

	Product A	Product B	Product C
Direct labor ($)	10.00	20.00	20.00
Direct material ($)	20.00	10.00	20.00

The company's annual projected overhead is $200,000 while labor and material costs are projected to be $100,000 and $400,000, respectively. The overhead rates to be applied are therefore:

Formula I) $200,000 / $100,000 = 2.0 × Labor
Formula II) $200,000 / $400,000 = 0.50 × Material
Formula III) $200,000 / $500,000 = 0.40 × (Material + Labor)

The total cost charged to each product and the product's sell price including a 10% markup is therefore:

	Product A	Product B	Product C
Direct labor ($)	10.00	20.00	20.00
Direct material ($)	20.00	10.00	20.00
Formula I			
Overhead ($)	20.00	40.00	40.00
Total cost ($)	50.00	70.00	80.00
Sell price ($)	*55.00*	*77.00*	*88.00*
Formula II			
Overhead ($)	10.00	5.00	10.00
Total cost ($)	40.00	35.00	50.00
Sell price ($)	*44.00*	*38.50*	*55.00*
Formula III			
Overhead ($)	12.00	12.00	16.00
Total cost ($)	42.00	42.00	56.00
Sell price ($)	*46.20*	*46.20*	*61.60*

As this tabulation shows, each product covers a considerable range in sell prices depending on the allocation formula used and the product's relative labor and material content. Nevertheless, if the sales and accounting departments have projected sales and costs accurately, the firm should see a profit at year's end regardless of which formula is used, provided, of course, that customers are willing to buy the products at the prices offered and in the quantities projected.

2.4 The Cost-Price Spiral

Cost-plus pricing can lead to some drastic consequences. In this section a real-life case will be presented. The company, Delta-Star, previously introduced in the Preface to *Pricing for Profit*, manufactured its products to order and used a more complex allocation formula than the ones described above. The basic version was in use for many years and similar formulas are most likely in use in various companies here and abroad today.

Illustrative Example: Delta-Star Electric Division

The Delta-Star Electric Company was established in 1908 on Chicago's West side to supply the electric power industry with products for the production, transmission, and distribution of electric power. The company's major product was a line of high-voltage outdoor air break disconnect switches for use by electric utility companies in their substations. In such facilities, the incoming high-voltage power is reduced (transformed) to the lower voltages required for commercial and household use.

Delta-Star's high-quality disconnect switches were much in demand for isolating the transformers, oil-filled circuit breakers, and other substation equipment from the power grid for periodic maintenance. In 1950, the company was taken over by the H. K. Porter Company of Pittsburgh and was renamed the Delta-Star Electric Division of H. K. Porter Company. Delta-Star continued to flourish but its fortunes changed and in 1980, after many years of unprofitable operations, the Delta-Star Division was closed down.

After its founding, Delta-Star had become a pioneer and innovator in high voltage technology and its products became the standard for the industry. The largest disconnect switches were rated at 750 kilovolts and motor-operated but the company also produced a line of high-capacity indoor switches as well as electrical connectors. The Chicago plant included complete manufacturing and assembly facilities and an adjoining high-voltage testing laboratory. Practically all of the country's largest electrical utilities including American Electric Power, Commonwealth Edison, Consolidated Edison, Duke Power, Florida Power & Light, Georgia Power, and Pacific Gas & Electric, were customers. Delta-Star's products were sold directly through company sales offices located close to the major utilities.

At the Delta-Star Electric Division, a cost-plus formula, developed by the corporate accounting department, was used to compute sell prices. These prices were strictly enforced by the parent company which required prior approval of all but the most trivial of quotations. To illustrate the pricing method, below is an actual and typical price computation in support of a quotation for a standard 3-pole, vertical break, manually operated disconnect switch.

Pricing Sheet for Pittsburgh Bid Approval

Product: MK-40A, 138 kilovolt /1600 ampere with swing handles less lugs less insulators.

1) Material	$600
2) Labor	200
3) Shop Burden @ 255% of Line 2	510
4) Total Shop Cost	1,310
5) Engineering @ 9.0% of Line 4	118
6) SG&A* @ 18.8% of Line 4	246
7) Total Cost	1,674
8) Net Profit @ 30%**	717
9) Freight @ 5.9% of Line 4	77
10) Suggested Quoted Price	2,468

  * Sales, General & Administrative expense
 ** Net profit = (Total cost / 1 – Percent net profit) – Total cost

The only pricing flexibility given the product manager was in the net profit level which ranged from a minimum of 15% for the largest orders to 30% for orders below a certain dollar value. To meet competition, this manager could and often did request to have the profit level requirements lowered.

Cost-plus pricing posed no major problems for Delta-Star until competitors started to enter the market with similar products. This development was, ironically, helped along by Delta-Star's own chief engineer who had aggressively pushed for more product standardization. As a member of the ANSI (American National Standards Institute) committee on disconnect switches, he helped standardize their design and performance. Establishment of these national standards was, as a whole, beneficial for the industry including Delta-Star. However, for the latter it had the disadvantage of allowing competitors to enter the market. By having their products tested and certified to meet the ANSI standards, Delta-Star's competitors could now request to be placed on the approved vendor lists at the various utilities which had previously not been possible.

As a result, Delta-Star's disconnect switches lost their unique and differentiated attributes. In the eyes of customers, these products were now an interchangeable commodity calling for a commodity price. As Delta-Star became ever less competitive price-wise, sales necessarily declined forcing the company to allocate its overhead costs to an ever diminishing output. As a result, overhead rates rose steadily along with the formula-computed prices.

The wounds that brought about Delta-Star's demise were largely self-inflicted because the company's management was unable to recognize and adjust to the changing conditions in the marketplace. Had it, instead of insisting that every sale carry its "fair" share of overhead, adopted a more flexible pricing approach, as did their competitors, the company might well have survived. The elimination of Delta-Star had unfavorable consequences for the electrical utilities industry as a whole because it lost a reliable supplier of innovative quality products and with fewer competitors in the market it eventually saw prices for these products rise as well.

2.5 Why "Cost-Plus" Remains Popular

Cost-plus pricing, despite its shortcomings, is still much in use, either by itself or in combination with other methods, and for some fairly good reasons. Among the benefits often cited are these:

* The method yields a definitive price which is not the case for value-oriented pricing which requires subjective estimates of customers' perceived values of products and services.

* Where the profit markups are reasonable, sell prices tend to be fair and equitable to both buyers and sellers.

* Computation and administration of sell prices is a simple routine requiring a minimum of time, effort, and expertise.

* Insofar as there are no major variances between actual and projected overhead costs and sales volumes, the firm will never incur a loss but always operate profitably.

* The firm can count on a steady, non-erratic stream of income as costs are fully and continuously recovered by ongoing sales.

* Prices are readily explained and, where necessary, justified to corporate buyers and government regulatory agencies.

* Provided costs remain relatively stable, cost-plus pricing fosters long-term price stability.

* Cost-plus pricing can be made responsive to market conditions by adjusting profit markups to make offerings more competitive.

Many of these benefits, unfortunately, seldom materialize because they are based on unrealistic and illusory assumptions.

2.6 The Case Against Cost-Plus Pricing

From a modern marketing point of view, cost-plus pricing makes little sense for a number of reasons. As we have seen in the previous section, overhead cost allocation is arbitrary resulting in distorted full costs and prices. But there is a deficiency that is even more fundamental and egregious. Thus, cost-plus pricing completely ignores all-important price-volume relationships, i. e., the fact that companies and individuals will buy less product from a specific supplier when prices are high and vice versa assuming, of course, that there are substitute products on the market. Also ignored are customers' value perceptions of products and services and their willingness to pay for these. The concept of value pricing is the subject of Chapter 9 (Market Oriented Pricing).

Another shortcoming is that sales volumes must be forecast even before the sell prices have been determined. That is obviously not realistic because the number of units of a products sold is heavily dependant on the prices charged. Furthermore, the method seeks to impose sell prices on the market based on the company's cost structure. That is possible only if the firm has acquired a monopoly position in the market it serves, i.e., it must be able to dictate to the market what customers buy and in what quantities and at what prices. That is generally not possible in a free-market economy.

Among the more specific deficiencies of cost-plus pricing are:

* The method, if judiciously applied, rejects all sales below the full-cost price thereby foregoing any contribution to overhead costs and profits on such sales.

* Premium pricing and profit opportunities from such factors as product uniqueness, customer value perceptions, and brand loyalty are not taken advantage of so that the firm is essentially "leaving money on the table" on many sales.

* Because of their cost-based nature, prices are in an inverse relationship with business activity in that they are too high during periods of low demand, i.e., weak markets, when downward pressure on prices is highest and too low in strong markets when sales are brisk and price sensitivity is low.

* There is the ever-present danger of what pricing experts Nagle et al have called a *death spiral* in which the firm prices itself out of the market because a price increase leads to lower sales which causes average unit costs to rise requiring a further price increase and so on.[3]

In summary, cost-plus pricing has some value in establishing a price level where no other benchmarks are available but it should never serve as the primary pricing tool inasmuch as it completely undermines the concept of pro-active, value-oriented and profitable pricing. Our next topic concerns cost and contribution which are both fundamental to understanding market oriented pricing.

Notes

1. Thomas Nagle, John Hogan, and Joseph Zale, *The Strategy and Tactics of Pricing*, 2.

2. For a more thorough discussion of overhead allocation, see Spencer Tucker, *Pricing for Higher Profit*, 43-49, and Kent Monroe, *Pricing*, 228-239. This topic is also treated in standard texts on cost accounting.

3. Thomas Nagle, John Hogan, and Joseph Zale, supra at 3.

3

Cost and Contribution

A fundamental principle in market-based pricing is to recognize that price is a statement of value, not a statement of costs.[1]

At this point readers should be convinced that pricing a product or service based on its costs is not the way to achieve profitability goals. Is cost, then, relevant at all in pricing and, if so, how relevant? This is one question we hope to answer in this chapter. But first, we want to examine the nature of costs and how they arise. The final topic is the contribution margin and how it allows marketers to recoup their companies' costs and earn a profit for their owners.

3.1 The Nature and Origin of Costs

A firm incurs costs in a number of ways and these may be divided into two broad categories—direct and indirect costs. Direct costs are, in turn, classified as variable or fixed. Marketers and pricers are mostly interested in the direct costs while top management will be more focused on the fixed costs. All executives and managers though will share the common goal of keeping all costs down to maintain and improve profitability.

3.1.1 Direct Costs

As their name implies, *direct costs* are costs that are directly attributable, traceable, and assignable to a profit entity whose profitability one wishes to examine such as a single product, a product line, a sales territory, a target market, an individual salesperson, or an individual customer account. These direct costs, which have also been called the *out-of-pocket costs* or *incremental costs*, are the *costs of doing business* and exist only because a specific product or other profit entity exists. If it did not exist or if it were to be discontinued, all associated direct costs would vanish.

Direct Variable Costs: For a product, *direct variable costs* increase in direct proportion to the number of units produced and sold and would include, but not be limited to, hourly labor and raw materials that went into the product, sales commissions, and royalties. Figure 3.1 (a) illustrates the relationship between direct variable cost and volume. As may be noted, at zero volume direct variable cost is zero and increases in direct proportion to sales volume.

Figure 3-1
Direct Variable and Fixed Costs

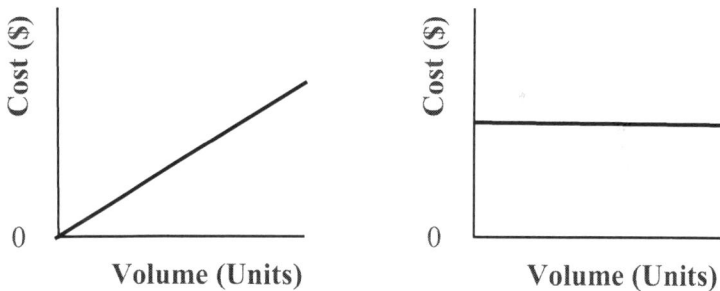

(a) Variable cost   (b) Fixed cost

Direct Fixed Costs: For a product, and unlike the variable costs, *direct fixed costs* do not increase with the number of units produced and sold but remain constant with volume. In other words, these costs are independent of the activity level and are not zero if production were to cease. These costs would look like Figure 3-1(b). Direct fixed costs, sometimes called *specific programmed costs*, would include costs incurred for a specific product such as modification or improvement, advertising and sales promotion, and warehousing. For example, suppose an advertising and promotional campaign was planned together with a price change to raise sales of a specific product, then the costs incurred must be charged to that product thereby reducing its profit by these costs after the price change. Or suppose the price of a product was reduced and the increased demand was expected to require an expansion in production capacity. Then the added costs, such as for machinery or fixtures, would be chargeable to this product. Similarly, suppose a hotel's management decided to combine several rooms to make a suit, the conversion costs would have to be taken into account in the new profit calculations.

3.1.2 Indirect Fixed (Common) Costs

Costs that are not directly attributable, traceable, and assignable to a specific product or other profit entity are known as *indirect fixed costs* or common costs. Sometimes they are referred to simply as *overhead* or *overhead costs*. These costs are shared by all the products and are therefore common costs or the *costs of being in business*. They cannot be changed in the short term for a number of reasons including legal and contractual, moral, and ethical. Common costs and expenses include salaries, general and administrative, sales and sales support, depreciation, mortgages, leases, rentals, loan interest, insurance, advertising and promotion, research and development, professional services, travel, and utilities. Clearly, these overhead costs cover a broader spectrum of costs than is the case for direct costs. Generally, the marketer is less involved with these costs because they play only a minor role in pricing.

The above is the most important information on costs a marketer and pricer needs to know. Typically, developing accurate cost data for pricing purposes, including a product's average unit variable cost, is the responsibility of the firm's cost accountants. For a more thorough and nuanced discussion of the topic, the interested reader may wish to consult the relevant literature including a text on cost accounting.[2]

3.2 The Basic Formulas

Profit is the difference between sales revenue and total cost and expressed symbolically:

$$I = R - C \qquad \text{Eq. (3.1)}$$

where,   I = Profit (before taxes)
          R = Sales revenue
          C = Total cost

Total cost consists, as we have seen, of variable and fixed cost components so that Equation (3.1) becomes:

$$I = R - V - F \qquad \text{Eq. (3.2)}$$

where,   V = Total variable cost
          F = Indirect fixed (overhead) cost

Revenue, in turn, is the product of the sell price and the number of units sold (sales volume):

$$R = P \times Q \qquad \text{Eq. (3.3)}$$

where,   P = Sell price
          Q = Sales volume (units)

while the total variable cost is:

$$V = VC \times Q \qquad \text{Eq. (3.4)}$$

where,   VC = Unit variable cost

Combining Equations (3.2) through (3.4), the general expression for profit is therefore:

$$I = (P - VC) Q - F \qquad \text{Eq. (3.5)}$$

As may be noted, Equation (3.5) makes no provisions for direct fixed, i.e., specific programmed costs. Nevertheless, unlike indirect fixed costs, programmed costs, if incurred in conjunction with a price change, must be included in the profit change computations. How net profits may be adjusted to account for these direct programmed costs is shown in Chapter 5 on contribution pricing. Unless otherwise noted, it is assumed that there are no programmed costs during an incremental price change.

3.3 How Important is Cost in Pricing?

While there is a consensus that costs must never be allowed to drive sell prices, one cannot ignore the fact that costs have a profound impact on profits. Equation (3.1) indicates that, as a first approximation, there are only two ways by which profits may be raised and that is by either raising sales revenue or reducing total cost. Now, as will be shown below, the relationship between profit and sales revenue is not a linear one, i.e., an increase in sales revenue does not guarantee an increase in profit. That leaves *cost reduction* as the only undisputable option for improving profitability. Clearly then, low total costs are of fundamental importance to profitable operations.

How relevant are costs then in incremental price changes meant to improve profitability? The answer is that it depends on which of the costs described above we mean. Take the case of the indirect fixed cost (overhead). For small price changes, overhead does not normally change with an incremental price change and therefore does not impact profits. If we are concerned only with profitability as a result of a price change, the overhead costs may therefore be ignored. Likewise, an incremental price change normally does not affect the product's unit variable cost and therefore not the change in profit. These two points can easily be demonstrated.

If we combine Equations (3.1), (3.2), and (3.4), and designate "0" as the parameters before a price change and "1" after the change, the profit before and after the change can be written as:

$$I_0 = R_0 - C_0 = R_0 - VC_0 Q_0 - F_0$$
$$I_1 = R_1 - C_1 = R_1 - VC_1 Q_1 - F_1$$

If one lets $VC_1 = VC_0$ and $F_1 = F_0$, as previously stipulated, and lets Δ stand for an incremental dollar change, then the incremental profit change as a result of an incremental price change is given by:

$$\Delta I = I_1 - I_0 = \Delta R - VC_0 \Delta Q \qquad \text{Eq. (3.6)}$$

In words, the incremental profit change following an incremental price change of an item equals the revenue change less the product of the item's unit variable cost and the change in sales volume. Since the overhead cost F does not appear in Eq. (3.6), indirect fixed (overhead) costs are *not relevant* in price change computations. This leads us to our first general pricing observation or proposition.

Pricing Proposition 1

Where indirect fixed (overhead) costs are the same before and after a price change, only direct costs (fixed and variable) are relevant in price change and price optimization computations.

Regarding the common notion that a revenue increase leads to improved profits, Equation (3.6) indicates that this is not necessarily the case.[3] This outcome can only hold if the second term on the right ($VC_0 \times \Delta Q$) is negative which means that, since VC_0 is always positive, ΔQ must also be negative. This, in turn, implies an incremental price increase ΔP. As will be shown later, incremental price increases can lead to profit increases as well as to profit losses. Clearly, the sales revenue versus profit relationship is more complex.

3.4 Contribution

By the term *contribution* is meant the amount of revenue remaining from the sale of a product or service after the direct variable costs have been deducted. This remainder will *contribute* to paying down indirect fixed (overhead) costs plus earning a profit. A company can begin earning such a profit only after sufficient contribution dollars have been generated to cover its overhead costs. Total contribution to overhead and profit is the difference between sales revenue and total variable cost:

$$K = R - V \qquad \text{Eq. (3.7)}$$

where, K = Total contribution

Inserting Equations (3.3) and (3.4) into Equation (3.7), total contribution may also be written as:

$$K = (P - VC)Q \qquad \text{Eq. (3.8)}$$

The expression in parentheses in Equations (3.5) and (3.8) is a key profitability metric known as the *unit contribution margin* which is defined as the difference between a product's sell price and its unit variable cost. Thus, the unit contribution margin expressed in dollars is given by:

$$\textbf{CM (\$)} = \textbf{P} - \textbf{VC} \qquad \text{Eq. (3.9)}$$

The dollar contribution margin may also be expressed as a percentage of the sell price:

$$\textbf{CM (\%)} = \frac{\textbf{P} - \textbf{VC}}{\textbf{P}} \qquad \text{Eq. (3.10)}$$

The actual percentage is obtained, as usual, by multiplying the right-hand side of Equation (3.10) by 100%. While the contribution margin can be expressed either as a dollar amount or as a percentage and distinguished by the two notations given above, we shall generally use CM to stand for both. Which one is meant becomes immediately clear from the context since any formula must be dimensionally correct.

The total contribution K earned by a firm with n products is simply the sum of the individual contributions:

$$K = (P_1 - VC_1)\, Q_1 + (P_2 - VC_2)\, Q_2 + \ldots\ (P_n - VC_n)\, Q_n$$

Example

Suppose Alpha Company has three products each with a different direct variable cost—$8 for product A, $5 for product B, and $2 for product C—but, for competitive reasons, each product is being sold at the same price of $10. The respective contribution margins are by Equations (3.9) and (3.10):

Product A: CM($) = $10 – $8 = $2 CM(%) = $2 / $10 = 20%
Product B: CM($) = $10 – $5 = $5 CM(%) = $5 / $10 = 50%
Product C: CM($) = $10 – $8 = $8 CM(%) = $8 / $10 = 80%

Clearly, Product C is the most profitable as every sale brings in $8 of contribution or 80% of the sell price. Product A is the least profitable with only 20% of the sell price available for contribution.

An easy way to understand contribution is to look on the unit contribution margin (P – VC) as the basic *building block* by which the firm can recover its overhead costs and earn a profit. Suppose we were required to build a wall of a certain dimension in a month's time. In our analogy, suppose that wall represented the firm's overhead costs. Assume further that we used these (P – VC) building blocks to build the wall. If we could complete the wall before the end of the month, any additional blocks could be used to build something else. In the business context, additional block would generate profits. If an insufficient number of block arrived in time, the wall would be left unfinished. For the business, the result would be a dollar loss for the month instead of profits. Clearly, success depends on the size of the building blocks (P – VC), their number (Q) and their rate of arrival. Ideally, the unit contribution margin and quantity would both be as large as possible and sales would be brisk.

3.5 Contribution or Profit?

Pricers, and marketers in general, talk more about contribution dollars than profits because, by Equation (3.2), calculating a profit requires one to know the indirect fixed (overhead) cost which, as we have seen in Chapter 2, involves allocation problems when considering individual products. Contribution K, on the other hand, can be calculated without knowledge of overhead costs. The relationship between profit I and contribution K is found by inserting Equation (3.7) into Equation (3.2):

$$I = K - F \qquad \text{Eq. (3.11)}$$

Thus, profit is simply total contribution less overhead costs meaning that total contribution must exceed overhead costs before a profit is made. This leads to a second pricing proposition:

Pricing Proposition 2

Achieving maximum total contribution dollars for its products and services ensures that the firm earns a profit provided that these exceed its indirect fixed (overhead) costs but, if they do not, they ensure that losses are minimized.

As was shown before, the overhead costs do not enter into incremental price change calculations provided these costs are the same before and after the change. Designating "0" before a price change and "1" after and letting $F_1 = F_0$, one has from Eq. (3.11):

$$I_1 - I_0 = K_1 - K_0 - F_0 + F_0$$

$$\Delta I = \Delta K \qquad \qquad \text{Eq. (3.12)}$$

This means that we can use the terms incremental contribution change and incremental profit change interchangeably since a dollar change in one results in an equal change in the other. In general. it is more practical to work with total contribution and total contribution changes rather than profit and profit changes since this avoids the overhead allocation problem.

Notes

1. Michael Morris and Gene Morris, *Market Oriented Pricing*, 2.

2. More information on costs and their role in pricing decisions may be found in Kent Monroe, *Pricing*, Chapter 7 and Thomas Nagle, John Hogan, and Joseph Zale, *The Strategy and Tactics of Pricing*, Chapter 9. For a textbook on cost accounting see, for example, Charles T. Horngren et al, *Cost Accounting: A Managerial Emphasis*.

3. Sometimes even well-known pricing texts leave the impression that profits may be improved by simply selling more product. For example, in André Gabor, *Pricing*, 30, one reads: "Even though exceptions are possible, increased sales generally mean improved profitability, that is to say, growth is not so much a rival aim as rather a means by which higher returns can be obtained."

4

Break-Even Analysis

In spite of its severe limitations, the break-even chart has not lost its relevance and deserves at least brief mention.[1]

Break-even analysis and, more specifically, the break-even chart, was a product of the Great Depression of the early 1930s at which time the very survival of many small businesses was at stake. Business owners and managers were encouraged to familiarize themselves with this simple yet powerful tool by which they could easily determine the necessary combination of costs, sell prices, and sales revenues that would avoid possibly disastrous losses and instead ensure profitable operations.

Before we construct a break-even chart, it will be useful to first review its mathematical underpinnings. A practical example will illustrate drawing and using the break-even chart and applying the break-even formulas to answer the questions posed in a feasibility study for a potential new product.

4.1 The Concept

The continuing popularity enjoyed by the break-even chart is mainly due to the fact that it is not only practical but easy to construct requiring the drawing of only two lines on a grid after which the break-even point can be read off directly. Furthermore, changes in the price and costs can be easily accommodated and their impact on the break-even point graphically demonstrated. While traditional break-even analysis ignores market-oriented factors such as product demand and competition and is therefore of limited usefulness in setting prices, it continues to be relevant in certain pricing situations. One of these is in product feasibility studies where, during the product conceptual stage, management needs to determine whether a proposed new product should be developed or dropped from further consideration.

Break-even analysis is based on the concept of contribution introduced in the previous chapter in which total product cost is separated into its two primary components, namely, a fixed cost that is independent of volume output and a total variable cost which increases in direct proportion to the number of units produced. The break-even point is reached when the sales revenue for the product just equals the product's total cost, i.e., the price-volume operating point at which profits are exactly zero.

4.2 The Break-Even Formulas

The basic equation relating a product's total cost, sales revenue and profits is from Equation (3.1) in the previous chapter:

$$I = R - C \qquad \text{Eq. (4.1)}$$

where, I = Profit ($)
              R = Sales revenue ($)
              C = Total product cost ($)

From Equation (3.5), the expanded form of this equation is:

$$I = (P - VC)\, Q - F \qquad \text{Eq. (4.2)}$$

where, P = Sell price ($)
              VC = Unit variable cost ($)
              Q = Sales volume (units)
              F = Indirect fixed (overhead) cost ($)

Solving Equation (4.2) for the sales volume, one obtains:

$$Q = \frac{I + F}{P - VC} \qquad \text{Eq. (4.3)}$$

Since by definition, the product's unit contribution margin is:

$$CM (\$) = P - VC \qquad \text{Eq. (4.4)}$$

one obtains:

$$Q_I = \frac{I + F}{CM (\$)} \qquad \text{Eq. (4.5)}$$

At the break-even point (BEP), the profit is zero ($I = 0$) so that the break- even quantity is:

$$\mathbf{Q_{BE}} = \frac{\mathbf{F}}{\mathbf{CM (\$)}} \qquad \text{Eq. (4.6)}$$

In words, the break-even quantity at which neither a profit is made nor a loss incurred for a given product is the product's fixed cost divided by its dollar contribution margin per unit. The break-even sales revenue is then:

$$R_{BE} = Q_{BE} \times P \qquad \text{Eq. (4.7)}$$

Sometimes it is desirable to know what the profit or loss is above or below the break-even point, respectively. If one lets:

$$I_{AB} = \text{Profit above or below the BEP}$$
$$I_{BE} = \text{Profit at the BEP}$$

one obtains, from Equation (4.5):

$$I = CM(\$) \times Q - F$$

$$I_{AB} - I_{BE} = CM(\$) \times Q_{AB} - F - CM(\$) \times Q_{BE} + F$$

But since at the BEP, the profit I_{BE} is zero, one has:

$$I_{AB} = (Q_{AB} - Q_{BE}) \times CM(\$) \qquad \text{Eq. (4.8)}$$

In words, the profit (or loss) outside the BEP is the product of the difference between the actual and break-even quantities and the product's unit dollar contribution margin.

The above formulas let a manager know how much product the company needs to sell and at what average price level during a given time period to ensure the firm's overhead is fully covered. The same formulas may also be used in new product introduction to determine what quantity must be sold and at what price level to ensure the direct fixed (programmed) costs in developing and marketing the new product are recovered. In that case, by conventional practice, the firm's overhead cost F now becomes the estimated direct (programmed) cost associated with developing and marketing the new product.

4.3 Application

An example will demonstrate the use of break-even analysis in a hypothetical feasibility study for a new product concept.

Illustrative Example: EMD Industries

EMD Industries is a medium-sized manufacturer of electro-mechanical devices such as automatic door and gate openers as used in senior living and health care facilities, and garage door openers for residential and commercial use. Recently, Felix, a new employee in the company's marketing department, came up with an exciting new product idea which he brought to Brian, the marketing manager, who immediately recognized the product's market and profit potential. Brian subsequently asked for a meeting of the new products committee composed of the president and managers of the accounting, engineering, finance, marketing, and production departments.

At the first meeting, some members objected to adding the product to the line since they considered it a bad fit. However, Brian was able to convince them that Product X could draw on the company's expertise in sensor technology, was relatively simple to develop and manufacture, and, furthermore, was compatible with one of their major distribution channels. At a later meeting, it was learned that Mail-A-Lert, the name Brian had chosen for Product X, would cost about $40,000 to develop and bring to market. This would include purchasing some additional machinery and shop fixtures, building a prototype, plus costs associated with an initial promotional campaign. Furthermore, there was a consensus that, once full-scale production was under way, Mail-A-Lert could be produced for as little as $20 per unit.

Since the product was unique, i.e., there was no substitute available on the market, and demand was expected to be high, Brian felt that he could market Mail-A-Lert to the home building industry at the premium price of $100. But before giving the green light, the new products committee needed to know what the chances were of the proposed new product becoming profitable within a year of market introduction. Brian responded by making a break-even analysis.

4.3.1 Break-Even Chart Solution

The Mail-A-Lert parameters were:

P   = $100
VC = $20
F   = $40,000

On the break-even chart shown in Figure 4.1, the horizontal (x) axis represents the number of units sold. The vertical (y) axis is simply labeled dollars. Now, from high school geometry we know that only two points are needed to draw a straight line. The sales revenue line begins at the origin where quantity and sales revenue are zero. For the second point, we can pick any quantity such as 600; it yields a sales revenue of $60,000 ($100 × 600 units). Connecting the origin with this second point gives us the sales revenue line.

The total cost is the sum of the fixed cost ($40,000) and the total variable cost. Our first point is therefore at $40,000 on the y-axis. At a quantity of 600, the total variable cost is $12,000 ($20 × 600 units). Adding the two costs, one obtains $52,000 which is the second point on this line. Connecting the two points gives us the total cost line.

Figure 4-1
Break-Even Chart for Mail-A-Lert

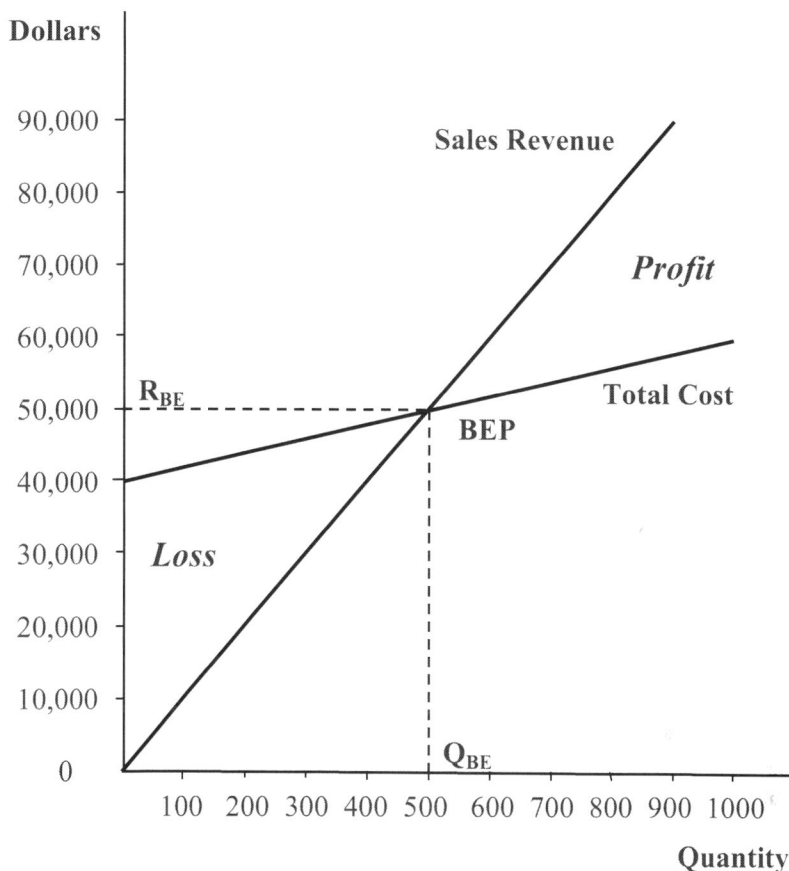

The break-even point (BEP) occurs where the sales revenue and total cost lines intersect. We note from the chart that the break-even quantity Q_{BE} and beak-even sales revenue R_{BE} are 500 units and $50,000, respectively. In the region where the sales revenue line lies below the total cost line, Mail-A-Lert will be unprofitable. To the right of the BEP, where sales revenue exceeds total cost, it will result in a profit. The amount of profit or loss is the vertical distance between the two lines. For example, if 600 units were sold, profits earned would be $8,000 ($60,000 − $52,000).

Besides the standard break-even chart shown, many variations have come into existence. Among these are composite break-even charts that allow the determination of a single break-even point for several products with different variable costs.[2]

4.3.2 Formula Solution

By Equation (4.4):

$$CM (\$) = \$100 - \$20 = \$80$$

By Equations (4.6) and (4.7), the break-even quantity and break-even sales revenue for the first year are therefore, respectively,

$$Q_{BE} = \frac{\$40,000}{\$80} = 500 \text{ units}$$

$$R_{BE} = \$100 \times 500 \text{ units} = \$50,000$$

This agrees with the chart solution.

Suppose the profit at a quantity of 600 units was desired. By Equation (4.8) one finds:

$$I_{AB} = (600 - 500) \times \$80 = \$8,000$$

If management decided that just breaking even did not suffice but that additional profits of $10,000 during the year were required, by Equation (4.5), the quantity to be produced and sold during this time period would rise to:

$$Q_I = \frac{\$40,000 + \$10,000}{\$80} = 625 \text{ units}$$

To further assist the new products committee, Brian prepared a table (not shown here) listing other price points and fixed costs and their associated break-even quantities and sales revenues. Thus, if EMD Industries had to reduce its price for Mail-A-Lert to $80 (a 20% reduction) to gain market acceptance, the break-even quantity would increase by a third. If the fixed cost had been underestimated by 20%, the break-even quantity would increase by an equal percentage.

Notes

1. André Gabor, *Pricing*, 59.
2. See, for example, Spencer Tucker, *Pricing for Higher Profit*, 101-117, and a discussion of his break-even system.

CHAPTER

5

Contribution Analysis

The underlying logic of contribution analysis is that a product or service should be held accountable only for those costs directly traceable to its production, sales, and distribution.[1]

It is not uncommon for management to be faced with the seeming paradox of increasing sales revenue but declining profits and vice versa. In this regard not much has changed since the mid-1930s when a company's president asked his controller for an explanation after sales had increased and profits declined by substantial amounts. The controller, Jonathan Harris by name, provided the answer by separating costs into volume dependant variable costs and volume independent fixed costs. This was the beginning of an accounting system known as *direct costing.*[2] It allowed management to study the profitability of individual products at different price and sales levels.

The concept of contribution was introduced in Section 3.4 of Chapter 3. The reader will recall from Equation (3.8) that total contribution is the difference between a product's sales revenue and its total variable cost:

$$K = R - V = (P - VC)\,Q \qquad \text{Eq. (5.1)}$$

where, $\quad K\ =\ $ Total contribution (\$)

$$R = \text{Sales revenue (\$)}$$
$$V = \text{Total variable cost (\$)}$$
$$P = \text{Sell price (\$)}$$
$$Q = \text{Sales volume (units)}$$
$$VC = \text{Unit variable cost (\$)}$$
$$P - VC = \text{Unit contribution margin (\$)}$$

The contribution income statement on which contribution analysis is based differs markedly from the typical income statement used for financial analysis. We begin by showing and comparing the two. Using an illustrative example, we next apply the contribution analysis in two situations where it is ideally suited. One is in determining the relative profitability of a firm's line of products. The other is in evaluating the profit impacts of various price change options for each product.

5.1 The Contribution Income Statement

The traditional quarterly or annual income statement is not suitable to a product profitability analysis because it lumps all costs, both direct and overhead, together under various aggregate cost categories. In somewhat simplified form such a *traditional income statement* would look like this:

	Sales revenue
Less:	Cost of goods sold
Less:	General sales & administrative expenses
Less:	Depreciation
	Operating profit
Less:	Other expenses
	Pretax profit

Such an income statement can also be very misleading because it strongly suggest that to improve the bottom line, a manager's best option, aside from reducing costs, is to increase sales revenue. We know, of course, from Chapter 3 that there is no direct unqualified relationship between sales revenue and total contribution and profit.

The *contribution income statement* does away with these problems and takes the following form:

	Sales revenue
Less:	Total variable cost
	Total contribution
Less:	Direct fixed cost
	Net contribution
Less:	Indirect fixed (overhead) cost
	Pretax profit

This income statement gives us the framework for a profitability analysis.

5.2 Profitability Analysis

Profitability analyses are not limited to individual products or product lines. Any profit entity such as a product-market segment, sales territory, salesperson, customer group, or customer account may be evaluated and compared with others in terms of contribution dollars generated as long as the underlying data are available. In this section, the profitability of three models of a product sold in three sales territories will be evaluated.

Illustrative Example: Maricopa Enterprises Ltd. (I)

Maricopa Enterprises was founded three years ago by some entrepreneurial individuals who, while still in college, decided to design, manufacture, and market a line of innovative products for the healthcare industry. While more products are still in the development stage, Maricopa Enterprise's only product on the market at this time is a portable medication organizer/dispenser called TimerX that holds a patient's daily supply of prescription medications and vitamins. This pocket dispenser, which includes a microprocessor, comes in three models for sale to three distinct market segments. The three models differ in several respects including the number of medication chambers and event alerts, the manner in which the medication events may be set (time interval or specific time of day), the length of time the medication alert stays on, the manner in which the patient is alerted to an event (visual, vibrating, or beep alarm), the construction (plastic or metal), and the warranty period (from one to three years).

The standard model TimerX-S includes all the features most in demand and sells for $100. Its unit variable cost is estimated to be $60. To attract the very price-sensitive segment of the market and compete with a bargain brand known as Pop-a-Pill, the economy model TimerX-E was introduced and is available for just $60 while its unit variable cost is $45. For patients who want a product with all the bells and whistles and do not mind paying $200, the premier TimerX-P can be had. Its variable cost per unit is $80. Maricopa Enterprise sells its products nationwide and maintains a company-owned sales office in each of its three primary sales territories—Atlantic, Central, and Pacific.

During the previous month, the company sold 3,000 units of the standard, 1,000 of the low-cost, and 500 of the premium-priced models yielding a monthly sales revenue of just under one-half million dollars. In line with modern pricing philosophy, the sell prices bear no direct relationship to the products' cost of manufacture, i. e., the direct variable cost, but rather are based on what management believes reflect their customers' value perceptions and their willingness to pay for each model. In fact, the unit variable cost differences among the three models are much less than their price differences.

The monthly contribution statement for the TimerX brand is shown in Table 5.1(a). The computations are straightforward and follow the contribution income statement shown in Section 5.1 above. During the month, the company expended $10,000 promoting the premium model TimerX-P including a targeted advertising campaign and showcasing the product at a trade show. Since this expenditure was specifically for the benefit of this model, it is a programmed cost and included as a direct fixed cost under the TimerX-P model reducing the total contribution by that amount.

As Table 5-1(a) also indicates, the premium model TimerX-P was the most profitable on a per unit basis with 60% of the sell price going to contribution. However, in terms of net contribution dollars the standard model was the most profitable bringing in $120,000 in net contribution dollars, or 65% of the total, followed by the premium model at $50,000. The company overhead, i. e., outlays which could not be directly assigned to any of the three models and were common to the firm and its products, was $100,000 leaving a pre-tax profit of $85,000 or 18.5% of sales revenue.

Summarizing the results of Table 5.1(a) one has:

	TimerX-E	TimerX-S	TimerX-P
% of Sales Revenue	13.0	65.2	21.8
% of Net Contribution	8.1	64.9	27.0

This information may also be presented in graphical form as in Figure 5-1 where sales revenue for the three models is shown together with the respective net contribution dollars earned after the total variable costs for the three models and the direct fixed cost for TimerX-P are deducted. This type of chart is very useful and recommended for general marketing and pricing analyses. Thus, where contribution dollars earned are much out of proportion with sales revenue for the product, the chart can point to possible pricing problems and necessary corrective measures.

Clearly, for the standard model, net contribution closely tracks sales revenue and both account for nearly two thirds of their totals. For the economy model, on the other hand, the percentage of contribution falls significantly below the percentage of sales revenue generated while both are relatively small. Why then would Maricopa Enterprises not simply drop TimerX-E from the line? The reasons are strategic. This model draws sales, however small, from the Pop-a-Pill brand and there is a good chance that, given a choice, customers will opt for the standard model which they see as a better value.

Figure 5-1
Sales Revenue and Net Contribution for TimerX Brand

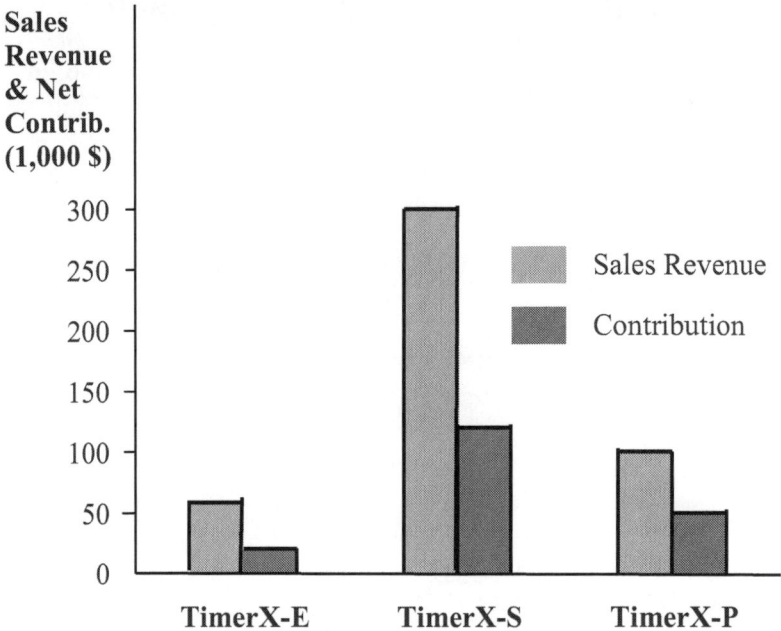

A second useful contribution statement breaks down sales and contribution by sales territory. Such a statement is shown in Table 5.1(b). In constructing this table, it was assumed that the Atlantic, Central, and Pacific territories generated 20%, 30%, and 50% of the $460,000 in total sales revenue, respectively. This would results from the fact that Maricopa Enterprises is located in a Southwestern state (Pacific territory) where its initial sales effort was focused before the two other sales offices were opened.

Assuming a similar percentage distribution in the sales revenue for each model across the three territories, one obtains the sales revenue for each model and territory. From this, the number of units sold for each model per territory could be determined and the total variable cost and total contribution for each territory computed. As one might expect, in this territorial statement the sales office expenditures appear as direct fixed costs. According to these calculations, the Pacific territory was the most profitable but by less than 2% over the Central territory.

5.3 Contribution Pricing

Of considerable interest to management is the profit impact of various price change options. To make such an analysis, the pricer needs to make some assumptions regarding the price-volume relationship and, specifically, he or she needs to estimate the percentage change in the quantity sold as a result of a percentage price change. In the following chapter we shall refer to this important price-volume relationship as the price elasticity of demand. An example, a continuation of the one introduced in the previous section, will illustrate the method.

Illustrative Example: Maricopa Enterprises Ltd. (II)

After reviewing the latest profitability statements for the TimerX brand, Maricopa Enterprises' management has decided to initiate some price changes to improve the bottom line. An informal pricing committee consisting of the president and the vice presidents for marketing & sales, and finance, wants to raise prices by up to 10% on each model. The committee is convinced that while a 10% price increase will cause a considerable drop in the number of units sold, the planned changes will still be profitable. These sales volume reductions are estimated to be 50%, 20%, and 10% for models TimerX-E, TimerX-S, and TimerX-P, respectively.

The assumed percentage drops in the number of units sold reflect management's belief that a price increase in the economy model will most heavily impact sales of that model because the competing Pop-a-Pill is already priced somewhat lower than the TimerX-E and buyers of both products are extremely price-sensitive. In stark contrast, the premier model is not expected to suffer significant sales volume losses because its buyers are more concerned about performance than the price they have to pay.

For illustrative purposes, we shall compute the contribution impact for just two incremental price increases, i.e., 5% and 10%. In actual practice, more and smaller price increments would be chosen for each model and not only price increases but also price reductions in order to locate the optimal price. As may be noted from the table, any incremental price increase is presumed to automatically lead to a corresponding sales volume reduction. That is in conformance with the law of demand stated in Section 6.2 of the following chapter. In the case of price cuts, an incremental price reduction would result in a proportional sales volume increase in line with that same law. The results of the analysis are given in Table 5-2.

Reviewing Table 5-2, the following can be concluded. For the economy model TimerX-E, a price increase of either 5% or 10% would be inadvisable because either would lead to substantial reductions in contribution and profits. One can only surmise that for this model a price reduction rather than an increase would be called for. For the standard model TimerX-S only a 5% price increase would add to contribution but only marginally, i.e., $1,500 or 1.2%. This could mean that we are close to or at the optimal price point already. The premier model TimerX-P, on the other hand, would add about 5% to contribution as a result of a 10% price increase. In fact, price increases beyond that price point are likely to increase contribution dollars even more. This all assumes, of course, that the estimated price-volume relationships at the present operating point (POP), prior to any price changes, are reasonably correct.

5.4 Contribution Log Pricing

One of the early proponents of contribution pricing, the management consultant and pricing expert Spencer Tucker, described the use of a cumulative *contribution log* to track incoming orders and the contribution dollars generated by each sale during a specific time period.[3] Specifically, for a chosen time period such as a month, for each sale the sales dollars would be recorded together with the total contribution from that sale plus the cumulative total contribution. By comparing the cumulative total contributions with the prorated overhead costs for the period, management could continuously determine how close it was to covering overhead costs and earning a profit during the period.

While Tucker did not specifically suggest it, such a contribution log could clearly be used as a pricing tool especially in job shop operations in which products are manufactured to fill specific orders. Thus, requests for quotations arriving early in the period could be priced low in order to fill manufacturing capacity and earn some contribution, however small. As more sales were made and the accumulated contribution dollars approached the prorated overhead costs for the period, prices and margins could be progressively raised as the danger of not having enough contribution dollars to cover overhead costs was waning.

Parenthetically, had such an approach be used at the Delta Star Electric Division discussed in Chapter 2, it might have saved that company from ruin provided, of course, it had been possible to persuade the company's upper management to give up its rigid cost-plus pricing method in favor of a more flexible one.

5.5 Establishing Price Limits

What should the lowest price be at which a product is offered for sale? In other words, what should be the *price floor*? Tucker makes the convincing argument that it should be the product's *out-of-pocket (oop)* cost.[4] These costs, according to Tucker, consist of direct labor, direct materials, and direct overhead cost, whether at the manufacturing or non-manufacturing level. Oop costs are specifically incurred for the particular order and/or sale and would not be incurred otherwise. We have previously called these the product's unit variable cost VC. Thus, in *Pricing for Profit* we shall define the price floor as:

$$P_F = VC \qquad \text{Eq. (5.2)}$$

In periods of business downturns, Tucker argues, selling at oop prices would allow a manufacturer to keep the doors open and retain a skeleton force of highly skilled labor until business improved. However, he also warns of the danger of selling at oop costs too often and too long since a business cannot survive if it does not find a way to eventually cover its overhead costs. Therefore, Equation (5.2) may be called the product's *short-term* price floor whereas the *long-term* price floor is the product's total unit cost (incremental plus fixed) which is neither easy to determine nor very useful for pricing purposes. This discussion leads us to a pricing rule of thumb:

Pricing Rule of Thumb

Under normal circumstances, no product or service should be sold below its average unit variable cost because no contribution to overhead and profit can be earned below this cost and price.

With the lower limit of a product's price thus established, what should be the upper limit? Should it simply be whatever the market will bear as some pricing experts have proposed? A better answer would be the price that either maximizes sales revenue or total contribution and profits depending on the marketing goal for the product. Any price points other than these optimal ones would lead to less than satisfactory results, i. e., sales revenues and total contributions and profits that are not at the maximum levels achievable under the prevailing price-volume conditions for the product. For the TimerX brand previously discussed, for example, one can distinguish among four price points—the price at the present operating point (POP), the price floor and the optimal prices for either sales revenue or profit maximization. These are:

	TimerX-E	TimerX-S	TimerX-P
P_0	$60.00	$100.00	$200.00
P_F	45.00	60.00	80.00
[P]	36.00	75.00	200.00
P*	58.50	105.00	240.00

where, P_0 = Sell price before a price change
        P_F = Price floor
        [P] = Sell price for maximum sales revenue
        P* = Sell price for maximum total contribution

Interestingly, for the economy model the optimal price for revenue maximization lies below the price floor. This is a good illustration for the often surprising realization of many managers, namely, that striving for maximum revenue and market share can be, and often is, fatal to the bottom line. Also, it may be noted, the price of the premium model is already optimal for sales revenue maximization. How these optimal prices were determined can be found in Chapters 13 and 14 of *Pricing for Profit* where price optimization for sales revenue and profit maximization, respectively, are covered.

Notes

1. Michael and Gene Morris, *Market Oriented Pricing*, 93.
2. Kent Monroe, *Pricing*, 160.
3. Spencer Tucker, *Pricing for Higher Profit*, 137-139.
4. Spencer Tucker, supra at 90-91.

Table 5-1 (a)

Contribution Statement for TimerX Brand by Product Model

Item	Product Model			Totals
	TimerX-E	TimerX-S	TimerX-P	
Sell price ($)	60.00	100.00	200.00	—
Unit variable cost ($)	45.00	60.00	80.00	—
Unit contribution margin ($)	15.00	40.00	120.00	—
Unit contribution margin (%)	25.0	40.0	60.0	—
Sales volume (units)	1,000	3,000	500	4,500
Sales revenue ($)	60,000	300,000	100,000	460,000
Total variable cost ($)	45,000	180,000	40,000	265,000
Total contribution ($)	15,000	120,000	60,000	195,000
Total contribution (%)	25.0	40.0	60.0	42.4
Direct fixed cost ($)	0	0	10,000	10,000
Net contribution ($)	15,000	120,000	50,000	185,000
Net contribution (%)	25.0	40.0	50.0	40.2
Common fixed cost ($)	—	—	—	100,000
Pretax profit ($)	—	—	—	85,000

Table 5-1 (b)
Contribution Statement for TimerX Brand by Sales Territory

Item	Sales Territory			Totals
	Atlantic	Central	Pacific	
Sales revenue ($)	92,000	138,000	230,000	460,000
TimerX-E	12,000	18,000	30,000	60,000
TimerX-S	60,000	90,000	150,000	300,000
TimerX-P	20,000	30,000	50,000	100,000
Total variable cost ($)	53,000	79,500	132,500	265,000
Total contribution ($)	39,000	58,500	97,500	195,000
Total contribution (%)	42.4	42.4	42.4	42.4
Direct fixed cost ($)	10,000	11,500	15,000	36,500
Salaries, commissions	4,000	5,000	6,000	15,000
Transportation	2,000	2,000	3,000	7,000
Rent	2,000	2,500	3,000	7,500
Other	2,000	2,000	3,000	7,000
Net contribution ($)	29,000	47,000	82,500	158,500
Net contribution (%)	31.5	34.1	35.9	34.5
Common fixed cost ($)	—	—	—	73,500
Pretax profit ($)	—	—	—	85,000

Table 5-2
Price Change Analysis for TimerX Brand

Model	TimerX-E		TimerX-S		TimerX-P	
Present sell price ($)	60.00	60.00	100.00	100.00	200.00	200.00
Price change (%)	5.00	10.0	5.0	10.0	5.0	10.0
New sell price ($)	63.00	66.00	105.00	110.00	210.00	220.00
Unit variable cost ($)	45.00	45.00	60.00	60.00	80.00	80.00
Unit contribution margin ($)	18.00	21.00	45.00	50.00	130.00	140.00
Present sales volume (units)	1000	1,000	3,000	3,000	500	500
Change in sales volume (%)	(25.0)	(50.0)	(10.0)	(20.0)	(5.0)	(10.0)
New sales volume (units)	750	500	2,700	2,400	475	450
Sales revenue ($)	47,250	33,000	283,500	264,000	99,750	99,000
Total variable cost ($)	33,750	22,500	162,000	144,000	38,000	36,000
Total contribution ($)	13,500	10,500	121,500	120,000	61,750	63,000
Present total contribution ($)	15,000	15,000	120,000	120,000	60,000	60,000
Change in contribution ($)	(1,500)	(4,500)	1,500	0	1,750	3,000
Change in contribution (%)	(10.0)	(30.0)	1.2	0.0	2.9	5.0

CHAPTER

6

Market Demand

Price-volume sensitivity or elasticity of demand is a valuable, strategic tool of pricing. Astute managers are aware of the demand elasticities of their various products and take advantage of this factor in their pricing policies.[1]

The focus of modern, market oriented pricing is on the buyer and specifically on his or her value perceptions of certain products and services and relative ability and willingness to pay for these. The present chapter introduces two very important concepts that are invaluable to the study of pricing, namely, the law of demand and the price elasticity of demand. Both originated with British neoclassical economist Alfred Marshall, one of the founders of that science, whose groundbreaking work *Principles of Economics* was first published in 1890 and remains relevant to this day.

The major part of this chapter will be devoted to the second of these concepts, namely, the price elasticity of demand (P.E.D.) since it is the real key to profitable pricing. In fact, it is doubtful that a marketing professional can effectively price a product or service without both a good understanding of its meaning and use and knowing something about the specific price sensitivities of the firm's products and services. This is not to say that the P.E.D. has found universal favor with marketers despite its provenance. Some pricing books, perhaps written for a less discerning audience, have either ignored or scoffed at the critical importance of this metric to marketers and pricers.[2] The chapter also includes information on how this key metric may be estimated either through formal research or from information within the firm. The chapter concludes with a discussion of another important metric known as the price cross elasticity of demand.

6.1 Marketing Terms

To ensure author and reader are on the same page, it might be useful to review some common marketing concepts and terms. An aggregate of buyers for a given product or service is described as a *market* for that product or service as opposed to an *industry* which is an aggregate of suppliers of such products or services. Thus one speaks of the automobile industry, the computer industry, or the entertainment industry. By *market demand* one means the number of units of a specific product sold or expected to be sold in a given time period.

Demand may be primary or selective. *Primary demand* is for a *product class* like automobiles while *selective demand* would be for a specific make or model of automobile. Primary demand must exist before selective demand can occur. For example, when a new product class like the cell phone first came on the market, the innovator's first task was to generate primary demand for it before shifting to selective demand for its particular brand of cell phones once competing models were being offered. In *Pricing for Profit*, we are mainly concerned with selective demand.

Marketers have long ago stopped speaking of markets and turned their attention to specific segments of an overall market. Market segmentation means partitioning a market into smaller submarkets or *market segments* composed of buyers with similar characteristics, product wants and needs, and the means and willingness to pay for these. Firms may choose one or more of these market segments to serve which become *target markets* for their marketing efforts. These efforts may then be focused on these segments with customized sets of marketing strategy variables—product, price, advertising and promotion, and distribution.

The focus in this book is, of course, on just one of these strategy variables, namely, the price charged for a specific product or service. Price can have many meanings—it could be the list price, the price charged by a distributor, a fully discounted price paid by the end-user, or some other price in the distribution chain. When a product's contribution margin (the difference between its price and direct variable cost) is determined, the price is the actual dollar amount received by the firm producing and marketing the product. If this price is overstated then, likewise, the product's profitability is overstated. Likewise, when we talk about the demand curve and the price elasticity of demand, the price is the actual, final price paid by the customer meaning the price he or she found acceptable for payment in exchange for the goods or services received. Neither case directly involves the price which the firm chose to list and advertise as the purchase price.

6.2 The Law of Demand

The *law of demand* states that, other things being equal (ceteris paribus), quantity demanded varies inversely with price or, stated differently, customers will buy more product at a lower than at a higher price.[3] Clearly, this economic principle only expresses what common sense and experience would dictate but it does have major practical and theoretical implications. A tabulation of sell price versus the number of units purchased at each price over a given time period is known as a *demand schedule*. A graphical representation of the law of demand is the *demand curve* which is illustrated in Figure 6-1. Curve DD represents the typical downward-sloping demand curve for some fictional product.

As may be noted, quantity appears on the horizontal and price on the vertical axis. This is the traditional Marshallian representation of the demand curve and is the reverse of a conventional curve which places the independent variable (price) on the horizontal x-axis and the dependent variable (quantity) on the vertical y-axis. Using a conventional representation, this curve is sometimes known as the *price response curve* (PRC). The curve's shape is the same in either case. We shall make use of both types of curves in *Pricing for Profit*.

While the demand curve is useful as a visual representation of the law of demand, it is of little practical use in pricing for at least two reasons. First, a marketer is not likely to know what the demand curves for his or her diverse products look like. All that is really known is the present price-volume operating point (P_0, Q_0) on Figure 6.1. All other points on the demand curve are unknown . If they were known, the marketer would be only one step away of being able to compute the optimal prices that would maximize sales revenue or profits.

Figure 6-1
Hypothetical and Linear Demand Curves

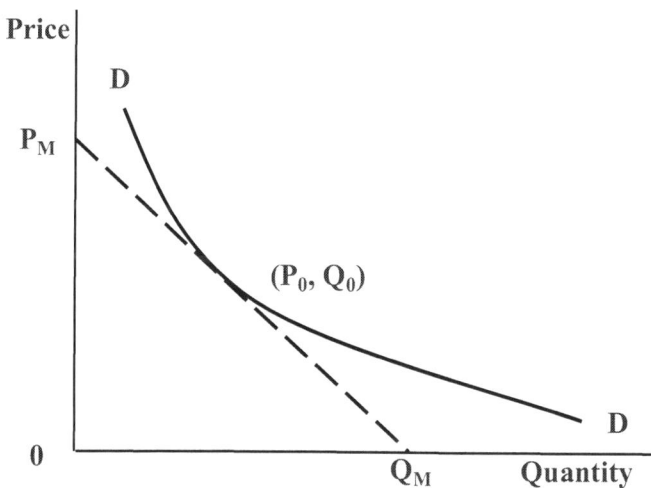

The second fundamental difficulty with the demand curve is that its location and shape is subject to frequent change due to factors both within and outside the firm. A point on the demand curve simply means that these are the number of units being sold during a given time period (month, quarter etc.) at this particular price. Movement along the present demand curve can occur only under ceteris paribus conditions, i.e., in the absence of any other major changes in another marketing strategy variable besides the product's price.

Changes that would significantly alter the shape of a product's demand curve include major product modifications, quality problems, deletions or additions to the line, raising or lowering the advertising budget, and any availability or delivery problems. Also impacting the product's demand curve would be major changes in a directly competing product such as in its purchase price or any other marketing strategy variable or product lineup of a competitor. For these reasons, the demand curve would be an unreliable guide for pricing purposes.

Below the demand curve in Figure 6-1 appears a straight-line approximation to this curve, known as a *linear demand curve*, which is drawn tangent (having the same slope) to the demand curve at the present price-volume operating point (P_0, Q_0). This curve, unlike the hypothetical demand curve, is very useful for both pricing purposes and establishing rules and guidelines of a general nature. The linear demand curve intersects the price axis at P_M, the maximum price a customer is willing to pay for the product. This parameter is sometimes known as the *reservation price*. The curve intersects the horizontal axis at Q_M, the maximum number of units of the product customers are willing to purchase during a given time period.

Is the law of demand always valid? The answer is "not always but nearly always." People buy more of a product if they can get it for less except in the case of certain luxury goods for which the high prices themselves are the source of their attraction. For some well-heeled buyers these satisfy a need to possess something so exclusive that only they and a few others can afford them. Thus, there have been instances where the prices of high-end products such as certain alcoholic beverages, perfumes, and clothing labels were reduced to stimulate demand when the opposite occurred, i.e., the quantities sold actually declined as their prices were lowered.

6.3 The Price Elasticity of Demand

In the absence of a useable demand curve, a product's price sensitivity at the present price-volume operating point (P_0, Q_0) can serve as a useful substitute for pricing purposes. Knowing the price elasticity of demand (P.E.D.), it can tell the marketer what sales volume changes to expect from a contemplated price change and predict its impact on sales revenue and profits. This P.E.D. too is not a fixed quantity and continuously subject to change over time for the same reasons as given for the demand curve.

6.3.1 The P.E.D. Formulas

A product's price elasticity of demand is defined as the relative responsiveness of quantity demanded to a change in price. If one lets the coefficient of price elasticity be denoted by the lowercase Greek epsilon (ϵ), the P.E.D. can be expressed as:

$$\epsilon = \frac{\text{Percentage change in quantity demanded}}{\text{Percentage change in price}} \qquad \text{Eq. (6.1)}$$

For small movements in price and volume, the *point price elasticity of demand*, or simply the *price elasticity of demand*, is defined as:[4]

$$\epsilon = -\frac{Q_1 - Q_0}{Q} \div \frac{P_1 - P_0}{P} \qquad \text{Eq. (6.2)}$$

where, P_0, P_1 = Price before and after a change, respectively
Q_0, Q_1 = Quantity before and after a price change, respectively

Letting the uppercase Greek delta (Δ) denote "the change in," this equation may be rewritten as:

$$\epsilon = -\frac{\Delta Q}{\Delta P} \times \frac{P}{Q} \qquad \text{Eq. (6.3)}$$

If the changes are sufficiently small (incremental), P and Q may be the original or changed prices and quantities, respectively, as the price elasticity of demand (P.E.D.) will be the same. If the changes are larger, the convention is to use the *lesser* of the two prices and quantities in computing the P.E.D..

The reader may wonder why the above two formulas are preceded by a negative sign. This is a convention introduced by Alfred Marshall. Since, by the law of demand, price and quantity vary inversely, the negative sign will ensure that the coefficient of price elasticity is always a *positive* number. We shall follow this convention throughout this book since it is much easier to relate to and manipulate positive numbers than negative ones. All one needs to remember is that a price *reduction* will *increase* the number of units sold and a price *increase* will *reduce* the quantity sold. In short, in *Pricing for Profit*, the P.E.D. will always be considered to be a *positive* number.

While the above formulas are useful for computing the P.E.D. given a hypothetical or linear demand curve, they are cumbersome to work with and, for the marketer, present no clear way to translate his or her knowledge of the price sensitivity of a product into an estimate of its P.E.D.. To correct this deficiency, throughout *Pricing for Profit* the following simplified notation for the P.E.D., based on Equation (6.1), will be employed:

$$\epsilon = - \frac{\blacktriangle Q}{\blacktriangle P} \qquad \text{Eq. (6.4)}$$

where, $\blacktriangle P$ = Percentage price change
   $\blacktriangle Q$ = Percentage quantity change

Using Equation (6.4), a marketer can estimate a product's price elasticity coefficient ϵ at the present price-volume operating point (P_0, Q_0) provided he or she has a good feel for the product's price sensitivity at that point. One way this coefficient can be determined is by the marketer, or more knowledgeable individuals within the firm, answering a simple question, namely, "What percentage sales volume change could one expect with a 10% price change?" If, for example, a 10% price reduction would increase sales volume by 25%, the product's P.E.D. would be 25% ÷ 10% or 2.5. Similarly, if a 10% price increase would cause sales volume to decline by 5%, the product's P.E.D. would be 5% ÷ 10% or 0.5. As may be noted, any negative signs may be ignored since, by definition, the P.E.D. will automatically be a positive number.

6.3.2 Sales Revenue and the P.E.D.

The size of the elasticity coefficient establishes whether demand is elastic or inelastic at the (P_0, Q_0) point. This lets the marketer know where on the product's linear demand curve this price-volume point is located which, in turn, gives him or her a good indication whether the sell price should be raised or lowered to improve sales revenue. The demand classification rule is:

If $\in$ is	Demand is
> 1.0	*elastic*
= 1.0	*unitary elastic*
< 1.0	*inelastic*

In addition to these three demand conditions, one can identify two special cases. Thus, when $\in = 0$, demand is said to be *perfectly inelastic* and when $\in = \infty$, demand is described as *perfectly elastic*.

If demand for the product is *inelastic* at the present price-volume operating point (P_0, Q_0), a small price change will produce a proportionally smaller change in sales volume whereas if it is *elastic*, the proportional sales volume change will be larger than the price change. At *unitary elasticity*, the change in sales volume will be in direct proportion to the price change. It can be shown that a product's demand elasticity at the present price-volume operating point is directly related to its sales revenue so that one can predict the direction of necessary price changes for raising sales revenue. [5]

Pricing Rule of Thumb

For sales revenue improvements, the following price changes are required:

If demand is	Price should be
Elastic ($\in > 1.0$)	*lowered*
Unitary elastic ($\in = 1.0$)	*held*
Inelastic ($\in < 1.0$)	*raised*

Clearly, the condition for sales revenue maximization is a sell price at which the coefficient of price elasticity of demand E equals 1.0. In the following section, this price-volume point will be shown to lie at the midpoint of the product's linear demand curve.

6.3.3 The Demand Curve and the P.E.D.

A product's linear demand curve is defined by the product's present price-volume operating point (P_0, Q_0) and the price elasticity of demand at that point. At least two common misconceptions about this curve exist and require clarification. The first is that the P.E.D., i.e., the coefficient of price elasticity, may be obtained by computing the slope of the linear demand line. That is not the case because the coefficient E is the *dimensionless* ratio of two *percentages* (quantity and price) and not simply the ratio of quantity and price. The latter ratio would not make E dimensionless.

The second misconception is that the demand curve for a specific product or service, and specifically the linear demand curve, is either elastic or inelastic. That is not correct either. It is, however, correct to speak of a demand curve as being more elastic or inelastic than another similar curve. For example, if a linear demand curve tends toward the horizontal one may correctly term demand for the product it represents to be elastic and, if this curve appears more vertical, one may speak of demand for this product to be inelastic. The typical demand curve is neither elastic nor inelastic. In fact, it is both. In the upper region of a linear demand curve, where the price is high and demand is low, demand is elastic. At the lower end, in the region of low prices and high demand, demand for the product is inelastic.

To illustrate this point, Figure 6-2 shows a typical linear demand curve on which five values of coefficient of price elasticity, from 0.5 to 5.0, have been posted. Parenthetically, these values may easily be determined by inspection.[6] As may be noted, the coefficient of price elasticity varies all along the demand curve with price elasticities increasing as one moves toward the left and higher price points and lower sales volumes. The dividing point is found at unitary price elasticity ($\mathsf{E} = 1.0$) where demand changes from inelastic to elastic. In other words, demand is elastic to the left and inelastic to the right of the price at which the P.E.D. equals one.

In the previous section it was noted that the maximum sales revenue is achieved at the price at which the P.E.D. is exactly 1.0.

Figure 6-2
Price Elasticities Along Linear Demand Curve

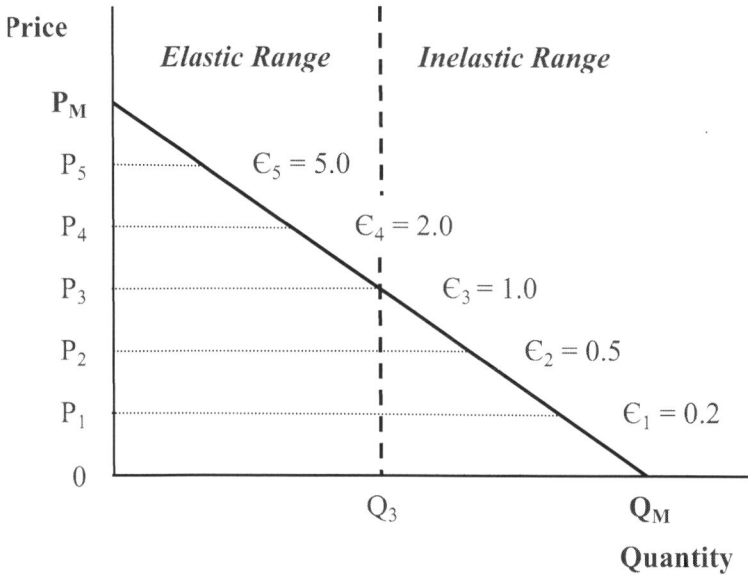

Figure 6-2 clearly shows why this is the case. Thus, if one selects any price on the y-axis and draws a line horizontally to the demand curve and from there draws a vertical line to the x-axis and multiplies the quantity found there by the selected price one obtains the sales revenue for that price and quantity. As may be noted, this product represents a rectangle within the triangle of the demand curve and the two axes. The largest possible rectangle and thus the maximum sales revenue is obtained where the P.E.D. is 1.0. In the diagram this maximum sales revenue is represented by the rectangle $P_3 \times Q_3$. All other rectangles that may be drawn within this space are smaller yielding smaller sales revenues.

An interesting point is that the triangular area under the linear demand curve is the sales revenue potential for this product, i.e., $R_P = \frac{1}{2} (P_M \times Q_M)$. The rectangle $P_3 \times Q_3$ mentioned above represents exactly one half of this potential sales revenue. The small triangles above and to the right of this rectangle represent the other half of R_P.

6.4 Price Sensitivity Estimation

Considering its importance to pricing, both in segmenting markets and in setting prices, it is perhaps not surprising that firms are much interested in the price sensitivities of their various products and services and consequently spend considerable amounts of effort, time, and money obtaining estimates. The marketing literature dealing with this topic is extensive and pricing books sometimes devote an entire chapter to price sensitivity analysis.[7] Marketing research is beyond the scope of *Pricing for Profit* and hence this section is confined to an overview of the diverse techniques and tests that have been devised. It ends with some suggestions on estimating price sensitivities using information available within the firm

6.4.1 Research Techniques

Several techniques have been devised for gauging the price sensitivities of potential buyers in terms of either actual purchases or intentions to purchase certain products. Pertinent information may be collected from the analysis of sales data, customer surveys, and sensitivity experiments.

An economical way of obtaining price sensitivity information is found in the analysis of historical sales data. Where a firm is linked to its retailers as part of an inventory management system, scanner data will allow tracking of sales volume changes in response to price changes that is especially timely and useful. Care must be taken that sales changes are truly reflective of the price changes and not some other variable. For this, the data are usually subjected to some statistical analysis.

Where a product is still in the planning stage, the measurement of product preferences and purchase intentions has proved useful. In the so-called *price response survey*, respondents in the target market are asked price related questions designed to elicit information on the willingness or probability of a purchase at various price points. From this data, a downward sloping curve may be constructed showing purchase probability on the vertical and price on the horizontal axis. The disadvantage of this technique is that with its focus on the purchase price, respondents may become unrealistically price conscious which could lead to distorted results.

In a controlled pricing experiment, the sell price (independent variable) is changed and its effect on the sales volume (dependent variable) is measured while all other variables that might influence the dependant variable are held constant. In a retail environment, such experiments may be conducted in stores or in a laboratory facility that closely duplicates the actual buying experience. In-store experiments are conducted without the buyers' knowledge and usually include a control store where prices are not changed so that possible extraneous non-price influences can be taken into account. A laboratory purchase experiment, on the other hand, has the advantage that the researcher can select the participants and control all variables that could impinge on the purchase decision.

Conjoint analysis, also known as *trade-off analysis* or *conjoint measurement*, is a relatively new and powerful experimental technique for new product development and pricing.[8] The heart of the technique is a sequential paired comparison in which respondents are asked to state their preferences between two product profiles with different attributes and attribute levels. The technique allows the marketer to assign a monetary value to any of a number of specific attributes and levels and rank product profiles to determine the one with the highest total value.

For a study on automobiles, for example, an attribute might be the brand name, engine horsepower, fuel consumption, environmental performance, or purchase price while the corresponding levels might be a number of actual makes and models of automobiles, typical horsepower ratings, various fuel consumptions in miles per gallon, contemplated purchase prices etc. Special conjoint software is required and expert guidance recommended in conducting the experiment and evaluating the data.

6.4.2 Internet Data

Firms and individuals that sell on the Internet can count on a veritable bonanza of quality price sensitivity information to guide their pricing decisions. The essence of P.E.D. determination for a product or service is, of course, finding the ratio of the percentage change in sales volume in response to a percentage change in price at the present price-volume operating point. The Internet seems tailor-made for the collection of this type of marketing data because prices can be changed almost continuously and the effects on sales volume found in real time which is something not possible any other way.[9] The Internet is also very cost-effective considering the huge outlays involved in traditional price-sensitivity research. In addition, some firms have successfully used the Internet to price-segment their market in order to serve these smaller segments more efficiently and profitably.

6.4.3 Internal Company Data

Other than the Internet, there is perhaps no better place for obtaining information on a product's P.E.D. than within the firm and specifically from the sales force, distributors and other distribution channel members, and loyal customers. Customer purchasing agents are known for telling salespeople something like this: "We like your product but you are simply not competitive. If you could drop your price by 5%, we would be willing to buy another x units per month from you." Sometimes a salesperson may tell his or her sales manager: "The people at Alpha Company really like our product and the best part is that we have no competition." Both scenarios reveal much about the relative price sensitivities for a company product at these two firms and offer clues about whether prices should be maintained at present levels or need to be adjusted to improve sales revenue or profits.

To obtain relevant P.E.D. information the pricer should question knowledgeable people within the firm and then apply some elementary statistics to this raw data to obtain a number that represents the best estimate available. Sales personnel will rarely be able to answer a direct question about the size of the P.E.D. which means that the pricer must frame the question so that this ratio may be computed from the responses. Two typical questions might be:

i) "If we were to lower our price for Product X by 10% today, how many more units could we expect to sell next month over this month? or,

ii) "If we were to raise our price for Product X by 10% today, how many fewer units could we expect to sell next month from this month?

To evaluate these responses, two simple statistical techniques, the *weighted average* and the *expected value*, may be used. If one were to tally the sales force, for example, it is likely that the sales manager and more experienced salespersons would be more knowledgeable than the others. Consequently, their assessment should carry more weight. Thus, if one lets ε_a, ε_b,......ε_n be the price elasticity coefficients computed from the responses of the individual sales persons and w_a, w_b,......w_n be the respective weights assigned to each, the *weighted average* would be:

$$\varepsilon = \frac{\varepsilon_a \times w_a + \varepsilon_b \times w_b + ... \varepsilon_n \times w_n}{w_a + w_b + ... w_n} \qquad \text{Eq. (6.5)}$$

An alternative way would be to select the most knowledgeable individual, presumable the sales manager, and let him or her assign probabilities P to estimates of the product's P.E.D.. The *expected value* would then be:

$$\varepsilon = \varepsilon_1 \times P_1 + \varepsilon_2 \times P_2 + ... \varepsilon_n \times P_n \qquad \text{Eq. (6.6)}$$

where, $P_1 + P_2 + ...P_n = 1.0$.

Example

Suppose Alpha Company's sales manger has been asked to estimate the P.E.D. of Product X at the present price-volume operating point (P_0, Q_0). Besides the sales manager, the sales force consists of two experienced salespeople, and two people in training.

The sales manager estimates the P.E.D to be 1.6, the two salespeople 1.3 and 1.6, and the two trainees 2.0 and 0.9, respectively. Furthermore, suppose their respective P.E.D. estimates have been assigned weights of 3.0 (sales manager), 2.0 (salespeople) , and 1.0 (trainees). Then, by Equation (6.5), one obtains:

$$\epsilon = \frac{1.6 \times 3.0 + 1.3 \times 2.0 + 1.6 \times 2.0 + 2.0 \times 1.0 + 0.9 \times 1.0}{3.0 \times 1 + 2.0 \times 2 + 1.0 \times 2}$$

$$\epsilon = 13.5 / 9.0 = 1.50$$

Thus, according to the company's sales force, Product X's present P.E.D. is 1.50 which means that demand for the product is somewhat elastic. A 5% price reduction, for example, would increase sales volume by 5% × 1.5 or 7.5%.

Using the sales manager's estimates only and the corresponding probabilities he or she assigned to each (10%, 20%, or 60%), one obtains by Equation (6.6):

ϵ	P	$\epsilon \times P$
1.4	0.1	0.14
1.5	0.2	0.30
1.6	0.6	0.96
1.7	0.1	0.17
	1.0	1.57

Thus, the sales manager's best estimate of Product X's price elasticity is slightly higher than that of the sales force as a whole.

6.5 The Price Cross-Elasticity of Demand

Another elasticity metric of interest to marketers is the so-called *price cross-elasticity of demand*. While the P.E.D. is a measure of the percentage sales volume change as a result of a percentage price change in the same product, the price cross-elasticity of demand (C.E.D.) relates the percentage price change in one product to the percentage sales volume change in another.

Thus, if a price reduction in one product causes a sales volume increase in another, the two products are considered *complements*. If a price reduction in one results in a sales volume decline in another, the two products are *substitutes*. The two products can belong to the same firm or one to one firm and the other to a competitor. Typical complementary products are razors and razor blades while pork and beef on a shopper's grocery list may be substitutes.

Analogous to Equation (6.3) for the P.E.D., the C.E.D. is defined as:[10]

$$\epsilon_X = \frac{\Delta Q_B}{\Delta P_A} \times \frac{P_A}{Q_B} \qquad \text{Eq. (6.7)}$$

where P_A is the price of product A and Q_B the demand for product B while Δ stands for "the change in."

One can determine whether two products complement each other or are substitutes by this classification rule:

If ϵ_X is   **The products are**

positive   *substitutes*
negative   *complements*

This is important for the marketer to know because if a product's price is lowered to increase demand, for example, it is not desirable to have it take away sales from another product unless, of course, the product is a competitor's.

Example

Armatec Company is a manufacturer of "smart guns" that allow safe storage of handguns at home by incorporating a locking mechanism that may only be released by entering a PIN code on a radio controlled device worn on the owner's wrist. Until recently, Pistol Model AP-1 sold for $100 with weekly sales of 1,000 units while the wrist unit Model RC-7 was available separately.

Clearly, models AP-1 and RC-7 are complementary products and a price change in the AP-1 would be followed by a sales volume change in both the AP-1 and RC-7, namely, upward in the case of a price reduction and downward for a price increase. Therefore, the ratio (ΔQ_B / ΔP_A) in Equation (6.7) will always be negative and $\epsilon_X < 0$. We therefore do not need to use Equation (6.7) to establish that the two models are complements.

The Armatec line also includes the more expensive Model AP-2. When its price was recently cut from $150 to $130, weekly sales of the AP-1 soon dropped to 800 units. How are the two models related, i.e., are they complements or substitutes? Letting "A" represent the Model AP-2 and "B" the Model AP-1 in Equation (6.7) one obtains:

$$\epsilon_X = \frac{1,000 - 800}{\$150 - \$130} \times \frac{\$150}{1,000} = 1.5$$

Since $\epsilon_X > 0$, the two models are considered substitutes. Clearly, as a result of the price reduction in the Model AP-2, some customers were willing to switch from the Model AP-1 to the Model AP-2. This could mean that with the price reduction the two models are no longer sufficiently differentiated in terms of features, functions and price so that some Armatec customers now considered the premium-priced model a better value.

Notes

1. Spencer Tucker, *Pricing for Higher Profit*, 12.

2 Dr. Mark Stiving, for example, in his *Impact Pricing*, 37, states: "Because the phrase price elasticity is so often misused and confused, I rarely use it in conversations and will not use it again in this text." In *The 1% Windfall*, 16, Dr. Rafi Mohammed writes: "Chances are that you have heard the term *elasticity* used in pricing. And for that reason, it's an important term to understand even though it isn't an integral component of setting the most profitable price. Elasticity answers the question, 'If quantity is changed, what will happen to revenue?'...Elasticity only focuses on revenues, not profits. While it's nice to know how revenues will be affected by changing price, most of us are more interested in what will happen to profits as price changes. This metric is the focus of a profit maximizer analysis."

3. J. P. Gould and C. E. Ferguson, *Microeconomic Theory*, 90.

4. J. P. Gould and C. E. Ferguson, supra at 94.

5. This simple rule of thumb follows directly from the relationship between the P.E.D. and sales revenue given in most microeconomic texts. See, for example, J. P. Gould and C. E. Ferguson, supra at 111.

6. The coefficient of price elasticity at a particular price P_X on the linear demand curve is the ratio of the distance on the y (price)-axis between 0 and P_X to the distance between P_X and the reservation price P_M. For example, in Figure 6-2 the coefficient of price elasticity at price P_2 is $\varepsilon_2 = P_0P_2 \div P_2P_M = 2 \div 4 = 0.5$. See J. P. Gould and C. E. Ferguson, supra at 97-99.

7. See, for example, Thomas Nagle, John Hogan, and Joseph Zale, *The Strategy and Tactics of Pricing*, Chapter 12 on "Measurement of Price Sensitivity," and Robert Dolan and Hermann Simon, *Power Pricing*, Chapter 3 on "Price Response Estimation."

8. For more thorough treatments of conjoint analysis with industry examples using trade-off techniques see, for example, Thomas Nagle, John Hogan, and Joseph Zale, supra at 289-294, and Robert Dolan and Hermann Simon, supra at 54-69.

9. Walter Baker, Michael Marn, and Craig Zawada, "Price Smarter on the Net," *Harvard Business Review on Pricing*, 158-165.

10. J. P. Gould and C. E. Ferguson, supra at 67-68.

CHAPTER

7

Isoprofit Analysis

They [the managers] decided upon the profit-maximizing combination [of price and volume] by use of a curve which, for lack of a better term, the author has called an "equal profit curve."[1]

Most products on the market have been there for enough time for sales revenues, market shares, operating profits, and competition to have stabilized. However, while sell prices too have become settled, this does not mean that price has lost its significance as a marketing strategy variable. On the contrary, managers of mature products are constantly trying to improve results by price adjustments.

Before changing an established price, be it up or down, a marketer needs to know whether such a move will be profitable or not. As is well known, a pricing error can lead to huge losses even though the price adjustment may have been relatively minor. This chapter introduces what has become the primary analytical tool by which a marketer can evaluate the relative profitabilities of contemplated price change options. The relevant isoprofit formulas are developed and two sets of tables presented by which this determination can be made without much time or effort. Based on the isoprofit formulas and two sets of graphs, some general comments and a pricing rules of thumb are given to assist in making these decision. The chapter ends with an example worked out to demonstrate use of the technique.

The presumptive originator of the technique presented here called it *equal profit analysis* while in the pricing literature it has variously become known as *break-even sales analysis* or simply as *break-even analysis*.[2] In *Pricing for Profit* the term isoprofit analysis is used because it is the name this author gave to the technique when he first came across it in the monograph cited below and developed the required formulas and also to avoid confusion with traditional break-even analysis which was the subject of Chapter 4.

7.1 Background

While isoprofit, equal profit, or break-even sales analysis is now widely known and used, its origin is obscure but presumably lies with a 1960 monograph written by a University of Michigan economist named Wilford J. Eiteman who sought to reconcile economic theory with business practice in regard to pricing. Eiteman researched the price setting procedures at various manufacturing firms in different industries by conducting personal interviews and found that business managers had little knowledge of economic theory beyond elementary price-volume relationships, namely, the intuitive understanding that higher prices led to lower demand and vice versa. Specifically, he found no evidence that that these managers made use of the economist's profit maximizing principle that seeks to equate marginal revenue with marginal cost.

What Eiteman did find was that in their attempt to maximize profits, managers envisioned a *hypothetical demand curve* for their product from which they could infer the volume change necessary as a result of a price change that would leave profits after the change the same as before. He called this relationship an *equal profit curve* which is a graphical representation of all the solutions to the equation

$$\frac{\text{Profit} + \text{Overhead}}{\text{Volume of Output (in units)}} + \text{Average Variable Cost} = \text{Price}$$

when profit plus overhead is held constant and the volume of output is a variable.[3] Using such curves, he could infer whether particular price changes would increase or reduce profits. Eiteman's formula has not proved particularly useful for evaluating price change options but one now in common use appears in Section 7.3 below together with a simple derivation.

Example

Suppose Alpha Company's management wanted to see an isoprofit curve for one of their products with these parameters: Price $P_0 = \$10$, direct variable cost $VC_0 = \$5$, and sales volume $Q_0 = 100$ units. Using Equation (7.8) below, the equation for this curve is:

$$Q_1 = 500 / (P_1 - 5)$$

The desired isoprofit curve for this product is shown in Figure 7-1.

Figure 7-1
Typical Isoprofit Curve

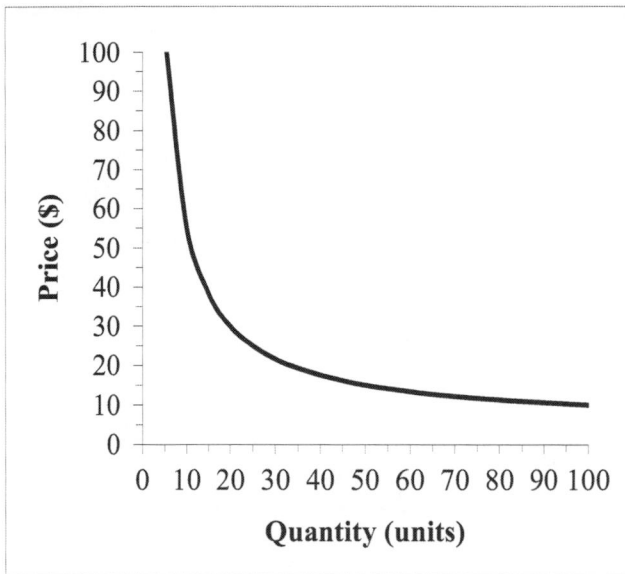

Not surprisingly, the shape of this curve is very similar to the hypothetical demand curve shown in the previous chapter, Figure 6-1.

As may easily be verified, all price-quantity points on this curve yield the same total contribution, namely, $500.

7.2 The Rationale

The concept of the demand curve and the law of demand was taken up in the previous chapter. Briefly, the law of demand simply says that more units of a product will be sold at a lower price than at a higher one. When a price is reduced, the number of units sold typically increases while an increase in the sell price will cause a drop in demand. Either a cut in the sell price or a price rise will thus change the sales volume in the opposite direction leading to a change in the total contribution level and profit as well. Isoprofit analysis is designed to answer two questions:

i) In the case of a contemplated *price reduction*:

What is the *minimum required sales volume increase* that will leave total contribution and profit unchanged.

ii) In the case of a contemplated *price increase*:

What is the *maximum allowable sales volume reduction* that will leave total contribution and profit unchanged.

This begs the question why a marketer would be interested to know what kind of price change would leave total contribution and profit the same as before the change. The answer is that isoprofit analysis sets the boundaries on profitable sales volume changes. Thus, in the case of a price reduction, the marketer can expect total contribution and profits to rise as long as the sales volume increase is larger than the minimum required. In the case of a price increase, the marketer can expect a total contribution and profit increase if the sales volume reduction is less than the maximum allowable. While the technique does not tell him or her by how much the sell price should be changed or what the contribution gain will be, it does tell the pricer the range of price changes which will be favorable and what changes must be avoided.

In most cases, isoprofit analysis is better suited to evaluating price change options than contribution analysis (Chapter 5) because instead of taking the proposed price change and "running it up the flagpole" (an expression used by engineering students) to arrive at an answer on profitability, the marketer is presented with the facts on which he or she can make an informed judgment whether the allowable or required sales volume changes can be expected to materialize. If not, the price change should not be implemented. The technique has another significant advantage in that the values on allowable and required sales volume changes as a function of price changes can be tabulated so that the marketer can simply look up the numbers and save considerable computation time and effort.

7.3 The Isoprofit Formulas

In developing the isoprofit formulas we proceed in the usual manner. In Chapter 3, Equation (3.8), we   defined the total contribution K as the product of the unit contribution margin $(P - VC)$ and the sales volume Q:

$$K = (P - VC) Q \qquad \text{Eq. (7.1)}$$

If one lets the subscripts 0 and 1 stand for a parameter before and after a price change, respectively, one obtains:

$$K_0 = (P_0 - VC_0) Q_0 \qquad \text{Eq. (7.2)}$$
$$K_1 = (P_1 - VC_1) Q_1 \qquad \text{Eq. (7.3)}$$

The change in total contribution as a result of a price change is then:

$$\Delta K = K_1 - K_0 \qquad \text{Eq. (7.4)}$$

But since, for isoprofit, the total contribution change $\Delta K = 0$:

$$K_1 = K_0 \qquad \text{Eq. (7.5)}$$

Combining Eq. (7.2), Eq. (7.3), and Eq. (7.5) and solving for the new sales volume, one obtains the basic isoprofit formulas:

$$Q_1 = Q_0 \times \frac{P_0 - VC_0}{P_1 - VC_1} \qquad \text{Eq. (7.6)}$$

and

$$Q_1 = Q_0 \times \frac{CM_0\ (\$)}{CM_1\ (\$)} \qquad \text{Eq. (7.7)}$$

In words, the isoprofit break-even sales volume after a price change is the product of the sales volume before the price change and the ratio of the original and new unit contribution margins.

In the special case where the direct variable cost VC does not change as a result of price and sales volume changes, Equation (7.6) becomes:

$$Q_1 = Q_0 \times \frac{P_0 - VC_0}{P_1 - VC_0} \qquad \text{Eq. (7.8)}$$

In order to put Equation (7.8) into a form suitable for tabulation, we need the sales volume change expressed as a percentage. Noting that

$$\blacktriangle Q = \frac{Q_1 - Q_0}{Q_0} = \frac{Q_1}{Q_0} - 1$$

and $\qquad \Delta P = P_1 - P_0$

and $\qquad VC_0 = P_0 - CM_0\,(\$)$

Equation (7.8) can be rewritten as:

$$\blacktriangle Q = -\frac{\Delta P}{\Delta P + CM_0\,(\$)} \qquad \text{Eq. (7.9)}$$

By dividing numerator and denominator on the right side of Eq. (7.9) by P_0 one obtains the percentage formula suitable for tabulation:

$$\blacktriangle Q = -\frac{\blacktriangle P}{\blacktriangle P + CM_0\,(\%)} \qquad \text{Eq. (7.10)}$$

where, $\qquad \blacktriangle Q$ = Percentage sales volume change
$\blacktriangle P$ = Percentage price change
$CM_0\,(\%)$ = Contribution margin prior to a price change

Equation (7.10) allows the marketer to compute the percentage of *required* sales volume increase in the case of a price reduction and the *allowable* sales volume decrease in the case of a price increase.

Example

Suppose Alpha Company's Product X has a percentage unit contribution margin of 45%. What would be the isoprofit volume changes for price changes of 5%, up and down? Using Equation (7.10) one finds:

i) For a 5% price reduction:
$$\Delta Q = -(-0.05) / (-0.05 + 0.45) = 0.125$$
Thus, a 5% price reduction would require a minimum sales volume change of $+0.125 \times 100\%$ or $+12.5\%$ to keep profits as before.

ii) For a 5% price increase:
$$\Delta Q = -(0.05) / (0.05 + 0.45) = -0.100$$
This means that for a 5% price increase the maximum allowable sales volume change would be $-0.100 \times 100\%$ or -10.0%.

7.4 Reference Tables

Doing the above exercise for every contemplated price change could become tedious and it is more convenient to rely on tabulations of isoprofit values.

7.4.1 Required and Allowable Sales Volume Changes

Table 7-1 lists the isoprofit sales volume changes in percent for unit contribution margins from 5% to 100% and contemplated price changes ranging from 1% to 30%.[4] Specifically, the *minimum required* percentage sales volume increase in the case of a price reduction is shown in Table 7-1(a) while Table 7-1(b) lists the *maximum allowable* percentage sales volume reduction for a price increase. For high price reductions at low margins, this formula can yield required sales volume increases above 100%. Since a doubling of the required sales volume in the absence of any cost changes (which these formulas presume) is not very realistic, these isoprofit points are excluded.

7.4.2 Required and Allowable P.E.D.s

The reader may have observed that when one computes the required or allowable percentage sales volume change for a given percentage price change one implicitly also determines the required or allowable price elasticity of demand since the percentage price and volume changes are directly related via the P.E.D.. Thus, in the example in Section 7.3 above, the minimum required P.E.D. for a 5% price reduction is 12.5% / 5% or 2.5. The maximum allowable P.E.D. for a 5% price increase is 10.0% / 5% or 2.0. This begs the question, Why not compute and tabulate the required or allowable P.E.D. as a result of a price change directly? Then the two questions of Section 7.2 could be rephrased thus:

i) In the case of a contemplated *price reduction*:

What is the *minimum required P.E.D.* that will leave total contribution and profit unchanged?

ii) In the case of a contemplated *price increase*:

What is the *maximum allowable P.E.D.* that will leave total contribution and profit unchanged?

The required formula is easily derived. In the previous chapter, Equation 6.4, the P.E.D. is defined as:

$$\varepsilon = -\,\Delta Q \;/\; \Delta P \qquad \text{Eq. (7.11)}$$

Combining equations (7.10) and (7.11) one obtains:

$$\varepsilon = \frac{1}{\Delta P + CM_0\,(\%)} \qquad \text{Eq. (7.12)}$$

Eq. (7.12) gives the *minimum required P.E.D.* for a price reduction and the *maximum allowable P.E.D.* for a price increase to leave total contribution and profits unchanged.

Based on Equation (7.12), Tables 7-2(a) and 7-2(b) list the isoprofit price elasticities of demand for unit contribution margins from 5% to 100% and contemplated price changes from 1% to 30%. Specifically, the *minimum required P.E.D.* for a price reduction appears in Table 7-2(a) while Table 7-2(b) lists the *maximum allowable P.E.D.* for a price increase.

Example

Returning to Alpha Company's Product X of Section 7.3 above and using Equation (7.12), one obtains:

i) For a 5% price reduction:

The minimum required P.E.D. is $1 / (- 0.05 + 0.45) = 2.5$

ii) For a 5% price increase:

The maximum allowable P.E.D. is $1 / (0.05 + 0.45) = 2.0$

These are the results obtained previously.

Figure 7-2(a)
Isoprofit Curves: Price Change vs. Sales Volume Change

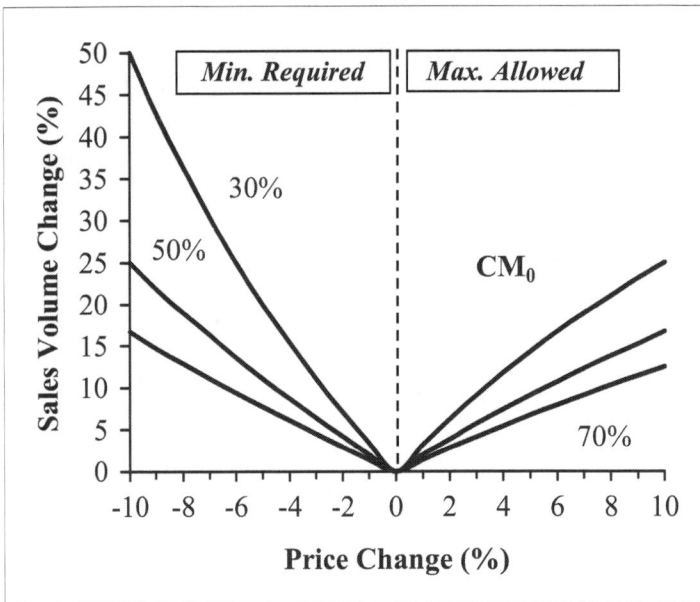

7.5 Pricing Guidelines (I)

For viewing trends and allowing for generalizations, a graphical representation of the data is often more useful than a mere tabulation of numbers. Figure 7-2(a) shows a graph of the isoprofit sales volume changes for price changes between −10% and +10% and unit contribution margins of 30%, 50%, and 70%. The region to the left of the vertical line at a zero price change, shows the minimum *required* sales volume increases and to the right the maximum *allowable* sales volume reduction. The graph in Figure 7-2(b) shows the price elasticity of demand required or allowed for a price reduction and increase, respectively, for three values of percentage unit contribution margin. Again, the region to the left of the vertical line at a zero price change shows the minimum *required* P.E.D. for a price reduction and to the right of this line the maximum *allowable* P.E.D. for a price increase.

Figure 7-2 (b)
Isoprofit Curves: Price Change vs. P.E.D.

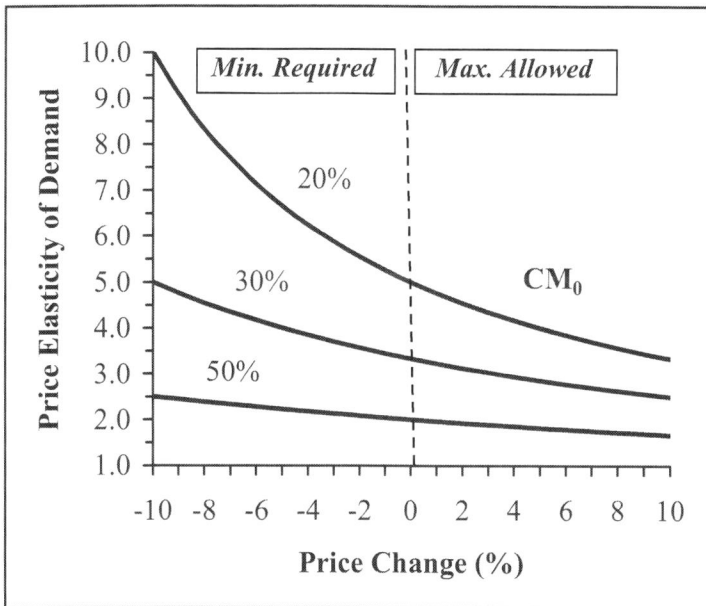

Of particular interest is the P.E.D. at which the percentage price change is zero. Letting ▲P = 0 in Equation (7.12) one obtains the optimal price elasticity of demand:

$$\epsilon^* = \frac{1}{CM_0 \ (\%)} \qquad \text{Eq. (7.13)}$$

Referring to Figure 7-2(b), for each percentage contribution margin CM_0 (%), the isoprofit P.E.D lies at the crossover point between negative and positive price changes. At that price point, no price change is needed and the present price should be held.

On hand of the isoprofit formulas of Equations (7.10), (7.12), and (7.13), and Figures 7-2(a) and 7-2(b), the following pricing propositions and pricing rule of thumb can stated:

Pricing Proposition 3

The lower a product's unit contribution margin, the higher must be the percentage sales volume increase and price elasticity of demand to make a price reduction profitable.

Pricing Proposition 4

The lower a product's unit contribution margin, the larger are the allowable percentage sales volume reduction and price elasticity of demand to make a price increase profitable.

Pricing Proposition 5

No price change for profit improvement is required where a product's price elasticity of demand is equal to the reciprocal of its unit contribution margin CM_0 (%).

Pricing Rule of Thumb

For total contribution and profit improvements, the required price changes are:

If the P.E.D. is	Price should be
$> 1 / CM_0$ (%)	*lowered*
$= 1 / CM_0$ (%)	*held*
$< 1 / CM_0$ (%)	*raised*

This simple decision rule allows the marketer to quickly determine whether the contemplated price change should be up or down. All that is required is to compare the reciprocal of the product's unit contribution margin with its estimated P.E.D. at the present price-volume operating point, and apply the above rule of thumb.

7.6 Application

The following example will demonstrate use of the technique.

Illustrative Example: Maricopa Enterprises Ltd. (III)

As may be recalled from Section 5.2 of Chapter 5 (Contribution Analysis), Maricopa Enterprises manufactures and markets a medication dispensing device known as TimerX which is sold in three versions—economy, standard, and premium. In Section 5.3 of that chapter we noted that the company's pricing committee had decided on a 10% across-the board price increase and estimated the resulting sales volume drops for the three models to be 50%, 20%, and 10%, respectively. By Equation (7.11) this is synonymous with saying that the economy, standard, and premium models had price elasticities of demand of 5.0, 2.0, and 1.0, respectively. The parameters for the three product models are therefore:

	TimerX-E	TimerX-S	TimerX-P
Sell price, P_0 ($)	60.00	100.00	200.00
Contribution margin, CM_0 (%)	0.25	0.40	0.60
Price elasticity, P.E.D.	5.0	2.0	1.0
Optimal P.E.D, $1 / CM_0$ (%)	4.0	2.5	1.7

Referring to the pricing rule of thumb above and Table 7-2, the range of profitable price changes are:

TimerX-E
Since the P.E.D. of 5.0 is larger than the optimal P.E.D. (ε^*) of 4.0, the price must be lowered (not raised). With a CM_0 (%) of 25% and a P.E.D. of 5.0, by Table 7-2(a), the maximum price reduction possible is 5%. Higher price reductions would require a higher P.E.D. Optimal price range: $57.00 to $60.00.

TimerX-S
Since the P.E.D. of 2.0 is smaller than the optimal P.E.D. ($\mathcal{E}^*$) of 2.5, the price should be raised. With a CM_0 (%) of 40% and a P.E.D. of 2.0, by Table 7-2(b), the price may be increased by up to 10%. Beyond that price, the maximum allowable P.E.D. drops below 2.0. Optimal price range: $100.00 to $110.00.

TimerX-P
Since the P.E.D. of 1.0 is smaller than the optimal P.E.D. ($\mathcal{E}^*$) of 1.7, the price should be raised. With a CM_0 (%) of 60% and a P.E.D of 1.0, by Table 7-2(b), the price may be increased by at least 30% since the allowable P.E.D.s always exceed 1.0 up to that price point. Optimal price range: $200.00 to $260.00.

7.7 Implementing Price Changes

Before committing herself or himself to any major price adjustment, the marketer is advised to carefully weigh a number of important factors with a bearing on the outcome It goes almost without saying that prices for a major product should not be changed too frequently lest the integrity of the sell price is adversely affected. While for buyers price reductions are obviously welcome news, customers generally do not like to see the prices of products they regularly purchase go up and down like a yo-yo. Prices should be believable, dependable, and predictable and not seem to have been set arbitrarily. *Price integrity* is very important in the marketplace.

Another important factor is *data validity*, i. e., the quality of the data available to the pricer and, specifically, the sell price, the unit contribution margin, and the price elasticity of demand prior to the planned price change. The product's net sell price and profit margin are data normally generated internal to the firm and should, in theory at least, present no major hurdle to being determined with a fair degree of accuracy. Price elasticity data, on the other hand, is a judgmental factor based on experience and, consequently, there is always a danger of significantly under- or overestimating the market's price sensitivity for a product. This is another reason for proceeding with caution.

While isoprofit analysis incorporates market demand and customer preferences through the price elasticity of demand, it makes no provision for *competitor responses* to price changes. Yet the most important factor that is likely to determine the success or failure of a price change is the reaction of competitors. Any permanent price change will to some degree disturb the equilibrium among competing brands in terms of sales revenue, market share, and profits. Depending on a number of factors, a competitor may decide to either ignore the price change or match it partially or fully. If the competitor feels threatened by an especially large price reduction, its management may retaliate with an even larger one. Thus, a competitor's response can fully or partially negate the hoped for benefits from the price change.

Clearly, price changes, especially significant ones, are fraught with risk and their size and timing require careful analyses. The risk may be ameliorated by first consulting isoprofit data such as those of Table 7-1 and Table 7-2 (or similar information found elsewhere) to check on the feasibility of a price adjustment. If a price change is not likely to lead to a profit improvement or even a profitability loss, the idea should be abandoned at least temporarily. Such a preliminary analysis can avoid any possible pricing and profitability debacles.

Also important to risk reduction is proper communication of impending pricing actions to both customers and, indirectly, to competitors as well. Competitors should have sufficient information that will assuage any major concerns that could lead to retaliatory actions especially in the case of significant and permanent price reductions. As will become clear in Chapter 15 of *Pricing for Profit* on the legal aspects of pricing, such communication must never be direct but can easily be accomplished through other means.

In the case of customers, they should be preconditioned to a price change, especially in the case of a significant price increase, and not be faced with a fait accompli whenever this is feasible. The general rule is that a price reduction calls for *price communication* while a price increase requires *value communication*.[5] The concept of *value*, a cornerstone of market-oriented pricing, is covered in Chapter 9.

Notes

1. Wilford J. Eiteman, *Price Determination in Oligopolistic and Monopolistic Situations*, 6.

2. See, for example, Thomas Nagle, John Hogan, and Joseph Zale, *The Strategy and Tactics of Pricing*, Chapter 10 (Financial Analysis).

3. Wilford J. Eiteman, supra at 33.

4. Table 7-1 is an adaptation of the author's 2-page flyer: H. P. Zell & Associates, *Iso-Profit Chart* (Oak Park, IL, 1983). (U.S. copyright registration no. TX 1-158-252 dated July 25, 1983).

5. Robert Dolan and Hermann Simon, *Power Pricing*, 319.

Table 7-1 (a)
Isoprofit Price Reduction: Minimum Required Sales Volume Increase (%)

CM₀ (%)	Price Change (%)													
	-1.0	-2.0	-3.0	-4.0	-5.0	-6.0	-7.0	-8.0	-9.0	-10.0	-15.0	-20.0	-25.0	-30.0
5	25.0	66.7	—	—	—	—	—	—	—	—	—	—	—	—
10	11.1	25.0	42.9	66.7	100.0	—	—	—	—	—	—	—	—	—
15	7.1	15.4	25.0	36.4	50.0	66.7	87.5	—	—	—	—	—	—	—
20	5.3	11.1	17.6	25.0	33.3	42.9	53.8	66.7	81.8	100.0	—	—	—	—
25	4.2	8.7	13.6	19.0	25.0	31.6	38.9	47.1	56.3	66.7	—	—	—	—
30	3.4	7.1	11.1	15.4	20.0	25.0	30.4	36.4	42.9	50.0	100.0	—	—	—
35	2.9	6.1	9.4	12.9	16.7	20.7	25.0	29.6	34.6	40.0	75.0	—	—	—
40	2.6	5.3	8.1	11.1	14.3	17.6	21.2	25.0	29.0	33.3	60.0	100.0	—	—
45	2.3	4.6	7.1	9.8	12.5	15.4	18.4	21.6	25.0	28.6	50.0	80.0	—	—
50	2.0	4.2	6.4	8.7	11.1	13.6	16.3	19.0	21.9	25.0	42.9	66.7	100.0	—
55	1.8	3.8	5.8	7.8	10.0	12.2	14.6	17.0	19.6	22.2	37.5	57.1	83.3	—
60	1.7	3.4	5.3	7.1	9.1	11.1	13.2	15.4	17.6	20.0	33.3	50.0	71.4	100.0
65	1.6	3.2	4.8	6.6	8.3	10.2	12.1	14.0	16.1	18.2	30.0	44.4	62.5	85.7
70	1.4	2.9	4.5	6.1	7.7	9.4	11.1	12.9	14.7	16.7	27.3	40.0	55.6	75.0
75	1.4	2.7	4.2	5.6	7.1	8.7	10.3	11.9	13.6	15.4	25.0	36.4	50.0	66.7
80	1.3	2.6	3.9	5.3	6.7	8.1	9.6	11.1	12.7	14.3	23.1	33.3	45.5	60.0
85	1.2	2.4	3.7	4.9	6.3	7.6	9.0	10.4	11.8	13.3	21.4	30.8	41.7	54.5
90	1.1	2.3	3.4	4.7	5.9	7.1	8.4	9.8	11.1	12.5	20.0	28.6	38.5	50.0
95	1.1	2.2	3.3	4.4	5.6	6.7	8.0	9.2	10.5	11.8	18.8	26.7	35.7	46.2
100	1.0	2.0	3.1	4.2	5.3	6.4	7.5	8.7	9.9	11.1	17.6	25.0	33.3	42.9

Table 7-1 (b)
Isoprofit Price Increase: Maximum Allowable Sales Volume Decrease (%)

CM_0 (%)	Price Change (%)													
	1.0	2.0	3.0	4.0	5.0	6.0	7.0	8.0	9.0	10.0	15.0	20.0	25.0	30.0
5	16.7	28.6	37.5	44.4	50.0	54.5	58.3	61.5	64.3	66.7	75.0	80.0	83.3	85.7
10	9.1	16.7	23.1	28.6	33.3	37.5	41.2	44.4	47.4	50.0	60.0	66.7	71.4	75.0
15	6.2	11.8	16.7	21.0	25.0	28.6	31.8	34.8	37.5	40.0	50.0	57.1	62.5	66.7
20	4.8	9.1	13.0	16.7	20.0	23.1	25.9	28.6	31.0	33.3	42.9	50.0	55.6	60.0
25	3.8	7.4	10.7	13.8	16.7	19.3	21.9	24.2	26.5	28.6	37.5	44.4	50.0	54.5
30	3.2	6.2	9.1	11.8	14.3	16.7	18.9	21.0	23.1	25.0	33.3	40.0	45.4	50.0
35	2.8	5.4	7.9	10.3	12.5	14.6	16.7	18.6	20.4	22.2	30.0	36.4	41.7	46.1
40	2.4	4.8	7.0	9.1	11.1	13.0	14.9	16.7	18.4	20.0	27.3	33.3	38.5	42.9
45	2.2	4.3	6.2	8.2	10.0	11.8	13.5	15.1	16.7	18.2	25.0	30.8	35.7	40.0
50	2.0	3.8	5.7	7.4	9.1	10.7	12.3	13.8	15.2	16.7	23.1	28.6	33.3	37.5
55	1.8	3.5	5.2	6.8	8.3	9.8	11.3	12.7	14.1	15.4	21.4	26.7	31.2	35.3
60	1.6	3.2	4.8	6.2	7.7	9.1	10.4	11.8	13.0	14.3	20.0	25.0	29.4	33.3
65	1.5	3.0	4.4	5.8	7.1	8.4	9.7	11.0	12.2	13.3	18.7	23.5	27.8	31.6
70	1.4	2.8	4.1	5.4	6.7	7.9	9.1	10.3	11.4	12.5	17.6	22.2	26.3	30.0
75	1.3	2.6	3.8	5.1	6.2	7.4	8.5	9.6	10.7	11.8	16.7	21.0	25.0	28.6
80	1.2	2.4	3.6	4.8	5.9	7.0	8.0	9.1	10.1	11.1	15.8	20.0	23.8	27.3
85	1.2	2.3	3.4	4.5	5.6	6.6	7.6	8.6	9.6	10.5	15.0	19.0	22.7	26.1
90	1.1	2.2	3.2	4.3	5.3	6.3	7.2	8.2	9.1	10.0	14.3	18.2	21.7	25.0
95	1.0	2.1	3.1	4.0	5.0	5.9	6.9	7.8	8.7	9.5	13.6	17.4	20.8	24.0
100	1.0	2.0	2.9	3.8	4.8	5.7	6.5	7.4	8.3	9.1	13.0	16.7	20.0	23.1

Table 7-2 (a)
Isoprofit Price Reduction: Minimum Required Price Elasticity of Demand (P.E.D.)

CM_0 (%)	Price Change (%)													
	-1.0	-2.0	-3.0	-4.0	-5.0	-6.0	-7.0	-8.0	-9.0	-10.0	-15.0	-20.0	-25.0	-30.0
5	25.0	33.3	—	—	—	—	—	—	—	—	—	—	—	—
10	11.1	12.5	14.3	16.7	20.0	—	—	—	—	—	—	—	—	—
15	7.1	7.7	8.3	9.1	10.0	11.1	12.5	—	—	—	—	—	—	—
20	5.3	5.6	5.9	6.3	6.7	7.1	7.7	8.3	9.1	10.0	—	—	—	—
25	4.2	4.3	4.5	4.8	5.0	5.3	5.6	5.9	6.3	6.7	—	—	—	—
30	3.4	3.6	3.7	3.8	4.0	4.2	4.3	4.5	4.8	5.0	6.7	—	—	—
35	2.9	3.0	3.1	3.2	3.3	3.4	3.6	3.7	3.8	4.0	5.0	—	—	—
40	2.6	2.6	2.7	2.8	2.9	2.9	3.0	3.1	3.2	3.3	4.0	5.0	—	—
45	2.3	2.3	2.4	2.4	2.5	2.6	2.6	2.7	2.8	2.9	3.3	4.0	—	—
50	2.0	2.1	2.1	2.2	2.2	2.3	2.3	2.4	2.4	2.5	2.9	3.3	4.0	—
55	1.9	1.9	1.9	2.0	2.0	2.0	2.1	2.1	2.2	2.2	2.5	2.9	3.3	—
60	1.7	1.7	1.8	1.8	1.8	1.9	1.9	1.9	2.0	2.0	2.2	2.5	2.9	3.3
65	1.6	1.6	1.6	1.6	1.7	1.7	1.7	1.8	1.8	1.8	2.0	2.2	2.5	2.9
70	1.4	1.5	1.5	1.5	1.5	1.6	1.6	1.6	1.6	1.7	1.8	2.0	2.2	2.5
75	1.4	1.4	1.4	1.4	1.4	1.4	1.5	1.5	1.5	1.5	1.7	1.8	2.0	2.2
80	1.3	1.3	1.3	1.3	1.3	1.4	1.4	1.4	1.4	1.4	1.5	1.7	1.8	2.0
85	1.2	1.2	1.2	1.2	1.3	1.3	1.3	1.3	1.3	1.3	1.4	1.5	1.7	1.8
90	1.1	1.1	1.1	1.2	1.2	1.2	1.2	1.2	1.2	1.3	1.3	1.4	1.5	1.7
95	1.1	1.1	1.1	1.1	1.1	1.1	1.1	1.1	1.2	1.2	1.3	1.3	1.4	1.5
100	1.0	1.0	1.0	1.0	1.1	1.1	1.1	1.1	1.1	1.1	1.2	1.3	1.3	1.4

Table 7-2(b)

Isoprofit Price Increase: Maximum Allowable Price Elasticity of Demand (P.E.D.)

CM_0 (%)	Price Change (%)													
	1.0	2.0	3.0	4.0	5.0	6.0	7.0	8.0	9.0	10.0	15.0	20.0	25.0	30.0
5	16.7	14.3	12.5	11.1	10.0	9.1	8.3	7.7	7.1	6.7	5.0	4.0	3.3	2.9
10	9.1	8.3	7.7	7.1	6.7	6.3	5.9	5.6	5.3	5.0	4.0	3.3	2.9	2.5
15	6.3	5.9	5.6	5.3	5.0	4.8	4.5	4.3	4.2	4.0	3.3	2.9	2.5	2.2
20	4.8	4.5	4.3	4.2	4.0	3.8	3.7	3.6	3.4	3.3	2.9	2.5	2.2	2.0
25	3.8	3.7	3.6	3.4	3.3	3.2	3.1	3.0	2.9	2.9	2.5	2.2	2.0	1.8
30	3.2	3.1	3.0	2.9	2.9	2.8	2.7	2.6	2.6	2.5	2.2	2.0	1.8	1.7
35	2.8	2.7	2.6	2.6	2.5	2.4	2.4	2.3	2.3	2.2	2.0	1.8	1.7	1.5
40	2.4	2.4	2.3	2.3	2.2	2.2	2.1	2.1	2.0	2.0	1.8	1.7	1.5	1.4
45	2.2	2.1	2.1	2.0	2.0	2.0	1.9	1.9	1.9	1.8	1.7	1.5	1.4	1.3
50	2.0	1.9	1.9	1.9	1.8	1.8	1.8	1.7	1.7	1.7	1.5	1.4	1.3	1.3
55	1.8	1.8	1.7	1.7	1.7	1.6	1.6	1.6	1.6	1.5	1.4	1.3	1.3	1.2
60	1.6	1.6	1.6	1.6	1.5	1.5	1.5	1.5	1.4	1.4	1.3	1.3	1.2	1.1
65	1.5	1.5	1.5	1.4	1.4	1.4	1.4	1.4	1.4	1.3	1.3	1.2	1.1	1.1
70	1.4	1.4	1.4	1.4	1.3	1.3	1.3	1.3	1.3	1.3	1.2	1.1	1.1	1.0
75	1.3	1.3	1.3	1.3	1.3	1.2	1.2	1.2	1.2	1.2	1.1	1.1	1.0	1.0
80	1.2	1.2	1.2	1.2	1.2	1.2	1.1	1.1	1.1	1.1	1.1	1.0	1.0	0.9
85	1.2	1.1	1.1	1.1	1.1	1.1	1.1	1.1	1.1	1.1	1.0	1.0	0.9	0.9
90	1.1	1.1	1.1	1.1	1.1	1.0	1.0	1.0	1.0	1.0	1.0	0.9	0.9	0.8
95	1.0	1.0	1.0	1.0	1.0	1.0	1.0	1.0	1.0	1.0	0.9	0.9	0.8	0.8
100	1.0	1.0	1.0	1.0	1.0	0.9	0.9	0.9	0.9	0.9	0.9	0.8	0.8	0.8

CHAPTER

8

Pricing Strategies

Although more than one strategy can achieve profitable results, even within the same industry, nearly all successful pricing strategies embody three principles. They are value-based, proactive, and profit-driven.[1]

$\mathbf{A}$ strategy is a comprehensive plan for attaining a given objective which, in a marketing and pricing context, is usually the maximization of either total contribution (profit), sales revenue, or market share. To be most effective, such a pricing strategy must be subordinate to the overall marketing strategy for each product-market or market segment the company has chosen to serve. Therefore, one may define a pricing strategy as a plan for directing and coordinating price-related activities in support of the chosen product-market strategy. In this chapter various pricing strategies and policies are discussed including general, life cycle, and industry-specific pricing strategies. The chapter ends with an overview of sealed-bid pricing where the customer is a single firm or government entity.

8.1 General Pricing Policies

Most business enterprises define themselves in terms of the markets and, specifically, the product-market segments they serve. In the case of manufacturing, some firms focus on highly unique and differentiated products for select market segments while others find opportunities in commodity type products that differ little from those of competitors but appeal to a broader customer base. Some companies have positioned themselves as suppliers of high-quality state-of-the-art products while still others choose to serve the more price sensitive portion of the market. Some retailers are considered upscale in terms of their merchandise offerings while others operate as general merchandisers or as discounters. How companies position themselves in the marketplace also defines their primary pricing strategies. These overall, governing pricing strategies may also be referred to as pricing policies.

Marketing theorists have identified three basic pricing strategies being employed by firms, namely, skim, penetration, and parity pricing. The first two were first proposed by the economist and business school professor Joel Dean as a guide to new product pricing.[2] They are still useful for that purpose but are of more general applicability as well because companies typically do not decide on a product-by-product basis on whether to skim or penetrate the market but use the same pricing policy, or action plan, for all of their products or services. Thus, for example, Starbucks, Apple, and DuPont are typical market skimmers while Amazon, Hyundai, and Target are known for penetration pricing.

8.1.1 Skim Pricing

In skim pricing a firm skims the cream of demand for its products or services by pricing these relatively high resulting in large unit contribution margins but at the expense of sales volumes and market shares. It is the policy of choice for firms whose products or services are highly unique and differentiated and, in the eyes of customers, have a high perceived value. Demand for such products and services tends to be relatively price inelastic, i.e., buyers are less concerned with the price they have to pay than the satisfaction they gain from ownership and use. Many manufacturers and retailers of such products, which typically carry well recognized brand names, use skim pricing to great advantage. Most luxury goods manufacturers such as BMW (automobiles), Gucci (fashion attire),

Rolex (watches), and Godiva (chocolates) successfully employ a market skimming policy.

8.1.2 Penetration Pricing

Penetration pricing, also called *volume pricing*, represents a policy that is most suitable for firms that have positioned themselves to serve the more price-sensitive segments of a larger market. Prices are kept relatively low to penetrate markets and generate volume at the expense of unit contribution margins. This strategy obviously works best for companies that have a cost advantage over competitors by the efficient management of their resources. A penetration price is not necessarily the lowest price for the product in the specific product-market served. Rather it is a low price in relation to a customer's value perception of the product. Among retailers, well-known penetration pricers are Amazon, Costco, Target, and Wal-Mart.

8.1.3 Parity Pricing

Parity or *neutral* pricing is the policy of choice for firms for which neither of the two extremes, skim or penetration pricing, seems appropriate in the product-markets they serve. A parity price is a middle price designed to generate good volume sales and, at the same time, respectable unit contribution margins. Successful parity pricers are likely to enjoy a significant cost advantage over competitors giving them good margins at even moderate prices. Such firms are also likely to be aggressive in the use of non-price marketing strategy variables such as product innovation, and advertising and sales promotion. Among the more successful parity pricers often cited are Samsung, Sony, and Toyota.

8.2 Life Cycle Strategies

One of the best known and most useful marketing concepts is that of the product life cycle (PLC) which maintains that every product on the market has a finite life much like humans and animals. It is furthermore postulated that every product passes through a number of distinct stages each of which represents challenges and opportunities that marketers must address to meet long term marketing and profitability goals. The concept had been around for some years when in a 1965 *Harvard Business Review* article Professor Theodore Levitt popularized it for use as a guide to strategic marketing decision making.[3]

The PLC concept has not gone unchallenged. In one often quoted paper, written by two advertising company executives, the major finding was that "[t]he PLC concept has little validity" especially if applied to individual brands.[4] The authors came to their conclusion after examining the shipment statistics for several diverse consumer goods over a number of years. Despite this, the idea that a product or service moves through distinct life cycle stages and pricing strategy must be adjusted accordingly, is intuitively plausible and hence the PLC has never lost its relevance for strategic pricing.

Four distinct stages for the PLC have been identified, namely, introduction, growth, maturity, and decline. A hypothetical product life cycle and its four stages appears in Figure 8-1. The horizontal (x) axis is labeled time and, depending on the particular product, could be measured in weeks, months, or years. Some new products and services are stillborn while others, often classified as fads, may have lives of only weeks or months while certain brands of durable consumer goods may be around for many years.

The vertical (y) axis has been labeled sales volume meaning the number of units of the product actually sold. In the marketing literature this axis is often simply labeled sales or sales revenue in dollars. That is not a sound practice because prices change over time and certain discounts may be offered diverse customer groups at various times. This will distort the shape of the PLC and obscure where each of the four stages begins and ends. Nor should one be plotting shipments leaving the factory floor but product actually purchased by the end user. Shipped goods may be stored and never be purchased and, in addition, there will be random time lags between shipments and between shipments and purchases.

The four PLC stages have been more fully described as follows.

8.2.1 The Introduction Stage

In most industries and markets new products and product innovations are an important factor for driving company growth and profits. More than that, product innovation is a necessity for survival especially for firms offering industrial or consumers products where technology is rapidly advancing. During the introductory PLC stage, sales start at zero and may languish there for some time before they begin to take off if they do so at all. For some products, such as a new version of an Apple iPhone, a Samsung Android phone, or another make of smart phone, the introductory stage is fairly short as many users of the previous model simply switch to the newer one as the old one is phased out. Pricing a new model presents no major problem since there is sufficient history to serve as a guide.

Figure 8-1
Hypothetical Product Life Cycle

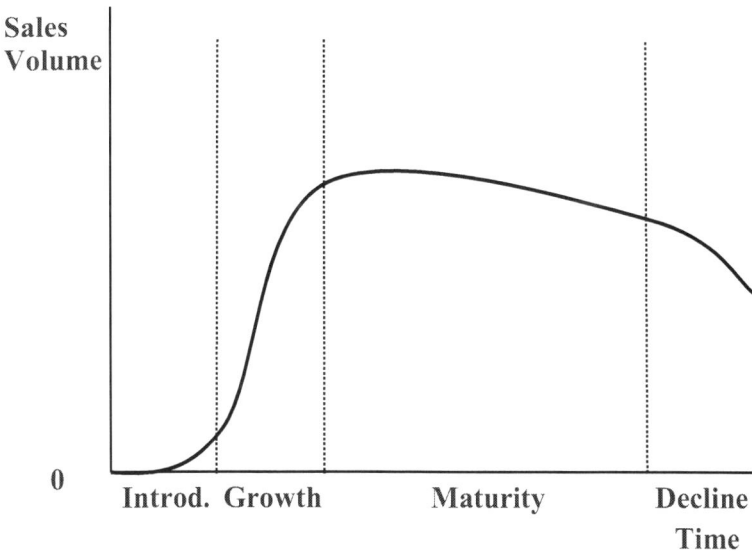

The situation is quite different in two other situations. One is the case for a true innovation, i.e., a product or service so new and different that the general public cannot yet relate to it. Examples of past innovations include the automobile replacing the horse and buggy, the refrigerator replacing the ice box, the airplane replacing the steamship for overseas travel, the compact disc replacing the gramophone record, and the cell phone replacing or supplementing the land line phone. For such products, the innovator's first task is to generate *primary demand* for the new product class by focusing the marketing effort on a customer group known as *early adopters*. For consumer goods, these are usually affluent young people receptive to new product ideas. Advertising and sales promotion must be geared to build product awareness and educate potential customers on product usage and benefits. The other situation is where the firm is entering a new product-market segment of a larger market in which it has no or little prior experience.

For an innovation during this introductory stage competition is minimal or small especially if it is protected by patents, trade secrets, and trademarks. Potential competitors with similar product concepts may watch from the sidelines to see whether the innovation catches on or fizzles before committing their own resources to product research and development. Due to relatively few sales and heavy advertising and promotional costs, this stage can be expected to show losses or minimal profits at best. Pricing an innovation can be difficult since there are no comparable products on the market to use as a guide. In the second case, where the company is entering a new product-market, the task of setting an appropriate introductory price is equally challenging. In both cases the two pricing options are skim and penetration pricing.

Skim Pricing

Skim pricing can be recommended where these conditions hold:

* Competitor entry will be difficult because of one or more entry barriers such as patent protection, required financial resources, manufacturing capabilities, and channel requirements.

* Demand can be expected to be relatively inelastic, i.e., potential buyers will not be overly sensitive to the purchase price.

* A high reference price is to be set to allow skim pricing for subsequent versions or models of the product.

* The market is to be split into market segments of increasing price sensitivity by the later introduction of lower-priced models.

* Initial production capacity is limited.

Penetration Pricing

A penetration pricing strategy would be the preferable approach where:

* A low price is needed to discourage competitor entry due to insufficient entry barriers such as patent protection.

* Product demand can be expected to be highly elastic from the start or become so shortly after introduction.

* The firm has no production capacity constraints.

* High volume production is likely to lead to scale and experience economies and a cost advantage for the firm.

* Large product usage will ensure that the innovator's technology will be adopted as the industry standard.

These two pricing strategies are not just theoretical abstractions but are being actively pursued by firms in diverse industries and markets. Two example will illustrate how important it is to get the introductory price right. Getting it right can lead to phenomenal success in terms of sales and profits while not getting it right can result in a financial disaster. The first case is a lesson in skimming and the firm the American chemical giant DuPont. When this long established company launched its leather substitute Corfam in 1963, management predicted that in twenty years the new product would be the major component in 25% of American shoes. The reality was that Corfam had to be withdrawn from the shoe leather market in 1971 after DuPont had invested $100 million in the ill-fated venture.

What went wrong? It was not the product which was described as comparable to leather in quality and features. In pricing Corfam, DuPont had used its traditional skim pricing strategy which involved initially pricing high and then, as competitors gained entry, rapidly dropping its prices. Consequently, Corfam was priced so high that Corfam shoes cost $25 which was two and one-half times the price of a leather shoe at the time. Despite subsequent discounting, the product never caught on. The lesson to be leaned was that skim pricing works only if demand is relatively inelastic and the American shoe market was highly elastic at the time and probably still is.

In a more recent example but with a happier outcome, in 1989 the Japanese automaker Toyota entered the luxury car market with its Lexus LS400 using a penetration strategy.[5] This was unusual for a luxury brand where skimming is the preferred pricing strategy. Management, however, knew that there was a large price-sensitive segment of the luxury car market that was not being served adequately and decided to compete in it with a quality vehicle. Excellent reviews in automotive magazines and *Consumer Reports*, heavy advertising and sales promotion, and positive word-of-mouth resulted in immediate market acceptance and a large surge in sales. Product demand was not only strong but became more inelastic so that five years after product introduction, the price of a Lexus LS400 had increased by nearly 50% from its original price of $35,000. Since then, Lexus has become well established successfully competing with older and more traditional luxury car brands.

Most new products or services that come on the market are not true innovations nor do they involve entry into a product-market new to the firm. These products will compete with brands and services already being offered. For such products and services a pricing strategy similar to *parity pricing* is appropriate in that the prices of competing brands are the major reference points. To determine an introductory price, management would normally draw up a grid listing the new product and all the directly competing models across the top and all the items potential buyers would be looking for down the left. For automobiles these items would include brand image, gas mileage, styling, horsepower rating, standard features and benefits, warranty terms, and financing options.

Weights would be assigned to each item, say from 1 to 10, based on how important buyers would likely find each item in their purchase decision. Each listed product would be rated and the total scores for each model compared. This would give a first order indication where the new product should be positioned price-wise among the competing products. As sales developed and demand elasticities became available, prices would be adjusted accordingly.

8.2.2 The Growth Stage

Most products that come on the market fail for one reason or another in that they do not sell well or not at all or their financial performance in terms of sales revenue or profits falls significantly below expectations. Such products must consequently be withdrawn to conserve and redirect company resources to more profitable ventures. The number of new product failures is legion with the most famous marketing disaster of all time being the Ford Edsel automobile launched in September 1957. Production was halted just two years later after the company had lost roughly $350 million on the project. Many factors caused the new product's demise but faulty pricing was a major one. Products that survive the introductory stage are, according to the standard PLC model, ready for a sharp and rapid expansion of sales volume, revenue, and profits. The growth stage has therefore also been called the *takeoff stage*.

During growth, several important things take place. For one, target customers have become fully aware of the product's existence, started using it and, having had a positive experience, become repeat buyers. In the case of an innovation, competitors who have been developing a similar product now rush in to claim their own share of the expanding market. The innovator's demand curve for the product now becomes more elastic (horizontal) while the company's advertising effort shifts from developing primary demand for the product class to *selective demand* for the firm's brand. With increasing sales, more distributors and retailers are willing to carry and stock the brand. Also, with increasing sales and declining variable costs, unit profit margins tend to be high. In fact, they are likely to peak at the inflection point leading to the maturity stage.

Prices during the growth stage are likely to be unstable. Some products may keep their introductory prices but others may see significant shifts as managers gain more experience with the new product. Companies have been known to drastically cut new product prices during this stage when they realized the product was overpriced and they needed to reduce prices to get sales off the ground. Another situation calling for price cuts, is where sales are below expectations resulting in overcapacity and large inventories of unsold product. Price increases are warranted where sales are so brisk that a firm cannot keep up with demand.

8.2.3 The Maturity Stage

Successful products typically spend most of their lives in the maturity stage as indicated by the relative length of this stage in the hypothetical PLC curve of Figure 8-1. By now, market conditions have stabilized in that demand for the new product is nearly flat and the major objective is to maintain or attain incremental increases in market shares, sales revenues, and profits. To this end, firms will make proactive use of the four marketing strategy variables, including the price, to maintain brand loyalty and encourage buyers to switch from competing brands.

In maturity, customers have become increasingly sophisticated in that they have developed strong value perceptions of competing brands. Buyers have become sensitive to the purchase prices of the competing brands and models and the demand curves of all have consequently tended more toward the horizontal. This increased price sensitivity has encouraged competitors to use price as a major competitive tool. Price adjustments are therefore the rule rather than the exception with a price change by one firm often countered by one or more competitors designed to negate the hoped for benefits.

Specifically, marketers of competing brands will *fine tune* sell prices to reach contribution dollar objectives. Because of the relative stable conditions of the maturity stage, managers can, for the first time, gauge their products' price elasticities of demand with some degree of accuracy. As we know, the P.E.D. is an all-important metric not only for evaluating the relative profitabilities of various price change options but also for computing optimal sell prices for sales revenue and profit maximization.

At this point it might be useful to review the two rules of thumb for sales revenue and contribution maximization given in Chapters 6 (Market Demand) and 7 (Isoprofit Analysis), respectively, because it is in a product's maturity stage where these rules may be most effectively employed. Both rules involve the price elasticity of demand at the present price-volume operating point (P_0, Q_0). Specifically, for sales revenue maximization, the optimal P.E.D., $[\mathcal{E}]$, is 1.0 while for profit maximization, the optimal P.E.D., $\mathcal{E}^*$, is $1 / CM_0$ (%). These two rules of thumb to optimize sell prices for the two pricing objectives are summarized in Table 8-1:

Table 8-1
Rules of Thumb for Price Optimization

Sales Revenue Maximization	Contribution Maximization	Required Price Change
If the P.E.D. is:	If the P.E.D. is:	-----------------
> 1.0	> $1 / CM_0$ (%)	*lower price*
= 1.0	= $1 / CM_0$ (%)	*hold price*
< 1.0	< $1 / CM_0$ (%)	*raise price*

Applying these simple rules allows the marketer to quickly determine whether a sell price should be lowered, raised or left unchanged to achieve either pricing goal. For maximizing total contribution, Table 8-2 is a listing of the optimal P.E.D.s ($\mathcal{E}^*$) for unit contribution margins from 2.5% to 100% in 2.5% increments. With this data the marketer can determine at a glance whether the optimal condition exists, i.e., whether or not $\mathcal{E}_0 = \mathcal{E}^*$ (hold price). If not, the pricing rule of thumb of Table 8-1 applies.

Extension Strategies

Long before the once new product enters the final decline stage of its life cycle, companies typically have another model or version ready for launch. In fact, even before the new product comes on the market, management should plan for its eventual demise and be ready with *life extension* or *market stretching* strategies.[6] With new versions or models, the decline stage shown in Figure 8-1 never materializes or is significantly delayed. Somewhere during the maturity stage another life cycle begins with a new S-shaped PLC curve superimposed on the old one. For a product such as the Apple

115

iPhone, Samsung Galaxy or other smartphone this process can continue indefinitely until a completely new technology and product concept replace the original one. Extension strategies may also involve finding new uses or new product-markets for a mature product or service.

Table 8-2
Optimal P.E.D. vs. Unit Contribution Margin

Contribution Margin (%)	Optimal P.E.D. (ε*)	Contribution Margin (%)	Optimal P.E.D. (ε*)
2.5	40.0	52.5	1.90
5.0	20.0	55.0	1.82
7.5	13.3	57.5	1.74
10.0	10.0	60.0	1.67
12.5	8.00	62.5	1.60
15.0	6.67	65.0	1.54
17.5	5.71	67.5	1.48
20.0	5.00	70.0	1.43
22.5	4.44	72.5	1.38
25.0	4.00	75.0	1.33
27.5	3.64	77.5	1.29
30.0	3.33	80.0	1.25
32.5	3.08	82.5	1.21
35.0	2.86	85.0	1.18
37.5	2.67	87.5	1.14
40.0	2.50	90.0	1.11
42.5	2.35	92.5	1.08
45.0	2.22	95.0	1.05
47.5	2.11	97.5	1.03
50.0	2.00	100.0	1.00

8.2.4 The Decline Stage

Eventually sales for the company's product enter a period of steep decline that even major product modification and drastic cost and price cutting is unable to halt. The product has now arrived at the decline stage of its PLC. During this stage, once loyal customers have lost interest in the product, drifted away, and begun buying competing brands. Typically, costs rise and profits decline along with sales revenue. To deal with this situation, three different strategies can be identified, namely, retrenchment, harvesting, and exit.

Retrenchment

A retrenchment strategy involves a continuing long-term commitment to the product combined with a partial market withdrawal. Specifically, product-market segments not well served in that sales and profits are below par, are abandoned and freed resources reassigned to more profitable segments. This strategy presupposes, of course, that the product is being sold in different versions to different customer groups with their own price-volume schedules and price sensitivities and that one or more of these is sufficiently profitable to justify keeping the product alive.

Harvest

With a harvesting strategy, management has decided to gradually withdraw from the market but do so in a manner that will generate maximum total contribution dollars over the product's remaining life. Prices are kept relatively high and major promotional and other marketing costs curtailed. As a result, unit contribution margins continue to be high even as some market share is surrendered to competitors. The company essentially treats its product as a *cash cow*. This strategy works best in cases where there remains a loyal customer base for the product or brand that can be profitably served for some time in the near future.

Exit

Where there is insufficient life left in the product and losses are mounting, management may decide to cut these losses by abandoning the market altogether. Production of the product is halted and the remaining inventory sold off at reduced prices. With the bargain basement prices, directly competing products may also be withdrawn unless managements are willing to hold on expecting to raise their prices again after their competitor has left the scene.

8.2.5 Summary

Keeping track of the number of units sold over time from the time of product introduction is a simple and cost-effective means for obtaining useful pricing and other marketing information. In fact, such PLC curves should be available for each brand, model, and product-market served. These curves are not likely to have the shape of the idealized PLC curve shown in Figure 8-1. The maturity stage, in particular, is likely to shows peaks and valleys like a camel's back (of the Bactrian kind) due to temporary price and sales promotions and other factors affecting product demand over time. Nevertheless, the product's progress over time and especially the onset of the critical decline stage should be clearly observable to alert management to needed remedial efforts as outlined above.

8.3 Industry Structure and Pricing Policy

The term industry, as previously noted, is applied to a group of manufacturers or service providers selling into the same market. Examples are the airline, automobile, banking, construction, entertainment, hospitality, fashion, fast foods, restaurant, and retail industries. Each of these industries is uniquely structured in terms of:

i) The number of competitors that comprise it;

ii) the relative market power of the competitors in terms of market share, growth rates, profitability, financial resources, etc.;

iii) the entry barriers to new competitors including investment requirement, cost structure, patents, trademarks, and preemption, if any, of scarce resources or distribution channels.

The reason marketers are interested in industry structure is that it much influences the primary pricing strategy prevalent in a particular industry. Understanding industry structure helps the marketer explain and predict the pricing behavior of competitors and understand the pricing limitations and opportunities facing his or her firm.

One defining element in industry structure and market organization is the level of competition. Economists view competition as a continuum that extends from *perfect competition* to *pure monopoly*. Few industries fit into either of these two extreme categories but they serve as good starting points for understanding market organization and pricing behavior. The three major forms of market organization are, according to economic theory, perfect competition, monopoly, and imperfect competition the latter of which includes monopolistic competition and oligopoly.[7]

Figure 8-2
Market Organization and Product Demand

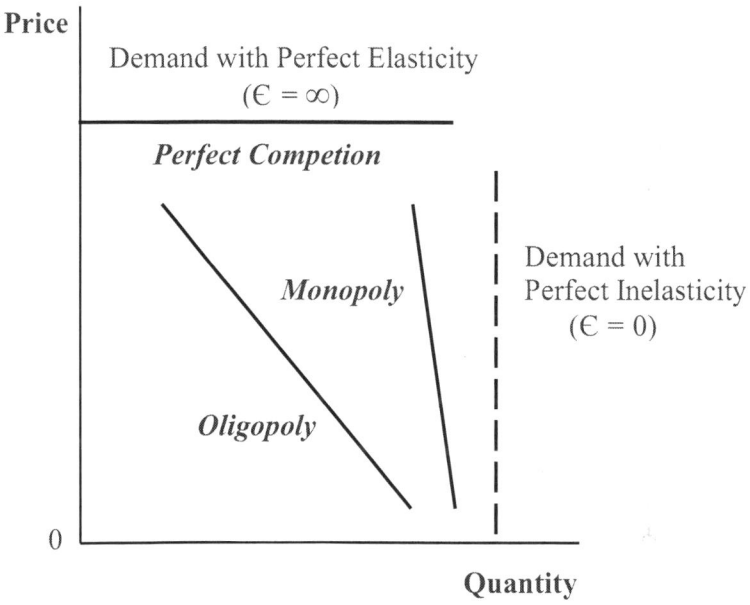

Price

Demand with Perfect Elasticity
$(\epsilon = \infty)$

Perfect Competion

Monopoly

Demand with
Perfect Inelasticity
$(\epsilon = 0)$

Oligopoly

0

Quantity

8.3.1 Perfect Competition

Perfect or pure competition is an economic model describing a market in which there are many firms selling an identical product with no one of them large enough relative to the entire market to influence the market price. In fact, each firm supplying this market is a *price taker* in that there is a market price for the usually undifferentiated product and the firm has no choice but to sell at that price. The demand curve for a firm in a perfectly competitive market is a horizontal line at the market price as shown in Figure 8-2. The firm cannot sell above the prevailing market price because there would be no buyers and to sell for less would be imprudent since this would not increase demand. Since a firm maximizes its profits when marginal revenue equals marginal cost and since marginal revenue in the case of perfect competition is the market price, a firm under these conditions would produce and sell at a quantity level where its marginal cost of production equals the market price.

Many companies manufacture and market undifferentiated products, commonly known as *commodities*, either for reasons of choice or their products are not easily amenable to differentiation. The most often cited example of firms in a purely competitive market are farmers growing wheat, corn, or some other crop. No farmer will be so dominant as to be able to influence the price and each can sell his or her product only at the prevailing market price.

8.3.2 Pure Monopoly

A market situation in which a single firm sells a product for which there are no good substitutes is called pure monopoly. It is the exact opposite of perfect competition and for a firm it is by far a more favorable position to be in since the monopolist can charge monopoly prices and earn monopoly profits without greatly affecting market demand for his or her product. The monopolist, however, will not charge any price but the one for which marginal revenue equals marginal cost. Pure monopolies are very rare with public utility companies and railroads hauling bulk raw materials like coal coming close to the ideal. A monopolist's demand curve is nearly vertical, as shown in Figure 8-2, but does include an upper elastic portion where the P.E.D. is larger than 1.0.

8.3.3 Monopolistic Competition

Monopolistic competition is characterized by the presence in the market of a large number of firms which vigorously compete with each other for sales and profits by offering differentiated and unique products and services. Generally speaking, these entities function *independently* of each other without tacit or overt collusion among them. Due to   product and brand uniqueness, usually based on product innovation, advertising and other non-price marketing strategy variable, they manage to achieve various degrees of market power. Most business firms, big and small, fit into this broad category. The product demand curves facing a firm under monopolistic competition typically have the standard downward-sloping form first shown in Chapter 6 (Figure 6-1). Their slopes depend on their relative competitive advantages vis-à-vis similar products on the market with steeper ones indicating that these products and services are highly differentiated and desirable for customers to own and use.

8.3.4 Oligopoly

An oligopolistic industry is one in which the number of sellers is small enough for the activities of a single seller to affect the other firms and for the activities of the other firms to affect that firm in turn. Typically, an oligopoly is characterized by strong *interdependence* among the firms regarding all product-market activities including the price. The demand curve of the *dominant* firm in an oligopoly is downward sloping as for monopolistic competition but somewhat steeper and inelastic so that it approaches that of a monopolist as shown in Figure 8-2 above. The reason for the relatively inelastic demand for their products and services is that, being few in number, oligopolistic firms have the market to themselves and manage to avoid overt price competition.

Many industries and markets in this country, Europe, and Asia are highly concentrated with just a few major firms, say three to five, sharing at least 50% and sometimes as much as 90% of the total market. A number of industries and the dominant players in each in terms of sales revenue and market share are listed in Table 8-3. Some of these firms are foreign-owned but they are all major players in the American market. This list is far from definitive or inclusive and presented primarily to illustrate the point that in most of these industries the number of participating firms is relatively small.

Firms of an oligopoly have a strong incentive to stay ahead of their competitors in terms of sales, market share, and profits. Most of them are equity financed and owned by investment firms and the

Table 8-3

Oligopolistic Market Structure in Selected Industries

Industry	*Companies*
Airlines	American, Delta, Southwest, United
Athletic shoes	Adidas, Nike, Puma, Reebok
Automobiles	Chrysler, Ford , General Motors, Toyota
Banks	Bank of America , Citigroup, JPMorgan
Brewers	Anheuser-Busch, MillerCoors, Pabst
Book publishers	HarperCollins, Penguin Random House
Book sellers	Amazon, Barnes & Noble
Breakfast cereals	General Mills, Kellogg, Post
Car rentals	Alamo, Avis, Budget, Enterprise, Hertz
Cigarettes	Philip Morris, Reynolds America
Coffee houses	Coffee Bean, Dunkin' Donuts, Starbucks
Commercial aircraft	Airbus, Boeing, Bombardier
Credit cards	American Express, MasterCard, Visa
Delivery services	DHL, FedEx, UPS, USPS
Department stores	Dillard's, JCPenney, Kohl's, Macy's, Sears
Digital cameras	Canon, Nikon, Olympus, Panasonic, Sony
E-readers	Amazon, Apple, Barnes & Noble
Elevators	Otis, Nippon, Schindler
Fast foods (burgers)	Burger King, McDonald's, Wendy's
Fast foods (chicken)	Chick-fil-A, Church's, KFC
Foods	General Mills, Kraft, Nestlé, Swift, Tyson
Farming equipment	International Harvester, John Deere
Gasoline stations	Chevron, ExxonMobil, Shell, Sunoco
Grocery stores	Albertsons, Kroger, Safeway, Wal-Mart
Home builders	PulteGroup, D.R. Horton, NVR
Insurance	Allianz, Allstate, Liberty Mut., State Farm
Jet engines	G.E., Pratt & Whitney, Rolls Royce
Men's jeans	Levi's, Rustler, T. Hilfiger, Wrangler
Movie studios	Disney, MGM, Paramount, Warner Bros.
Office supplies	Staples, OfficeMax, Office Depot
Pharmaceuticals	Abbott, J & J, Merck, Pfizer, Roche
Railroads	BNSF, CSX, Norfolk South., Union Pacific
Smart phones	Apple, Nokia, Samsung
Television sets	LG, Panasonic, Samsung, Sharp, Sony
Wireless carriers	AT&T, Sprint, T-Mobile, Verizon

general public which are both keenly interested to have the value of their investments rise along with the quarterly dividend payouts. Not surprisingly, oligopolistic companies proactively use most of the marketing tools available to them to reach their goals. Continuous product innovation is one characteristic of oligopolistic industries. Indeed, these firms are typically large and financially strong enough to fund the costs involved in financing technological breakthroughs and product innovations on a large scale. It has even been persuasively argued that research and development which drives technological advances and economic growth, thrives only in oligopolistic markets.[8]

Oligopolistic firms typically spend millions of dollars yearly on advertising and sales promotion in order to stimulate selective demand for their products and services and turn potential customers into buyers. All firms in the industry are more or less obliged to participate with each firm trying to outdo the others in the originality and intensity of print and television advertising. Because of their interdependence, firms in an industry with an oligopolistic market structure are characterized by some unique behavioral patterns in terms of pricing including:

i) Price fixing: This pricing practice involves collusion in the form of an agreement among the members of an oligopoly to establish uniform prices to avoid price competition. Price fixing is the most egregious of antitrust violations and will be treated in Chapter 15.

ii) Predatory pricing: Another pricing practice associated with oligopolies is predatory pricing by which a dominant firm may temporarily charge exceedingly low prices, often below its products' direct variable costs, with the intent of driving one or more competitors from the market leaving it in a monopoly position. This practice too is proscribed by law and further discussed in Chapter 15.

iii) Price wars: Price wars among members of an oligopoly are a persistent danger and may erupt for a number of reasons. They can be destructive of an entire industry because the depressed prices may substantially shrink its size and force some members into bankruptcy. Price wars are discussed in Chapter 11.

iv) Leadership pricing: Price leadership and cooperative pricing is a form of tacit collusion among firms in an oligopoly that avoids direct price competition. The practice is not illegal because there is no verbal, written, or implied agreement among the firms.

8.4 Leadership Pricing

Perhaps the most unique feature of oligopolistic competition is the *absence* of competition in one very important area—the price. Most real competition is confined to the non-price strategy variables in the marketing mix. As economists J. P. Gould and C. E. Ferguson noted: "Practically speaking, active price competition is seldom if ever observed in oligopolistic markets. To be sure, price wars occasionally erupt; but this does not indicate price competition. A price war indicates that the (probably implicit) communication channels among firms in the market are temporarily out of repair. In the normal course of events, the pre-price-war situation is quickly restored."[9]

Price competition is avoided by a practice known as *price leadership* in which one dominant firm in the industry sets the price and all others are expected to follow its lead.[10] In economic theory, the dominant firm uses the market demand curve for all competing products including its own to set an optimal price that maximizes its own profit. The price leader's optimal price becomes the market price for all competing products especially in the absence of effective product differentiation, i.e., if customers view the competing products as commodities or close substitutes. Specifically, as one economist has observed: "In an oligopolistic situation the price that maximizes the profits of the price leader will always be lower than the price (or prices) that maximizes the profits of the price followers."[11]

The price leader typically not only sets the price but initiates price changes which the other firms are expected to follow. Once the price leader has set the price, each of the other competitors of the oligopoly faces a highly elastic demand curve for its product meaning that it can sell all it wants at that price but little above it. If a company tries to sell its product significantly below this price, it is subject to sanctions by the price leader who may retaliate by dropping its price even further. The situation becomes more complicated when there is more than one dominant firm in the market and one of these tries to challenge the price leader and assume its role. Other difficulties may arise when the price leader attempts to initiate a price change and the others refuse to follow with similar changes or a firm other than the price leader initiates a major price change. The result may be either a short pricing skirmish or an all-out price war.

How does a firm in an oligopolistic industry become its price leader? Typically the price leader is the largest firm in terms of sales revenue and market share and the most profitable. The reasons for its leadership position vary. Sometimes the price leader was the first in the industry and established its brand as the standard of comparison. It may be the firm with the greatest technological prowess that brings out a continuous stream of advanced new products unmatched by its rivals. At other times the price leader has a significant cost advantage so that it can produce more economically and efficiently and set its prices accordingly. Other possible competitive advantages may lie in a superior distribution network or a more effective advertising and promotional effort. More often than not, it is a combination of all.

It should be noted that not all or even most industries with an oligopolistic market structure follow the practice of price leadership or other forms of tacit collusion especially where the competing products are highly differentiated. They not only vigorously compete using all the non-price marketing strategy variables available to them but also on price. It is only that firms that are part of an oligopoly are more susceptible to collusive practices and therefore face more scrutiny from state and federal agencies concerned with competition or the lack thereof.

8.5 Pricing Strategies with Cost Economies

In certain industries companies base their pricing strategies on cost advantages they enjoy over their marketplace rivals. Large companies benefit from *economies of scale* which result from the well-known fact that in almost every business activity including purchasing, manufacturing, distribution, and marketing, direct incremental and fixed costs tend to decline with increasing volume.

These cost advantages can lead to *price leadership* in oligopolistic industries and the ability to set prices and terms most profitable to the price leader and which smaller firms are obliged to follow.

Another cost advantage comes from so-called *economies of experience* first popularized in the early 1970s by the Boston Consulting Group.[12] Unlike economies of scale which depend on cost reductions due to current output volume, experience economies are the result of cost reductions due to the *accumulated* volume of output. The effect results from experience—the more a company produces the more it learns to do so more efficiently. Specifically, Boston Consulting found that due to the experience effect, every doubling of accumulated output results in a predictable percentage decrease in a product's total unit cost in constant dollars. By plotting total unit cost as a function of cumulative volume one obtains a so-called *experience curve* which, if plotted on log-log paper, is a straight line. Its slope typically ranges between 10 and 30 percent with 20 to 30 percent being the most common. For a ninety percent experience curve, for example, unit costs will decrease by 10 percent with each doubling of cumulative volume.

This finding and a related one, namely, that firms with dominant market shares are more profitable than their smaller competitors, led Boston Consulting to recommend a daring new pricing strategy. Their clients companies were advised not to wait for cost reductions before cutting prices but to project future costs based on the experience effect and reduce prices prior to and in anticipation of these lower costs. The result would be a faster doubling of cumulative volume and a dominant and sustainable market share with superior profits. Experience curve pricing soon became a fad touted by many consultants. However, the strategy proved disastrous for many firms and sometimes, in their quest for market share, led to skirmishes and price wars. The reason was that the conditions necessary for experience curve pricing had not been met.

Pricing on the experience curve can be profitable but may fail for a number of reasons including buyers who are insufficiently price sensitive, insufficient added value in the end-product to justify a price reduction, the experience effect may not be proprietary with the

126

firm, and the firm's competitors will match any price-cut to maintain market share. A quantitative analysis suggests that for experience curve pricing to be viable at least three conditions must be met:[13]

i) The product's demand must be highly price elastic, i.e., buyers must base their purchase decision mainly on the price variable;

ii) the market for the product must be growing with growth rates that are large and increasing with time;

iii) the firm must actively pursue a cost reduction program to improve productivity and efficiency in all areas of its business.

In general, for most firms buying market share by price reductions is not a viable option for the long term. A far more effective strategy is to reduce incremental and fixed costs for all products and services, increase the perceived values of these products and services in the eyes of customers, and charge prices commensurate with these values.

8.6 Combination Strategies

This chapter has focused on pricing strategies but firms obviously use others to reach their goals and price may be just one of the four marketing strategy variable employed. Some companies such as Apple, Samsung, and Microsoft have attained their goals by a strategy of aggressive product innovation resulting in a continuous stream of must-have products and services. These products enjoy steep demand curves making them price-insensitive so that firms can successfully employ skim pricing and thereby reap the huge rewards associated with product innovation in consumer electronics.

In the retail and fast foods industries another combination strategy that may be called *market saturation* is evident because member firms completely saturate their markets with huge numbers of retail outlets and restaurants around the globe. Thus, as of this writing, McDonald's, Starbucks, and Wal-Mart operate over 34,000, 21,000, and 11,000 retail outlets, respectively, world-wide. While saturation strategies are not illegal, they nevertheless include strong anticompetitive elements because they drive out local competition making such firms the dominant players in their territories by way of sheer numbers. Their focus is on the marketing strategy variable concerned with "Place," namely, location, logistics, and distribution. Interestingly, the three companies mentioned employ different pricing strategies with two being known for penetration and the other for a skimming strategy.

The business models employed by these firms, including the franchise concept, has been successfully exported overseas where it has even changed lifestyles. European coffee aficionados used to sit in locally owned cafés hours at a time over a can of gourmet coffee while reading or people watching. Starbucks has much changed that culture by putting their restaurants at the most strategic locations throughout Europe's major towns and cities forcing many of these traditional coffee houses out of business. Sometimes the standard model had to be modified. Thus, McDonald's was obliged to sell beer in its European restaurants and redo their standard menu in Asia to make their system work.

In some cases the standard corporate model has not worked at all. Thus, Wal-Mart, the world's largest retailer, had to withdraw from Germany and South Korea and more recently India. As Kotler and Keller noted: "Wal-Mart's tried-and-true formula of low prices, tight inventory control, and big selection doesn't always pay off in markets where consumers have different shopping habits, discount competitors are already entrenched, and employees and suppliers are less subservient."[14] The company left Germany, Europe's largest economy, in 2006 after ten years of continuous losses estimated at three billion dollars. Even the world's most successful and sophisticated companies cannot always succeed.

8.7 Competitive Bid Pricing

An interesting pricing and profit opportunity area is competitive bid pricing which comes into play when the buyer is a government entity or other regulated body although large business firms sometimes use this practice as well. It assures the buyer that the product or project requirements are fully met at the lowest possible price. Competitive bidding is a specialized field and beyond the scope of this book.[15] However, a few words about it appear in order.

A buyer may issue a *request for quotation* (RFQ) for purchases involving just a few thousand dollars such as in the case of a government agency or firm buying its yearly requirements of office supplies, or millions in the case of a state for the building of a new highway or bridge or similar construction project, or billions in the case of an airline buying a new fleet of airplanes. For certain companies, such as those in the defense industry, competitive bidding may represent the only type of sales and purchase transaction engaged in.

Competitive bid contracts can be a very profitable source of sales revenue and profits for businesses in diverse industries and markets. Nevertheless, many managements eschew it because of the costs involved in getting on a buyer's *approved bidders list*, in processing bid requests, and in administering the contract in the case of a successful bid. The purpose of the approved bidders list is to ensure that only qualified firms submit bids while any bids by spurious suppliers who may not be able to fulfill the contractual obligations are eliminated. An item often overlooked by potential bidders is the cost savings that usually accrue such as from the diminished need for advertising and sales promotion.

Due to the bidding costs and the uncertainty of the outcomes, firms typically rely on *probabilistic models* and other statistical methods to assist them in preparing bids that are most likely to both win the contract and also be profitable. The most common fixed-price competitive bid model is known as the *specific opponent approach*. It applies when a firm knows its competitors which are typically the firms on the buyer's approved bidders list. Using this model, each bidder keeps careful track of the bidding history of its competitors on similar projects by noting how many times these companies submitted bids above the *bid ratio* defined as the ratio of the bid price to the estimated project cost.

To obtain this bid ratio, each firm estimates its opponents' costs based on its own estimated project cost while the bid prices are those normally published by the buyer after the award is made. These bid ratios are then used in a probability analysis to determine the company's best bid, i.e., the bid with the highest expected value.

Notes

1. Thomas Nagle et al, *The Strategy and Tactics of Pricing*, 6.

2. Joel Dean, "Pricing Policies for New Products," *Harvard Business Review on Pricing*, 114-120.

3. Theodore Levitt, "Exploit the Product Life Cycle," *Harvard Business Review*, Nov.-Dec. 1965, 1-15. See also Theodore Levitt, "Exploiting the Product Life Cycle," *The Marketing Mode*, 28-52.

4. Nariman K. Dhalla and Sonia Yuspeh, "Forget the Product Life Cycle Concept!," *Harvard Business Review*, January-February 1976, 102-111. These two advertising agency executives plotted shipments of such consumer staples as cereals, cigarettes, and toilet tissue between 1955 and 1974 as reported in *Advertising Age* and other external and internal company sources and found little resemblance to the postulated PLC curves. The fact that bulk manufacturer shipments were used in their sales plots rather than actual product sales most probably accounted for their findings.

5. Robert Dolan and Hermann Simon, *Power Pricing*, 278-279.

6. Theodore Levitt, *The Marketing Mode*, 40-52.

7. Ross Eckert and Richard Leftwich, *The Price System and Resource Allocation*, 208-215.

8. J. P. Gould and C. E. Ferguson, *Microeconomic Theory*, 344.

9. J. P. Gould and C. E. Ferguson, supra at 342.

10. For a discussion of the economic theory behind price leadership see, for example, Ross Eckert and Richard Leftwich, supra at 409-411, and J. P. Gould and C. E. Ferguson, supra at 338-342.

11. Wilford Eiteman, *Price Determination in Oligopolistic and Monopolistic Situations*, 40.

12. Thomas Nagle and Reed Holden, *The Strategy and Tactics of Pricing*, 312-315.

13. Kent Monroe, *Pricing*, 254-264.

14. Philip Kotler and Kevin Keller, *Marketing Management*, 619. The problems encountered by Wal-Mart in Germany would have involved all three factors mentioned by the authors not the least of which would have been the presence of Aldi which has dominated the German discount foods business for decades. The company also operates Aldi stores in the U.S. where it owns Trader Joe's. In a sure sign that deep discounting based on cost advantages can be very profitable, the owners of Aldi, the Albrechts, are, like the Waltons of Wal-Mart, multi-billionaires.

15. For a good introduction to fixed-price competitive bidding see, for example, Kent Monroe, supra at 411-428.

CHAPTER

9

Market Oriented Pricing

The only valid pricing objective in today's uncertain environment is to ask the customer to pay for the "perceived value" of what he is buying. That holds for products or services, consumer or industrial goods.[1]

Market oriented and specifically *perceived value pricing* with its focus on the customer's perception of a product's value is a radical departure from the cost-plus approach in which the focus was on the product's cost of manufacture. For marketers, market oriented pricing has opened up entirely new opportunities for proactive and creative pricing methods and techniques which help to significantly expand growth and profit opportunities for their firms. Witness, for example, the enormous profits being generated by some high-tech consumer products and services companies in the field of wireless communications which would have been unimaginable by firms using the traditional cost-driven pricing methods of the past.

This chapter opens with a discussion of the concept of perceived value including a customer purchase model and the seller's response in the products and services offered. The psychological aspects involved in a potential buyer's purchase decision, such as the reference price, price-quality and other effects, are covered next. This is followed by some common pricing practices and techniques used by market oriented pricers.

9.1 Customers and the Perception of Value

Before a company can effectively price a product or service it must know what value the customer, and more specifically, the target group of customers, places in that product or service. Since individual customers and customer groups have their own value systems, value is a very subjective quantity and marketers speak of the *perceived value* rather than the more definitive value.

What then is perceived value? Dan Nimer, a former business executive turned pricing consultant and one of the earliest and best-known proponents of perceived value pricing, defined it as "what the customer is willing to pay for the 'bundle' of benefits offered by the supplier."[2] The term bundle is to emphasize that the customer is evaluating not only the physical product or service but many other factors that go into the purchase decision such as product quality, availability, and service. A justified price, according to Nimer, is "one that represents the value the buyer puts on what he buys."[3] The larger the product's perceived value, the higher should be the asking price.

A buyer's purchase decision is a complex one that may be simplified somewhat if one looks at the mental exercise she or he typically performs to arrive at it. Specifically, the customer is expected to weigh the benefits of owning and using the product or service against the total cost likely to be incurred. This evaluation may be expressed thus:

Perceived value = Perceived benefits − Perceived cost

It is only when the perceived benefits outweigh the perceived cost yielding a positive *customer perceived value* (CPV) that a purchase transaction will take place. Again, it is the *perceived* benefits and cost and not necessarily the real ones from the standpoint of a disinterested observer.

Consider, for example, some of the factors the buyer of a new automobile is likely to weigh before reaching a decision to buy or not to buy a particular brand and model.

i) Perceived benefits: Brand image, style, special features, standard and available accessories, reliability, engine performance, gas mileage, roominess, interior décor, trunk space, safety features, available financing, warranty terms, location and reputation of dealership, and personal relationships with the sales staff.

ii) Perceived cost: Net purchase price after applicable dealer discounts and trade-in value of present car, operating expenses, maintenance costs, financing costs, and insurance premiums.

Sometimes the customer has made up her or his mind on which brand and model to purchase to the exclusion of any others from further consideration. In most situations, however, the customer is likely to visit other car dealerships offering similar brands and models of interest and make this mental assessment:

$$\frac{\text{Perceived Value Product A}}{\text{Perceived Value Product B}} = k$$

If the customer were to rate the perceived value of each brand or model from 1 to 10, then a purchase of Product A is likely only if the *perceived value index* $k > 1.0$ and especially if this index is much larger than 1.0.

For the seller, this buyer model suggests a series of steps to profitably engage the target market including value assessment, value creation, value communication, and value recoupment.

9.1.1 Value Assessment

Value assessment for a new product or service should begin even before the development stage. Management must select a target market and determine the wants and needs of that market segment. This requires that the value system of these target customers become known. In other words, what design, performance and other factors are important to these buyers and what are not. This assessment must include a range of possible prices the product or service should be offered at. Next a feasibility analysis is required to determine whether, based on anticipated manufacturing and marketing costs and sales volume, the firm can profitably develop and market the new product or service. If not, another product-market segment may be more suitable or else the project may have to be abandoned. The following chapter discusses market segmentation, especially price segmentation, in more detail.

9.1.2 Value Creation

Business firms exist to create value. They create value for their owners and equity holders in profits earned, their employees in salaries and wages paid, their suppliers in products and services purchased, and their communities in taxes paid. Most importantly, companies create value in the products and services they develop and market. As previously mentioned, this value goes beyond the physical product and includes the entire package offered including warranties, payment terms, and customer service. Firms differ in their relative success for value creation with the most profitable ones continuously creating the highest perceived value in terms of innovative new products and services or in terms of cost reductions that make their products and services more affordable.

9.1.3 Value Communication

An important part of perceived value pricing is to convey a *value message* to potential customers of a product or service. The most popular and effective way for conveying such a message is through advertising and sales promotion. One way this marketing strategy variable may be used is to enhance a firm's image and raise the perceived value of all its products and services. Not surprisingly, the most successful companies and brands also are the ones most prolific in using this important tool. However, most print, television, and other media advertising focuses on the features and benefits of specific models to enhance their perceived value in the eyes of potential buyers. In the absence of effective value communication the purchase decision will default to the price variable. Price competition is generally not conducive to maximizing contribution and profits.

In this author's opinion there is undoubtedly a strong social component in all advertising in that the reader or viewer is well aware that he or she is part of a much larger audience. In the buyer's mind, this public and transparent aspect of advertising legitimizes and strengthens the message conveyed. What is well-known and popular is also desirable. An especially powerful form of advertising is *word-of-mouth*. A satisfied or dissatisfied customer, especially one close to the potential buyer or one whose judgment and veracity can be trusted, can have a very profound influence on a potential buyer's value perception and purchase decision. Firms are well advised to follow up on any product or service complaints because word will get around. By word of mouth one must also include the Internet and especially the social media such as Facebook and Twitter.

9.1.4 Value Recoupment

A firm recoups its expenditures in value creation and communication by way of the purchase prices for its products and services. This is where the firm gets rewarded for its efforts on behalf of the customers it serves. Unlike cost-plus pricing, value-based pricing has no simple rules and formulas to follow. In theory, the firm's *price discretion* extends from the price floor, which we have previously identified as the product's average unit variable cost, to the product's or service's perceived value expressed in monitory terms.

A business does not have the market to itself, of course, and if it does, it is likely to be for only a short time. It must content with rival firms which puts an upper limit on the prices it can charge. It is also true that the customer typically does not want to pay the full price at which she or he values the product or service. Like the seller, the buyer seeks to make a profit on the transaction and do so by paying a price below his or her perceived value price where possible.

9.2 Psychological Aspects of Pricing

There is a strong human element in peoples' perception of value and the prices they are willing to pay for certain products and services. These emotional factors can exert a strong influence on buyer behavior especially if the purchase is a major one in terms of financial commitment or social status. Buyers show certain repetitive behavioral patterns in their evaluation of product and service offerings and marketers must take these into account to be able to price profitably. Specifically, these factors strongly impact the demand curves and the P.E.D. levels. Pricing experts and authors Nagle and Holden identified nine psychological factors that influence the perception of value which they termed *effects*: i) Reference price effect, ii) difficult comparison effect, iii) switching cost effect, iv) price-quality effect, v) expenditure effect, vi) end-benefit effect, vii) shared cost effect, viii) fairness effect, and ix) framing effect.[4] The following describes a few of these and other important effects.

9.2.1 The Reference Price Effect

Except in the case of an innovation that is completely new to the market, a customer is likely to have internalized a purchase price that he or she considers fair and reasonable especially in the case of a frequently purchased item. In other words, the customer has a reference price with which offerings of the same or competing products may be compared. This is known as the *reference price effect*. Thus, the buyer of groceries is likely to know the approximate prices of a number of items and expects to pay these prices on subsequent purchases. Prices that are out of line with these reference or expected prices are likely to be questioned and even rejected with the customer looking for alternatives. This puts strong limits on a marketer's pricing discretion.

Marketers can and do influence reference prices in a number of ways. For example, a reference price may be raised by adding a premium-priced product to the line which will make a mid-priced product more acceptable. It may also encourage buyers to *trade up* to the more expensive model. Retailers try to influence reference prices by advertising manufacturers' suggested retail prices or the higher prices of competitors along with the lower store prices. The behavioral finding that the first price buyers see or hear mentioned becomes the reference price has given rise to *top-down selling*. Here, the seller of a product or service quotes a higher price first which is followed by a price more acceptable to the buyer.

The reference price effect also has important ramifications for new product pricing. Once the product is on the market and made available at a specific price, that price is likely to become the reference price unless it is made known to potential customers that the price is a special introductory price which will be raised to its normal level on a future date. Because it is more difficult to raise prices than lower them, it is often advisable to premium-price a new product and effectively communicate its value to potential customers rather than enter the market with a low price unless rapid market penetration is found more favorable to long term profits.

9.2.2 The Price-Quality Effect

Where the prospective buyer is unfamiliar with a class of products or services, the purchase decision will likely depend on the relative price level for a specific product or service. The reason is that customers intuitively believe this price to be fair and equitable (as when derived by a cost-plus formula) and that it is a reflection of its worth and quality. In other words, the higher the price of a product or service, the higher must be its quality. This notion finds expression in the old adage "you get what you pay for." To marketers, this in known as the *price-quality effect*. It too has important pricing ramifications. It can work for or against a product or service. If a product or service is premium-priced it may convey a message of high quality but a price perceived too low may signal shoddy quality and be rejected even though the two products or services may be of comparable quality.

In fact, Gabor has suggested that a potential buyer for a given product or service enters the market with two price limits in mind, namely, an upper and a lower limit.[5] A price beyond the upper limit will be viewed as too expensive and the product or service eliminated from further consideration. If the price falls below the lower limit, the customer will suspect the quality and he or she will again reject the product or service. Both limits are quality assessments, of course, in that a price above the upper limit is viewed as a quality level that is higher than required. Customers, therefore, operate within a *price band* of acceptable prices beyond which no purchase will take place.

The price-quality effect is especially important in the pricing of services because, unlike material goods, these cannot be inspected before the purchase.[6] This is especially true of specialized, non-standardized services such as advertising, accounting, health care, law, and management consulting. The size of the retainer or hourly fee is perceived as a strong indicator of quality. For this reason lawyers and business consultants charge new potential clients a small fixed fee for a first session which is subsequently credited to the account if the prospect is satisfied and becomes a client. The price-quality effect is of less importance in the case of standardized services such as car washes, laundries, and dry cleaning. Here the customer has a fairly good notion of the quality level of the service ahead of time and does not need to rely on the price as an indicator.

Scenario A

Monica is a successful regional sales manager for an up-and-coming high-tech consumer products company and hopes to be considered for the newly created position of vice-president of marketing and sales. To smooth the way she and husband Ken have decided to invite the company's president Haley and husband Bill to dinner. They would like to serve a good wine with the meal but neither knows anything about wines. At their favorite supermarket, which carries a large selection of French wines, Monica spots an especially pricey bottle labeled Châteauneuf-du-Pape and says to Ken "Get a load of this, this must be really good stuff."

The couple picks up a couple of bottles of their discovery and take it home. Neither is aware that this particular wine, known as the wine of the popes, has a very rustic, tannic character that is not to many people's taste. After dinner, the guests complement their hosts on their excellent choice of wine. Fortunately, it seems, Haley and Bill know as much about wine as their hosts do. Monica tops it off by turning to her husband saying "It's our favorite, isn't it Ken?"

9.2.3 The Prestige Effect

What may be called the *image* or *prestige effect* is quite different from the price-quality effect in that in this case the product or service is well-known to the customer and he or she can come to a purchase decision without speculating on its quality. Here the customer chooses a product or service not for its intrinsic value but for the status image or prestige it conveys in its possession and use. Because of the product's usually lofty price tag, its perceived value is very high to a select group of customers who find satisfaction in its exclusiveness and in knowing that few others can afford it.

Many luxury brands such as Armani, Cartier, Coach, Dior, Gucci, Hermes, Louis Vuitton, and Rolex benefit from this effect and their owners tend to be exceptionally profitable. This is why, for example, an Armani T-shirt may cost a few hundred dollars, a Louis Vuitton handbag over a thousand, a Cartier watch several thousand, and a Leica camera over ten thousand dollars when other brands that are equally functional, stylish, and high-quality may be had for a fraction of these prices. The demand curve for these sought-after luxury brands are typically very steep allowing the marketer extensive price discretion. While most customers will say "Why pay more when I can get it for less?" to the delight of marketers there is a substantial portion of the populace which seems guided by the motto "Why pay less when I can get it for more?"

Scenario B

Sadie is a supervisor at a prestigious Manhattan investment bank. In the morning she and her partner Robin never seem to have enough time for breakfast together so on the way to work Sadie stops by a Starbucks restaurant and picks up a cup of café latte plus a pastry which she carries to the bank. On the way she passes a Dunkin' Donuts restaurant and, although she likes their coffee better and would prefer not to keep paying the starry prices of their competitor but use the extra bucks to buy some other things she needs, she never gets breakfast there. That's because Sadie highly values that Starbucks logo on her cup. To walk around the office with a Dunkin' Donuts cup would just not be the in thing for someone in her position, she feels, and so she keeps to her customary early morning routine.

Scenario C

Joe Blitzinger is a retiree from the U.S. State Department where he specialized in Chinese-American relations. After writing a couple of books on the subject which brought him critical acclaim and much publicity, he was contacted by a member of the staff of the Harry Walker Agency, reputedly the country's largest lecture bureau, to join its roster of speakers. The company's clients include former U.S. presidents, captains of industry, Noble laureates, bestselling authors, Hollywood stars, and many other celebrities. Speaking fees are typically in the 4-5 figure range with the agency taking about a one-third cut for its services.[7] Joe did not hesitate to accept the proposal. He was fairly well off financially but could use the extra money. He also felt that by his talks he would be making a real contribution by educating the American public about an ascendant China and the pivotal role it is destined to play in the twenty-first century.

Joe had never been known for an extravagant life style. He had been wearing suits off the rack, a nondescript watch, and driven an older model car. With his new position, income, and the audiences he would be addressing, Joe realized he had to reinvent himself and project an image of affluence and sophistication. Joe now sports Armani suits, Prada shoes, and a Rolex watch. He arrives at his speaking assignments in a chauffeured limo. Joe's new attire does not fit or look much better than what he had been wearing before nor does his new watch give better time. What he has gained are symbols of status in line with the expectations of his discriminating audiences. These legitimize the fees he is being paid since they demonstrate success made possibly by other businesses and organizations which highly value his services as well.

9.2.4 The Shared Cost Effect

People are more likely to purchase a product or service and are less sensitive to its price when they pay only part or none of it. Examples of this *shared cost effect* abound and companies in the transportation and hospitality industries such as airlines, car rental companies, hotels, restaurants, and travel bureaus take full advantage of it. Senators, representatives, and heads of federal departments and agencies regularly make consultation and fact-finding trips to foreign capitals and less prominent places while state governors and mayors travel overseas to promote trade. Needless to say, when these government officials and their entourages are out of town they do not fly economy class, stay in one-star hotels, or dine at McDonald's. Similarly, when an insurance company pays for all or most of the cost of health care, or reimburses for damage suffered to a home or automobile, service providers can be expected to be much more in the premium pricing mode than otherwise.

Many other examples abound. Major business firms routinely send key employees to seminars and executive training programs to improve their business skills. This is beneficial to both companies and employees but is normally fully paid for by the employers. In particular, business schools at major universities offer accelerated MBA programs that are considerably more expensive per semester hour than for regular students. Trade fairs, exhibitions, congresses, conventions, and seminars paid for by other than the attendees are a boon to many businesses. Finally, many professionals are required to keep current in their field to retain their state licenses. Such expenses are tax deductible which means that these people too will not be overly cautious regarding their expenditures.

9.2.5 The Captive Customer Effect

Accessories typically command premium prices because if a customer has already purchased the basic product he or she is not likely to buy another brand to accessorize it. Thus, if a customer of a certain brand of camera is in the market for an interchangeable lens, he or she is most likely to buy it from the camera maker and not from some other source especially if the customer is an amateur and not a professional photographer. Needless to say, the lenses and other accessories will cost the customer more than if they had been part of the original purchase. Countless other examples may be cited for what may be called the *captive customer effect*.

Replacement parts and tie-in products are other examples of the captive customer effect. Manufacturers and dealers charge considerably more for replacement parts because the price sensitivity for these is relatively low unless the identical part is available from another vendor at a much cheaper price. An example of a tie-in product would be the ink cartridge for a printer. Thus, Hewlett-Packard, for example, is known to use penetration pricing for its printers but skim the market for the ink cartridges it recommends for use with its products.

The service industry is well-known for taking advantage of the captive customer effect. Banks and credit card companies obtain a substantial part of their income from overdraft charges, late payment fees, and similar fees and charges. For airlines, charges for checked baggage and flight schedule changes are a large source of profits. Movie theaters typically make more money on their concession operations than on the tickets they sell and usually forbid patrons from bringing their own snacks and drinks onto the premises. Vacationers traveling in Western Europe know that whenever one of the numerous trade shows or conventions is in town, the prices of hotel rooms skyrocket as hoteliers cash in on the temporary surge in demand for accommodations. In each of these cases the customer has no or very limited alternatives to paying the going rate.

9.2.6 The Unique Benefits Effect

Where a product or service stands out among competing ones for one or more characteristics or features potential customers perceive to offer some unique benefit or benefits, it is more likely to attract customer attention and a willingness to buy. As usual, by product is meant the entire "package" not just the physical product itself. Differentiated products are more price inelastic meaning customers are less sensitive to the purchase price which, in turn, gives firms more pricing discretion. The *unique benefits effect* can be seen in most of the products and services on the market today as companies try to *differentiate* their products and services from those of competitors. In fact, based on the previous discussion on the demand curve and the P.E.D., the following pricing proposition can safely be stated.

Pricing Proposition 6

The more unique and differentiated a product or service is the steeper will be its demand curve and the less sensitive it will be to price changes while the more undifferentiated and commodity-like a product or service is the flatter will be its demand curve and the more price-sensitive it will be.

9.2.7 The Weber-Fechner Effect

A behavioral effect that is especially useful in *product line pricing*, i.e., the pricing of different models or versions of the same basic product is the *Weber-Fechner effect*. Weber, and later Fechner, were behavioral scientists who found that the relationship between a stimulus S and the resulting response R takes this form:

$$R = k \log S + a \qquad \text{(Eq. 9.1)}$$

where k and a are constants. Equation 9-1 is known as the Weber-Fechner Law. In a pricing context, S would be the price and R the market response to that price. This law can be interpreted to mean that price perception follows a logarithmic rather than a linear scale. In other words, price differentials between models of the line should become wider as one approaches the highest priced model.

Monroe gives two formulas by which the price of any model j may be computed based on the Weber-Fechner effect.[8]

$$Pj = P_L k^{j-1} \qquad \text{(Eq. 9.2)}$$

where P_L is the price of the lowest-priced model and k the ratio to be applied for the price of each succeeding model. Also, one has:

$$\log k = \frac{1}{n-1} (\log P_H - \log P_L) \qquad \text{(Eq. 9.3)}$$

where n is the number of models in the line and P_H the price of the highest-priced model. The low and high end prices *anchor* the product line price-wise and must be chosen carefully and preferably for maximum sales revenue or contribution dollars.

Illustrative Example: Droneco Ltd. (I)

Droneco Ltd. was started to manufacture and market small surveillance drones for governmental and private use and the first line of the Droneco brand of products is now ready for market introduction. During the product planning stage, a number of target markets were identified including i) national parks and state forestry services for use in spotting wildfires before they could do any significant damage, ii) western cattle ranchers, whose herds are spread over large areas, for keeping   track of their livestock, iii) governmental agencies to patrol their countries' borders to prevent illegal immigration or the smuggling of goods, and iv) African game reserves, such as ones to protect endangered elephants or rhinos, for locating and apprehending poachers before they can reach their targets.

Droneco's market study revealed that potential customers were willing to invest as little as $5,000 or as much as $30,000 per vehicle and the line of five models was designed with these two end prices in mind. These drone versions differ mainly in their speed and maneuverability, their range of operation, the length of time they can stay afloat, and the quality of their sensor systems. Droneco's marketing department is familiar with the Weber-Fechner effect and wants to price the Droneco line to take advantage of it. The actual features and benefits of each model would then be brought in line with these prices to maximize overall contribution from the line.

By Equation (9.3) one has:

$\log k = 1 / 4 \times (\log 30{,}000 - \log 5{,}000) = 0.25 \times (4.4771 - 3.6990)$
$\log k = 0.25 \times 0.7781 = 0.1945$
$k = 1.565$

Using this ratio in Equation (9.2) for the five models one obtains:

$P_1 = \$5{,}000$
$P_2 = \$5{,}000 \times 1.565 = \$7{,}825$
$P_3 = \$7{,}825 \times 1.565 = \$12{,}246$
$P_4 = \$12{,}246 \times 1.565 = \$19{,}165$
$P_5 = \$19{,}165 \times 1.565 = \$30{,}000$

The marketing department is also familiar with odd-number pricing (see Subsection 9.4.4 below) and will most likely offer the five models at these prices: $4,999.95, $7,824.95, $12,245.95, $19,164.95, and $29,999.95.

9.3 Setting an Initial Price

While it is a fact that value-based pricing has no rules or formulas to offer by which an initial price that is both profitable for the firm and acceptable to buyers may be determined, some guidelines do exist for the case where a similar product or service is already on the market. The general approach is to use a competitor's price for a similar product or service as a reference and adjust that price to account for differences in the features and benefits supplied by the two competing brands or models. In other words, the marketer adds positive differential values to the reference price and subtracts negative ones to obtain a net differential value which, when converted to a dollar figure, will give at least a ball park estimate for an appropriate price point for the new product. To ensure that the comparison is made with a directly competing brand or model, it is often advisable to find out from potential customers who they would buy from if not from the marketer's firm.

Nagle et al recommend a three-stage price setting process that consists of: i) Defining a price window for each served market segment; ii) setting the initial price for that segment; and iii) communicating the price to the market.[9] The price window is defined by the ceiling, the highest allowable price point, and the price floor. Price ceiling and floor depend on the differential value (positive and negative) vis-à-vis the closest competing product and the relevant costs of the product. Setting the initial price point depends on the pricing objectives, price sensitivity considerations, and the price-volume tradeoffs with their impact on profitability. The communication stage is to ensure that the price is perceived to be fair. The obvious problem with this approach is that it will be difficult to assign a dollar (economic) value to the positive and negative differential values of the competing products.

Pricing consultant Mark Stiving recommends the following five-step approach:[10] i) Identify your customer's second-best option to your product; ii) determine the price of the second-best option; iii) list your advantages and disadvantages relative to the second-best option; iv) estimate in dollars and cents the value of each advantage and disadvantage; and v) calculate your price:

$$\text{Price} = \text{Price of second-best option} + \text{Value of}$$
$$\text{advantages} - \text{Value of disadvantages}$$

Concerning step iii), the author notes, one easily overlooked differentiating feature is the brand name. Buyers normally have a favorite brand and this can have a dominant impact on the purchase decision. It must therefore be given extra weight in the analysis. Regarding the fourth step, i.e., estimating the dollar value of each advantage and disadvantage, "This is hard," the author admits. "Not only is it subjective, it's difficult to convince a marketer to be honest about this." Stiving suggests use of some statistical techniques such as conjoint analysis or, more simply, asking potential buyers how they value the different features and benefits of the product or service.

A third approach to setting a value-based price is offered by pricing consultant Rafi Mohammed who recommends a four-step technique:[11] i) Identify the next-best alternative and use it as a base price; ii) determine the product's differences; iii) create a demand curve; and iv) undertake a "profit maximizer analysis." The most difficult step is obviously the third—the demand curve. Estimating a demand curve showing the trade-off between price and sales volume for a new product is probably one of the most challenging assignment in marketing. The author suggests constructing one by use of diverse tools such as market research including conjoint analysis, internal company data on sales volume at various price points, and experienced judgment. The profit maximizer analysis consists of using the demand curve and computing the sales revenue, total cost, and profit at various price points and selecting the price at which the profit is maximized.

Summarizing, none of the above procedures and techniques are without serious flaws. However, the basic premise of most, namely, that all prices must be market and perceived value oriented and tailored to specific market segments is valid. For a new product or service that must compete with those already on the market, the prices of competitors can serve as useful reference prices. The firm's price must be adjusted up or down to take into account the perceived value differences, both negative and positive, between the firm's product and the competing ones. Translating these perceived differences into dollars to arrive at a price will be a major challenge. If there is a question on whether to price high or low, the former can be recommended because it is always less problematic to lower a price than raise it once the product or service has come on the market.

9.4 Pricing Practices and Techniques

Market oriented pricing has given rise to a number of pricing practices and techniques the most common ones of which are discussed below.

9.4.1 Price Bundling and Unbundling

Price bundling, also known as *product bundling*, is popular in every type of industry or market and for both consumer and industrial products and services since it is beneficial to sellers and buyers alike. With bundling a firm offers two or more of its products or services at a total price that is lower than if the customer purchased each product or service separately. For the firm, bundling increases sales revenue and strengthens brand loyalty by encouraging the purchase of additional products and services the customer may not have purchased at all or elsewhere while the customer benefits from lower prices. *Unbundling* is the reverse practice where products and services previously offered only as bundles, a practice known as *pure bundling*, now become available separately.

Sometimes pure bundling makes good sense in the case of an innovative and complex new product where the potential buyer may have difficulty in putting all the elements of a working system together. A case in point was IBM's successful introduction in 1964 of the System/360 digital computer for business use by offering lease or sales contracts that included hardware, software, systems engineering, maintenance, and employee training as one bundle. This marketing strategy was very successful for about five years when the U.S. Department of Justice sued IBM alleging attempts to monopolize the digital computer system market in violation of the Sherman Antitrust Act. Later that same year (1969), IBM decided to unbundle by charging for hardware, software, and services separately. Most bundling today goes by the term *mixed bundling* where the customer has the choice of buying either a bundle or each component à la carte.

Bundling is part of most peoples' everyday experiences. In restaurants, the diner can purchase individual food items à la carte or a complete meal including entrée, dessert, and drinks for a lesser price. McDonald's sells hamburger and chicken products individually or as a "meal deal" including French fries and a soft drink that costs less than the sum of the individual items. Hotels may bundle breakfast and some services with the room price at a discount. Cable companies usually offer cable, telephone, and Internet services at a special bundle price. Insurance companies allow their customers a special discount if they purchase both homeowners and auto insurance. Travel bureaus put together special packages that may include the flight or cruise ticket, hotel accommodations, meals, and travel guide expenses. Many other examples of bundling could be cited.

In a price-sensitive market when price competition becomes fierce, companies may decide that *unbundling* of previously bundled products and services is more profitable. Air travel provides the perfect example. A complimentary meal used to be included on most long distance flights. To reduce costs and improve profitability, this practice has been largely discontinues and meals are now available at an extra charge. Similarly, a traveler's baggage used to be checked in free while now only one piece of luggage is so treated. Interestingly, in line with our previous discussion on oligopolies and their coordinated behavior, practically all the air lines follow these same practices in what antitrust lawyers call conscious parallelism.

Bundling, if not handled properly, can lead to customer ill will and his or her decision to split purchases among competing service providers. Consider the customer who had been receiving a special bundle price for cable, telephone, and Internet services and whose monthly bill suddenly takes a twenty percent or more jump. On checking with the cable company, the customer is told that the bundle price was a promotional feature that expired after one year. In the meantime, the customer has budgeted for this amount and cannot understand why this price should not continue to be available since the reason she or he decided to obtain all services from one provider was the expected cost savings.

Clearly, bundling raises a customer expectancy of more favorable treatment price-wise on a continuing basis which should be honored. The company, after all, continues to benefit from bundling its products as a result of cost savings and customer loyalty. For the service provider this means it should consider not promoting the bundle with a large upfront discount but instead offering a smaller one without a time limit. This bundle discount should appear on the customer's monthly bill as a constant reminder of the benefits received by using all of the provider's services.

9.4.2 Private Label and Store Brands

National brands are typically marketed to the whole country. Because they are heavily advertised and obliged to meet high quality standards, such products tend to be relatively expensive. To appeal to a more price-sensitive market segment, private label brands, also known as *store brands*, have become a major part of the retail scene and are believed to now account for at least twenty percent of supermarket sales. Store brands are typically priced below the *national brands* which they are designed to imitate. According to Gabor, offering store brands can be a successful policy where i) the national brands are burdened by high marketing costs, ii) the quality of the national and store brands are comparable, and iii) the store has a favorable image in the eyes of the customer.[12]

Like price bundling, the use of private label or store brands brings benefits to all parties in the sales chain from producer to user including manufacturers, distributors, retailers, and customers. For customers the benefits are obvious in the cost-savings involved in buying a lower-priced store brand of good quality. For the retailer it has the benefit of drawing more price-sensitive shoppers into the store who are then likely to also buy from the more standard product offering carrying higher markups.

The benefits for the manufacturer of private label brands are also significant. It allows manufacturing at peak capacity thereby holding unit variable costs to a minimum. While sales at the lower prices and margins may not be very profitable, a steady stream of contribution dollars will help cover the firm's overhead costs. Where overcapacity exists, this is one way of dealing with it. A number of cost savings will accrue as well. Thus, since private label products are not advertised on a national level, the firm need not budget for this item. Most of these expenses are born by the retail chains. Additional cost savings may accrue from diminished quality and service levels. In fact, by selling under a private label a firm can protect the quality image of its name brand offerings.

Some companies employ private labels as *fighting brands* against price-aggressive competitors.[13] Consider a manufacturer of high quality, large-margin leather goods whose best seller is Product A. Suppose further, that an import from a low-cost manufacturer, Product B, has become available that not only simulates the company's product A in looks and style but is of a comparable quality and, most importantly, costs significantly less. The company may answer the challenge by offering a Product C under a private label to directly compete with Product B. Its low price may not make sales of Product C profitable but it will protect Product A by preventing the competitor from drawing price-sensitive customers away from Product A to Product B. Competition will now take place between Products B and C which the company can turn in its favor by positively differentiating Product C from Product B to raise its perceived value vis-à-vis its competition.

9.4.3 Price Lining

Price lining is the practice of offering an entire inventory of a class of products at a number of specific but limited prices.[14] It is not uncommon for a department store or other retailer to have a policy to carry merchandise only at specific price points. For the retailer, this tends to simplify the purchase, inventory, and pricing process. For these retailers the normal pricing procedure is reversed in that the store's buyers search for merchandise that can be sold at the set prices. To make the method work, a minimum of three basic price points is recommended which should roughly correspond to "good," "better," and "best." Also, these should be sufficiently far apart to suggest differences in quality. For example, a clothier's inventory of men's neckties might be sold at $20, $30, and $50 depending on type of material and quality.

The main argument for *price lining* for shoppers is that it makes it easier for them to make their selections since there are only a limited number of merchandise categories and associated price points to choose from. This pricing model could be especially useful for certain specialty retailers such as gift and jewelry shops since shoppers will normally have a price range for the intended gift in mind and price lining would make it easier to zero in on a suitable item. The drawback to price lining is, of course, that merchandise that shoppers may want to buy is often not available.

9.4.4 Odd-Number Pricing

Another pricing technique popular with retailers is to use a price that ends with an odd number because it is believed this is more attractive to shoppers than an even number. Also, this number should be slightly less than the closest round number. That is why most prices end in a 5 or 9 but never in a 6, 8 or 0. Thus, bananas may be priced at 59 cents a pound and not at 60 cents, a paperback novel at $19.95 rather than $20.00, and a television set at $499.95 rather than at $500.00. Customers undoubtedly focus on the left-most, the most significant, number in the price and give less regard to the remainder. They perceive a price just below a round number as being lower than it actually is, i.e., rather than rounding up to the nearest higher denomination, shoppers substantially exaggerate what may only be a marginal difference downward.[15] Here again, perception plays a key role in purchase behavior.

The practice must have a very beneficial impact on sales or it would not find almost universal favor with sellers of products and services. To the average shopper, merchandise priced at $9.95 is perceived to be a much better deal than something priced at $10.00 and a product priced at $3,995.95 is more attractively priced than the same product at $4,000.00. In either case, the customer perceives the lower price to be a bargain even though the actual price differential is negligibly small. A price ending in less than a full dollar would also signal to the price-sensitive shopper that it has been cut to the bare bone further reinforcing the bargain message.

9.4.5 "Raising the Price Without Raising the Price"

Raising prices for consumer or industrial products to adjust for cost increases or some other reason is as unpopular with sellers as it is with buyers. This is especially true where demand for the product is highly price elastic and the product is frequently purchased so that any price change will be instantly noticed. In such situations firms often "raise prices without raising prices" by such techniques as:[16]

* Changing the physical characteristics of the product
* Revising the discount structure
* Changing the payment terms
* Charging for delivery
* Raising the minimum acceptable order size
* Charging for special services such as rush orders
* Collecting interest on delinquent accounts

There are obviously many other creative ways by which prices may effectively be raised without the necessity of announcing a price increase.

Notes

1. Daniel A. Nimer, "Pricing The Profitable Sale Has A Lot To Do With Perception," *Sales Management / Special Report*, 1971,13.

2. Ibid.

3. Daniel A. Nimer, "Developing a Strategy for Pricing," *Management Review*, November 1971, 43.

4. Thomas Nagle and Reed Holden, *The Strategy and Tactics of Pricing*, 82-104.

5. André Gabor, *Pricing*, 254.

6. André Gabor, supra at 195.

7. Ross Eckert and Richard Leftwich, *The Price System and Resource Allocation*, 380-381.

8. Kent Monroe, *Pricing*, 308-312.

9. Thomas Nagle, John Hogan, and Joseph Zale, *The Strategy and Tactics of Pricing*, 118-140.

10. Mark Stiving, *Impact Pricing*, 41-52.

11. Rafi Mohammed, *The 1% Windfall*, 3-19.

12. André Gabor, supra at 166.

13. Robert Dolan and Hermann Simon, *Power Pricing*, 213-214.

14. André Gabor, supra at 158-162.

15. Michael and Gene Morris, *Market Oriented Pricing*, 66-68.

16. From a handout at the Nimer pricing seminar (see Preface).

CHAPTER

10

Marketing and Pricing Dynamics

The key to profitable pricing is building and sustaining competitive advantage.[1]

Businesses thrive when customer oriented marketing and market oriented pricing come together in a synergistic union that is the envy of competitors and the delight of owners and shareholders, customers, employees, suppliers, and the public at large. This chapter focusers on the marketing and pricing dynamics necessary to achieve such results. A key component of modern marketing is market segmentation and that topic is covered first. It will be shown how this practice, and especially price customization, can significantly increase sales revenue and profitability. This is followed by a discussion on how a firm may consistently outperform its competitors and achieve optimum results by a number of means all designed to reduce the price sensitivity of products and services and thereby increasing their profit potentials.

10.1 Market Segmentation

Manufacturers have historically treated their markets as an undifferentiated *mass market* of buyers with uniform needs and wants. The object was to produce a standard product at the lowest

155

possible cost and promote and sell it for maximum profits. All business activity was essentially company, production, and product oriented and marketing meant selling what the company had to offer. The business philosophy of the day was exemplified by a quote from Henry Ford's autobiography which has been paraphrased as "People can have the Model T in any color they want so long as it's black."

Even as late as the early 1970s, Professor Philip Kotler's now classic *Marketing Management* called market segmentation "a relatively recent and revolutionary concept in business circles." He defined *market segmentation* as the "subdividing of a market into homogeneous subsets of customers, where any subset may conceivably be selected as a market target to be reached with a distinct marketing mix."[2] This still serves as a good definition for the then new and now conventional marketing concept. The focus has clearly shifted away from the needs and wants of the seller (the firm) to the needs and wants of the buyer (the customer).

Segmenting markets into component customer groups which share common needs and wants in terms of products or services and price expectations brings obvious advantages for both the selling firm and the buying customer. Instead of using a shotgun approach to marketing, companies now can focus on their *target markets*, which are *market segments* the firm has chosen to serve, and channel their efforts and limited human and financial resources to serving these in the most efficient and profitable manner possible. Sometimes these standard market segments are subdivided further into so-called *market niches* to serve customers with more specialized wants and needs.

An important marketing function is therefore dividing a market into component segments and choosing those segment and niches which the firm can most profitably serve. This should be based on the firm's resources and capabilities, the size, sales and profit potential of each segment, and the competition in that segment. Each of a firm's target markets is typically supported by its own tailor-made set of marketing strategy variables including product, price, advertising and sales promotion, and distribution. Customers benefit from this concept in that their specific needs and wants are satisfied with diverse products and services at prices they are able and willing to pay.

Kotler and Keller give four criteria for segmenting consumer markets—geographic, demographic, psychographic, and behavioral.[3] Geographical segmentation is based on such factors as region of the country, urban or rural area, city size, and climate. Demographic segmentation takes into account customer age and life-cycle stage, gender, marital status, education, income, occupation, race, religion, and social class. In psychographic segmentation customers are divided according to psychological and personality traits such as lifestyle, core values and whether they are culture oriented, or sports fans. Behavioral segmentation involves the relationship between buyers and the product such as product knowledge, benefits, usage rate, and attitude toward the product. The authors list a total of twenty-five of these variables for segmenting markets.

Market segmentation has become the norm in most industries. In automobiles, some manufacturers operate in the luxury segment, others market more low-priced designs while still others offer a complete line of vehicles that appeals to different market segments from busy singles to style- and comfort-oriented family folks to status-conscious corporate executives. Some hotels cater only to the most discriminating patrons while others seek out business travelers, families with children, or budget-minded tourists. Department stores and shopping centers may carry only brand name luxury goods or they may offer merchandise of more traditional appeal. Numerous specialty retailers and boutiques cater to the needs and wants of select groups of buyers.

10.2 Price Customization

Customers differ significantly in their value perceptions and ability and willingness to pay for the same or similar products and services. Take, for example, a consumer product like a novel of a given title and author. One reader will want an e-book version while another will opt to download an audio book. Two other readers will buy only print copies. These, in turn, will have a choice of buying a paperback or a hardcopy. All four of these fiction aficionados are willing to pay different prices for essentially the same product in terms of information content. The only difference lies in the packaging.

Other examples abound. Two auto buyers will purchase the same brand and model but one will get the stripped down version while the other will add several options. Even though the cost differential to the manufacturer may be minimal, the two buyers will pay significantly different prices. Or take an industrial fastener like a simple nail of a certain make and dimension. A building contractor will buy it by the bagful, a carpenter or cabinet maker may need only a hundred or less, while a hobbyist just a few. The packaging may be different but it is essentially the same nail sold to different market segments but at significantly different prices.

Given the varying price sensitivities among customers, price is one of the most important variables by which sellers can and do segment markets. The practice is known as *price segmentation* or *price customization*. One speaks of *versioning* where a product or service is modified, with or without cost differences, to accommodate price customization. To be sure, this practice represents blatant price discrimination and may be illegal under certain circumstances but it is nevertheless a fact of life. As will be shown below, charging different customers with varying price sensitivities different prices for the same or similar product or service is the only way a firm can capture the full sales potential for that product or service and thereby optimize sales revenue or contribution.

Price discrimination as described requires a special mechanism by which more affluent and so-called "price buyers" can be kept apart. Otherwise all of them would buy at the lowest possible price and the company would forego more profitable sales. This mechanism is known as a *price fence*. Price fences are criteria set by the seller which a buyer must meet in order to qualify for a lower price. Nagle et al identify four main price fences—buyer identification, purchase location, time of purchase, and purchase quantity.[4]

Some of the more common price fences are based on age or status. Thus, seniors and school age children typically do not pay the full price on public transportation, in museums, or movie theaters and similar venues and may be readily identified as belonging to that special price-sensitive class. If the market is segmented by family income, for example, a mail order firm may do one mailing to high income ZIP codes with one set of prices and another with lower prices to less affluent areas even though the products in the two catalogs are identical or very similar. If the company mailed out just one catalog, the high income customers would buy at the lower prices meant for the more price-sensitive buyers and the company would forego additional sales revenue and profits.

Airlines erect price fences by charging different prices for the same seats depending on the day and time of travel. Restaurants may have lunch and dinner menus with identical meals but the evening meal will be more expensive than the one at noon. Electric utilities will charge more for peak than off-peak energy usage. In the business-to-business (B2B) sector, a firm may qualify for a quantity or order size discount only if it meets the dollar or purchase quantity criteria. Needless to say, price fences are not always perfect barriers. How could one, for example, keep a Warren Buffett or Bill Gates from using a senior discount card to see a movie at their local theater? That is not to say, of course, that either would ever want to do that.

The benefits of price customization are best demonstrated on hand of Figure 10-1. The drawing shows a price response curve (PRC), the downward sloping line Q_M–P_M, which is a version of the typical Marshallian demand curve but with the price and quantity axes reversed. As previously noted, Q_M represents the maximum quantity customers will take if the price is reduced to zero while P_M is the maximum price customers are willing to pay, i.e., the reservation price. As usual, [P] and [Q] represent the optimum price and quantity for *sales revenue* maximization, and P^* and Q^* the optimum price and quantity for *total contribution* maximization, respectively. P_F is the price floor and Q_F the quantity taken at that price. Price customization can be analyzed in terms of whether a product's sales revenue or total contribution is to be maximized.

Figure 10-1
Optimal Prices for Maximum Revenue and Contribution

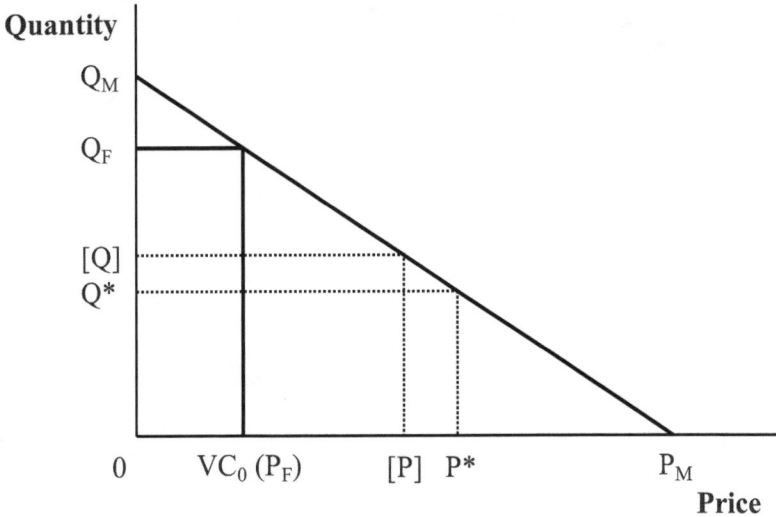

10.2.1 Customizing for Maximum Sales Revenue

The reader will recall that sales revenue for a product or service is obtained by multiplying the price by the quantity sold. The PRC shows the quantity that can be sold at each price. In fact, the area under this curve (the right-triangle P_M–Q_M) is the maximum sales revenue that can be generated from this particular product or service. This sales potential is given by $R_P = \frac{1}{2} \times P_M \times Q_M$.

Since the firm cannot charge a multitude of prices for the same product but must decide on one, the question is, What is the best price to capture the maximum amount of this potential sales revenue? As may easily be shown, it is the price [P] which lies midway between 0 and P_M.[5] Projecting upward from [P] to the PRC, we note that it bisects this curve, i.e., it lies at its midpoint where the price elasticity of demand ε for the product or service equals one ($\varepsilon = 1.0$). Projecting left from there to the quantity axis, we find [Q] which is the quantity for sales revenue maximization. The area [R] = [P] × [Q] represents the largest rectangle that can be enclosed within the right-triangle of the PRC and is the maximum sales revenue achievable with just one price point.

The area of this rectangle and therefore the maximum sales revenue [R] is seen to be only one half (50%) of the potential sales revenue R_P. The other half of potential sales revenue R_P is lost to the firm for two reasons. Sales represented by triangle Q_M-[Q]-[P] do not materialize because at the combination of price and quantity in that region no buyers may be found since their value perception of the product falls below these price-volume levels. Triangle [Q]-[P]-P_M similarly represents lost sales because potential customers who would take the quantities at the associated higher prices cannot do so because the product is available at only the lower price of [P]. In other words, their value perception of the product is significantly higher than that of the other group of potential customers.

The firm is not likely to be satisfied with this result and look for another option. This option is to add two more versions of the product or service with price points midway between O and [P] and midway between [P] and P_M, respectively. This three-product, three-price solution will add another fifty percent to the sales revenue achievable with just one product price and bring the total to 75%. The following illustrative example will further clarify the point.

Illustrative Example: Roboco Enterprises

Roboco Enterprises is the brainchild of Emily Bolingbroke, a retired robotics engineer. Emily designs and markets costumed action robots for the amusement of young children. Her present customers are mostly the parents of small boys but she would like to appeal to little girls as well to stimulate their interest in science and technology. Her toys are constructed from plastic components and include a microprocessor, a battery-run motor, and a remote control unit. Emily's latest design, the Model EB7, is a miniature robot dressed as a circus clown that can do all sorts of gymnastic exercises including rollovers, handstands, pushups, sit-ups, and somersaults.

Emily would like to sell the Model EB7 to some toy stores in her area for around $80 to $100 each. She has been told that the maximum she can hope to get for the toy is about $160. Maximum monthly sales are estimated at about 200 units at an extremely low price near zero. What advice can one give Emily? Should she sell just one version and at what price or should she offer additional versions and, if so, at what prices? The cost differences between models would be negligible. Her goal is to maximize sales revenue.

Figure 10-2
Sales Revenue Without and With Versioning
for Roboco's Model EB7 Toy Robot

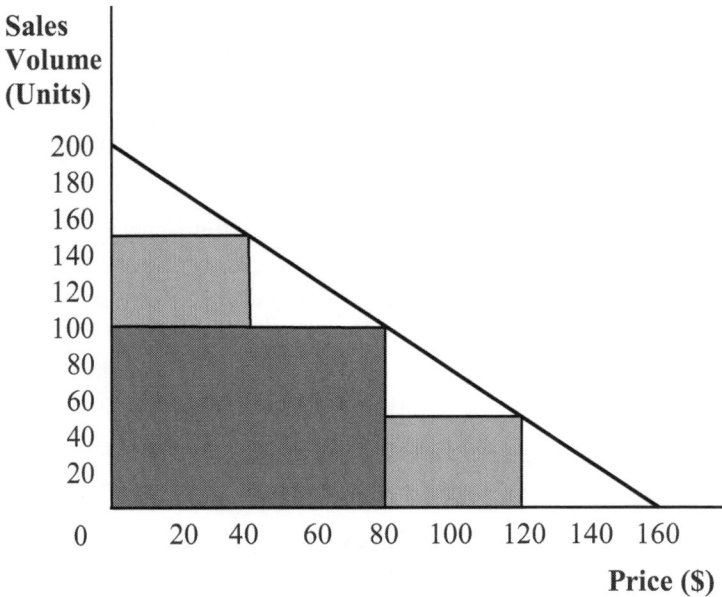

With the maximum possible sales volume Q_M given as 200 units and the maximum price P_M as $160, one can draw the price response curve as shown in Figure 10-2. The optimal price [P], which is one-half the maximum $160, is therefore $80. This is the price Emily must charge for maximum sales revenue [R]. Thus, [R] = $80 × 100 or $8,000 which corresponds to the darkly shaded area in Figure 10-2. This revenue is just one-half of the potential sales revenue of $R_P = \frac{1}{2} \times \$160 /$ unit $\times 200$ units $= \$16,000$.

Suppose Emily added two more versions of the Model EB7, with one at half the price of the $80 version and the other at $120, which is halfway between $80 and $160. This would add another $2 \times 40 / unit $\times 50$ units or $4,000 to sales revenue. (See the lightly shaded rectangles in Figure 10-2). Total sales revenue would now be $R = $8,000 + $4,000 = $12,000$. Clearly, by adding two more versions, an economy and a premium one with each model differing in looks and performance capabilities, Emily would have added another 50% to sales revenue bringing the total to 75% of the potential sales revenue of $16,000. This process could be extended, except that too many versions with only minor differences between them could confuse customers and be detrimental to overall sales. Emily could, however, sell other versions through different venues.

10.2.2 Customizing for Maximum Total Contribution

Returning to Figure 10-1 above, the reader will recall that contribution K is the difference between sales revenue R and the total direct variable cost V where V is given by the area $VC_0 \times Q_F$. Therefore, the right-triangle bounded by Q_F, VC_0, and P_M represents the maximum contribution K_P achievable with this product. The question again is, What price must the firm charge to capture the maximum of this potential contribution? It can be shown that the optimal price P* for contribution maximization lies at the midpoint between VC_0 and P_M.[6] As in the case of sales revenue maximization above, this price yields just 50% of the potential contribution K_P. The other half is again lost because potential customers are either not willing to purchase the product in the quantities required by the PRC below the optimal price P* while others would pay more than P* if the firm offered the product at a higher price.

The company will again meet this challenge by adding two more product versions with two more price points to the line. These three products will roughly correspond to "good," "better," and "best" and might be called "economy," "standard," and "premium" models. The two additional prices will lie midway between VC_0, the product's unit variable cost, and the optimal price P* for contribution maximization, and between P* and the maximum price P_M, respectively. These additions will add another 50% to contribution bringing total contribution to 75% of the maximum potential contribution K_P.

A three-product offering, or rather three-class seating, has become standard in the airline industry. This makes intuitive sense because of the different needs and wants of travelers. The leisure passenger will book long in advance of the flight, is more interested in the price than any amenities, and is more likely to cancel out. For this customer *economy class* is the answer. The corporate executive traveling in *business class* is likely to book shortly before a scheduled flight, is less interested in the ticket cost because her or his employer will pay the fare, and wants to travel in relative comfort. The *first-class* passenger can afford and is willing to pay for all the amenities the airline has to offer. Clearly, the price sensitivity and willingness to pay differs much among the three market segments. The following analysis will further clarify these points.

Illustrative Example: Jubilee Airlines

Jubilee Airlines is a charter air service which specializes in transporting seniors from their retirement homes in the United States and Canada to various places around the globe that are of special cultural and historical interest.[7] The airline has recently added three Boeing 787-8 *Dreamliners* to its fleet but has not yet decided whether to fly these in a one-class configuration or have the traditional three-class seating arrangement of regular commercial airlines that includes economy class, economy plus (or business) class, and first class.

The Boeing 787-8 *Dreamliner* seats about 240 in a three-class seating arrangement. The incremental variable costs of transporting each additional passenger are small, here assumed to be just $100, while the maximum price a senior would pay for a round-trip ticket to the intended destination is estimated to be $1,300. Jubilee Airlines' goal is to maximize the dollar contribution from each trip. From this information the PRC of Figure 10-3 can be drawn.

The maximum potential total contribution from this particular flight would be $K_P = \frac{1}{2} \times (\$1,300 - \$100) \times 240 = \$144,000$. If the airline set its price at $700, which is halfway between $100 and $1,300, it would maximize its contribution at K = ($700 – $100) × 120 = $72,000. This area, indicated by the large dark square, represents just 50% of the maximum potential contribution K_P. Thus, the "load factor" which is the percentage of capacity utilization is just 0.50. Adding two more classes priced at $400 and $1,000 would add another K = ($400 – $100) × 60 + ($1,000 – $700) × 60 = $18,000 + $18,000 = $36,000. (See the two lightly shaded areas in Figure 10-3). Total contribution would therefore be K = $72,000 + $36,000 = $108,00 which is 75% of the maximum potential contribution K_P of $144,000 giving a load factor of 0.75.

Figure 10-3
Contribution With Single and Three Class Seating
for Julilee Airline's Boeing 787 Dreamliner

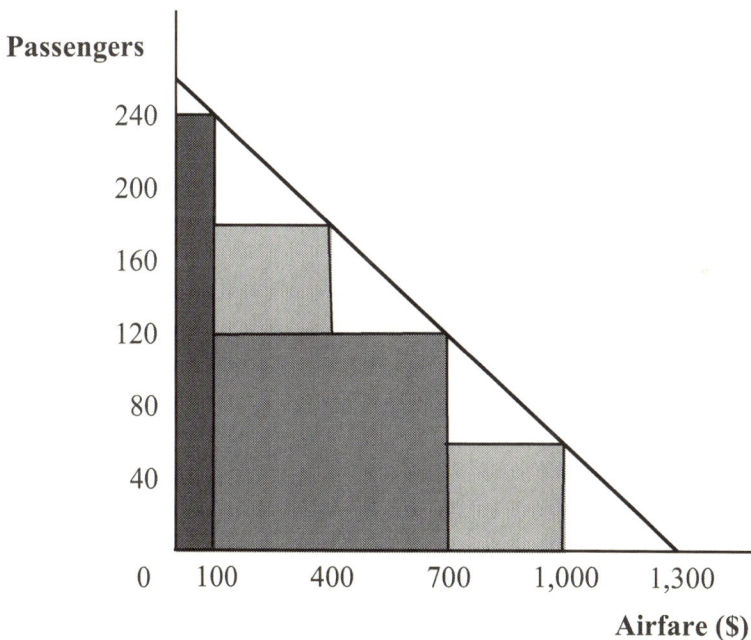

While the above analysis is useful for demonstrating the advantages of a three-tier seating arrangement, it is not totally realistic because more than the 240 seats would become available if Jubilee flew just one (economy) class. In fact, maximum seating for the 787-8 is about 380 passengers. Thus, the maximum potential contribution from this flight with economy class only would rise to $K = \frac{1}{2} \times (\$1,300 - \$100) \times 380 = \$228,000$. Yet the actual total contribution would be $K = \$600 \times 190 = \$114,000$ which is just $6,000 more than with 3-class seating. The load factor would still be only 0.50 meaning one-half the seats would remain empty.

While we have demonstrated the advantage of offering versions of the same product at different prices using toy and airline industry examples, the same holds true for any other product or service in any industry. In fact, one may generalize and offer this further pricing proposition:

Pricing Proposition 7

Sales revenue and total contribution (profit) will be significantly improved when a product or service is offered in two or more versions and associated prices rather than just one version at one price.

10.3 Yield Management

Yield management, also known as *revenue management*, was developed at American Airlines soon after the Airline Deregulation Act of 1978 (which ended government control over fares and routes) to address the industry-specific marketing and profitability problems faced by airlines. In the airline industry, the seats available on a flight are referred to as inventory and whenever a flight leaves the gate with empty seats sales from those unoccupied seats are lost and cannot be replaced. The inventory is thus said to be *perishable*. Yield management was designed to ensure that all seats on each flight are filled on take-off and that each seat has been sold at the maximum obtainable price.

An airline's objective is to maximize sales revenue on each flight by astute management of discounted and full fare prices offered to the public. In the context of our pervious analysis (see the PRC of Figure 10-1), the goal is to cover the entire area (ticket prices times number of passengers) under the price response curve and thus the total sales revenue achievable from each flight. Since for airlines, the total direct variable costs are minimal in comparison to the fixed costs, maximizing sales revenue is nearly equivalent to maximizing contribution to fixed costs and profits.

Yield management is made possible by use of high speed digital computer systems which can track historical bookings for all flights and instantly adjust fares on upcoming flights accordingly. In fact, for any given flight the airline knows at any time of day prior to flight time how many passengers it had booked the previous year (or years) and compare this bookings rate with that for the next scheduled flight. If fewer flights have been booked for, say, economy class, when the request for ticket price information is received than in the previous year, it will indicate a drop in demand and more seats will be made available at a lower fare. The reverse is true if the present bookings rate is higher in which case the cost of tickets in economy class will go up because more travelers are willing to pay more and the chance of empty seats by flight time has become less.

While yield management's advantages in terms of load factor and profits are apparent, it is still not a perfect system. For example, once a flight has been booked it cannot be resold later when some travelers would be willing to pay more to get on that particular flight. There is also much opportunity for customer alienation. In order to deal with flight cancellations and no-shows, airlines typically overbook, i.e., they sell more tickets than there are seats available. This can be bad news for someone whose seat has been resold because of a later than required appearance at the gate. The typically large disparity in ticket prices can also be a source of customer discontent and is only mitigated by the fact that travelers do not normally ask the person next to them how much they paid for their seat. Fare differences among comparable seats can be very large.

Yield management is ideally suited to certain firms operating in the service sector.[8] Not surprisingly, the system has also been adopted by large hotel chains, car rental companies, and even some hospitals. The conditions suitable to its use include:

* Capacity is relatively fixed
* Inventory is perishable
* Demand fluctuates
* Price sensitivity is variable
* Fixed cost is high w.r.t. total cost
* Booking occurs in advance of use
* Arbitrage (resale) is negligible

Clearly, these conditions are met by airlines and the other service providers mentioned.

10.4 "Raising the Flagpole" (RTF)

The reader will recall our discussion in Chapter 8 on pricing strategies and specifically Figure 8-2 showing the demand curves faced by different firms based on industry and market structure. Specifically, a demand curve labeled *monopoly* is shown which is very steep approaching perfectly inelastic demand where the P.E.D. for the product or service is, by definition, perfectly inelastic ($\epsilon = 0$). It was pointed out that while this condition is very desirable because of the very high profits achievable, it was rarely met in practice because of competition and other factors. In fact, firms in a monopoly position often face government scrutiny for possible antitrust violations. There are, however, perfectly legal means by which a near-monopoly position may be achieved.

First of all, let us focus on why such a monopoly position is so desirable. Consider the four linear demand curves of Figure 10-4. These are for different products or services with the same maximum quantity Q_M that can be sold when the price approaches zero and the same unit variable cost VC_0. The only difference between them is their different price elasticities of demand resulting from the different maximum prices P_M that customers are willing to pay. The four curves are in ascending order of inelasticity with demand curve P_{M1}-Q_M being the most elastic and P_{M4}-Q_M the most inelastic.

As before, the area within the right triangle formed by the demand curve and the quantity axis represents the maximum potential sales revenue while the area within the right triangle formed by the demand curve and the unit variable cost line VC_0 represents the maximum potential contribution. We also know from Figure 10-1 that the optimal price P* for contribution maximization lies at the midpoint between VC_0 and P_M of each curve. These optimal prices appear in Figure 10-4 as P_1* through P_4*.

Figure 10-4
Contribution Maximization by "Raising the Flagpole"

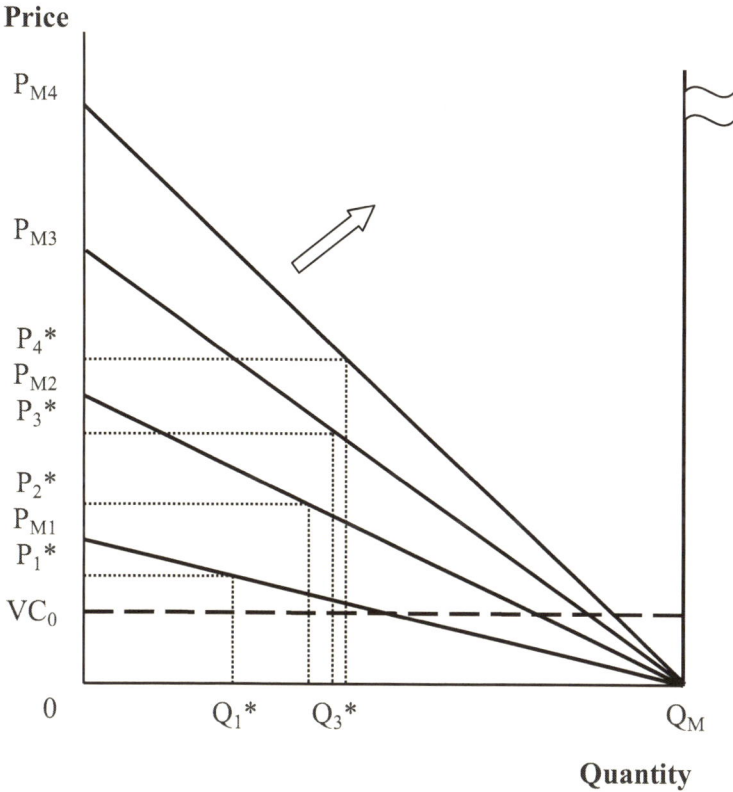

Clearly noticeable in Figure 10-4 is the fact that as the demand curve gets steeper, i.e., rises towards the vertical indicating more inelastic demand, the optimal sell prices also increase from P_1* to P_4* meaning that the firm can and should charge higher prices. At the same time, the triangle under each demand curve gets larger as well meaning that the total contribution potential as well as the actual total contribution increase proportionately. If one were to look on the demand curve as a "flagpole" (for raising the profit banner perhaps), one could speak of *raising the flagpole*. This leads to the following pricing proposition.

Pricing Proposition 8

The steeper (more vertical) the demand curve for a product or service, the higher is the optimal price for total contribution maximization and the larger the achievable total dollar contribution to fixed (overhead) cost and profit from this product or service.

10.5 Implementing RTF

How then does one *raise the flagpole* to attain these superior results in terms of improved margins and more contribution dollars? Among the measures managers and marketers will want to pay special attention to are such marketing activities as market segmentation, product innovation, product differentiation, patenting, branding, and advertising and sales promotion. Each will be briefly discussed in turn.

10.5.1 Market Segmentation

Market segmentation, more fully discussed in Section 10.1 above, plays a central role in how well a firm does in the marketplace. If marketing is all about finding a need and filling it at a profit, then finding a segment of the market whose needs and wants have not yet been met and targeting it with an effective marketing mix of strategy variables can be very profitable. Relatively large enterprises are very good at this exercise because they have the marketing and financial resources for identifying new market segments and target markets. Often overlooked by the larger firms are the many market niches made up of customers with special needs and wants that are not part of the mainstream

Niche marketing is very much the province of smaller firms both in the consumer and industrial goods sectors. These often family owned and bank financed businesses are found all over this country,

Europe, and Asia. Each has found a small part of the market with specialized needs and wants and has the expertise to develop innovative and unique new products to fill them. Sometimes the innovation is so new and unique that no demand for it has existed before. Demand for these specialized products and services tends to be very inelastic allowing firms to charge premium prices because there are no direct substitutes on the market. Niche markets are often difficult to find and identify but they are there and can be a way for young entrepreneurs to get a start in the business world. *Internet niching* has become a popular way for them to go.

10.5.2 Product Innovation

Strictly speaking, to be called an innovation a product or service should be so unique and different that there is nothing comparable on the market when it is introduced. Among the most successful and popular digital consumer product innovations of the recent past have been the Apple-1 (1976), the videocassette recorder (1976), the digital camera (1976), the compact disc (1979), the camcorder (1981), the cell phone (1984), the Internet (1985), Windows (1985), the digital video disc (1993), high-definition television (1996), the iPhone (2007), and the iPad (2010). Similar developments are found in many other industries and markets.

For most of these products the innovators envisioned a potential market long before the general public expressed any need for or desire to own such a product. In the case of the personal computer for example, the major computer makers at the time were focused on the business community and long rejected the notion of a computer for home use until Steve Jobs and Steve Wozniak appeared on the scene to prove them wrong. Their innovations opened up huge new markets with billions of dollars in sales and employment opportunities for tens of thousands. Successful innovations typically have the steepest demand curves as customers buy them in large quantities despite the premium prices they command.

More commonly, the term product innovation is applied to the process of bringing out new models and versions of products already on the market. In that sense, innovation has become an imperative for survival for many firms especially in industries and markets of rapidly changing technologies. Product life cycles are getting ever shorter and companies must innovate or risk losing out to more aggressive competitors. Thus, to keep a competitive edge both Apple and Samsung continuously introduce new models of the iPhone and Galaxy smartphones, respectively, while companies in diverse industries serving both the consumer and industrial sectors keep modifying their product offerings to keep up with changes in technology and/or customer wants and tastes.

Not surprisingly, among the world's most successful and profitable companies are also the most innovative including Apple, BMW, Disney, General Electric, Google, IBM, Microsoft, Proctor & Gamble, Samsung, and Toyota. In general, product innovation ensures that demand curves remain inelastic allowing manufacturers and marketers the maximum amount of pricing discretion.

10.5.3 Product Differentiation

Historically, differentiating products and services from those of competitors has been the traditional means of decreasing price sensitivity for ones own products and services. The technique is well-established and profitable and predates some other marketing concepts like market segmentation and perceived value pricing. The object is to make the product or service as unique and different as possible from other products and services on the market. Product differentiation is a more general and less focused approach than found in market segmentation where products and services are developed and marketed specifically for the firm's target market or markets.

Product differentiation became necessary after the proliferation of competing products and services that all served to meet the same customer needs and wants. An undifferentiated product is much like a *commodity* with a horizontal demand curve such as the one labeled *perfect competition* in Figure 8-2 of Chapter 8 on pricing strategies. For a company it is not a good position to be in because it leaves the marketer with few if any pricing options. Since all products are essentially the same, customers simply use price as the only selection criteria.

Products and services differ in their abilities to be differentiated. Some are natural commodities with little opportunity for differentiation such as aspirin, potatoes, salt, or chicken parts. Yet even here, manufacturers attempt to do so. Thus, aspirin maker Bayer (which developed the "wonder drug") promotes Bayer aspirin to distinguish it from other makes. Potatoes are labeled Idaho potatoes if they come from that state and it's Morton salt that contains the nutrient Iodine. Most products and services, however, are readily differentiated by design, style, size, packaging, and many other factors to ensure that they have downward-sloping demand curves.

10.5.4 Patents and Trademarks

Patents, trademarks and other intellectual property rights have been called "the crown jewels" of a company. For many firms, especially in the high-tech field, they are the source of most of their economic power. In order to promote inventions and innovation, the United States and other governments grant their citizens an exclusive right to exploit their inventions commercially for a given number of years. In other words, the inventors are granted monopoly powers that would otherwise be violations of the antitrust laws. Under American patent law (Title 35 of the United States Code) the term is twenty years from the earliest claimed filing date. For the marketer, a product protected by a patent can have a very steep demand curve meaning that it is amenable to premium pricing if there are no close substitutes available on the market.

A trademark is a sign, design, or phrase used to identify a particular manufacturer or seller's products and distinguish them from the products of another. (Title 12 of the U.S.C.). Its function is to prevent buyers from being confused or deceived as to the origin of the goods. Trademark registration is not required by law but highly recommended. In order to qualify for registration a mark must be *distinctive*. This means it must be i) *arbitrary* or *fanciful* or ii) *suggestive* of the underlying product. A *descriptive* mark may be registrable under certain circumstances but a *generic* mark will not be. Examples of the latter would be "salt" for table salt or "golfcart" for the two-seater popular with golfers. One can acquire trademark rights by being the first to use the mark in commerce or being the first to register it with the U.S. Patent and Trademark Office (PTO).

10.5.5 Branding

Brands and trademarks are complementary concepts in that a brand is a marketing tool used in promoting a product or service while a trademark is an intellectual property right allowing brands to be bought and sold and defended against infringement. While the practice of branding goes back to antiquity such concepts as branding, brand equity, and brand marketing are relatively new. *Branding* has been defined as endowing products and services with the power of a brand while *brand equity* is the value added to a trademark as a result of the brand name. Brand names should be i) memorable (easy to remember and recognize), ii) meaningful (relate to the product), iii) likeable (pleasurable), iv) transferable (to other products), v) adaptable (to changing tastes), and vi) protectable (by intellectual property law).[9] The first of these is especially important and the ancient adage *nomen est omen* often applies.

Companies use different strategies in selecting brand names. Some firms simply rely on the company name to identify its products such as Campbell for its soups. Others choose a brand name for each product category such as Sears with its lines of Kenmore appliances and Craftsman tools. Still others use individual brand names for their major lines. Thus, in the luxury segment of the auto industry General Motors has its Cadillac brand, Ford the Lincoln, Toyota the Lexus, and Volkswagen the Audi. Table 10-1 is a listing of the top thirty brands as compiled by *Forbes* magazine and *Interbrand* with each using its own rating criteria.[10] While there are some differences as to the exact ranking of each brand, there is nevertheless a general consensus on which brands are the most popular and powerful.

Both the owners of brands and customers benefit from branding. Recognized and popular brands can create intense emotional bonds with customers leading to strong brand loyalties. Since buyers are familiar with and trust a favorite brand, the risk factor is reduced simplifying the purchase decision. For the firm, branding is a powerful means of gaining a competitive advantage

Table 10-1
Top Global Brands

Rank	*Forbes*	*Interbrand*
1	Apple	Apple
2	Microsoft	Google
3	Coca-Cola	Coca-Cola
4	IBM	IBM
5	Google	Microsoft
6	McDonald's	General Electric
7	General Electric	McDonald's
8	Intel	Samsung
9	Samsung	Intel
10	Louis Vuitton	Toyota
11	BMW	Mercedes-Benz
12	Cisco	BMW
13	Oracle	Cisco
14	Toyota	Disney
15	AT&T	Hewlett-Packard
16	Mercedes-Benz	Gillette
17	Disney	Louis Vuitton
18	Wal-Mart	Oracle
19	Budweiser	Amazon
20	Honda	Honda
21	SAP	H & M
22	Verizon	Pepsi
23	Gillette	American Express
24	Nike	Nike
25	Pepsi	SAP
26	American Express	Ikea
27	Nescafe	UPS
28	L'Oréal	Ebay
29	Marlboro	Pampers
30	H & M	Kellogg's

because brand loyalty effectively creates a barrier to competitor entry when buyers consider their options among competing brands. Most importantly, in a pricing context, brand-loyal customers are willing to pay premium prices. From pricing studies and everyday experience we know that these price differentials can be very substantial.

10.5.6 Advertising and Sales Promotion

A strong and popular brand supported by an imaginative and effective advertising and sales promotion effort is a winning combination that can result in an unusually strong competitive advantage. The reason is that this third element in the mix of marketing strategy variables can substantially increases perceived value in the brand and the underlying products and services and help *raise the flagpole* which we have decided is the gateway to higher profits. Advertising and sales promotion are two communication platforms that are part of *marketing communication* which also includes special events, public relations, direct and interactive marketing, word-of-mouth, and personal selling.

Advertising is by far the most important of these platforms and includes various media types each with its own advantages and limitations. Kotler and Keller identify eleven of these: [11] Newspapers, television, direct mail, radio, magazines, outdoor, yellow pages, newsletters, brochures, telephone, and the Internet. Newspapers are cited for their timeliness and good market coverage but suffer from a short life and a small "pass-along" audience. Magazines have the advantage of a long life and good "pass-along" readership but are disadvantaged by long ad purchase lead times. Television, the most popular advertising medium, combines sight, sound and motion to attract attention but has the limitation of only fleeting exposure and a high absolute cost.

All marketing communication efforts are designed to guide a prospective buyer through the various stages of the buying process from unawareness of the company's brand or brands to awareness, to liking, to preference, to purchase intention, and finally to actual purchase. As companies attempt to rise above the din of the marketplace with hundreds of brands vying for buyer attention, they are willing to spend huge amounts on advertising their products and services. These expenditures add, of course, to the company's indirect fixed costs (overhead) and may or may not be fully justified based on results achieved in terms of sales revenues, market shares, and profits.

How much companies value the power of advertising is demonstrated by the fact that in 2012, U.S. advertising expenditures reached $139.5 billion. According to Kantar Media, an advertising research firm, the top ten advertisers spent over $15.3 billion led by Proctor & Gamble, the world's largest consumer products company, with $2.8 billion. This represented about 3.3 % of sales revenue of $83.7 billion for that year. Included in the list are General Motors with $1.6 billion, L'Oreal with $1.5 billion, and Toyota Motor with $1.2 billion.[12] Undoubtedly many of these outlays produced no or only marginal benefits in terms of actual sales and profits except for the advertising agencies themselves but paraphrasing John Wanamaker, an early marketing pioneer, who once lamented "I know half the money I spend on advertising is wasted but the trouble is I don't know which half," it behooves managements to closely monitor costs versus benefits.

Notes

1. Thomas Nagle, John Hogan and Joseph Zale. *The Strategy and Tactics of Pricing*, 267.
2. Philip Kotler, *Marketing Management*, 165-166.
3. Philip Kotler and Kevin Keller, *Marketing Management*, 213-226.
4. Thomas Nagle, John Hogan, and Joseph Zale, supra at 63-70.
5. For a proof, see Appendix I. "Formula Derivations: A. Optimal Prices on Price Response Curve."
6. Ibid.
7. This airline scenario was suggested by an example given in Robert Dolan and Hermann Simon, *Power Pricing*, 118-126, to explain the rationale behind customized pricing in the airline industry. The seating capacity and fare structure as well as some other aspects of their analysis have been changed. The authors correctly noted (without proof) that on a price response curve the optimal price for profit maximization is located exactly at the midpoint between the product's unit variable cost and its reservation (maximum) price.
8. Frederic Voneche, "Yield Management in the Airline Industry," <http://www.ieor.berkely.edu> (28 Feb. 2005).
9. Philip Kotler and Kevin Keller, supra at 246.
10. Forbes: A listing of 100 brands based on average earnings for the past three years and other financial statistics. The brands must have a presence on the American market to be included in the list. Over one-half of the listed brands are American. The brand value for first-ranked Apple is estimated at $104.3 billion, for tenth-ranked Louis Vuitton $28.4 billion, and for last-ranked Estee Lauder $5.4 billion. *Forbes*, "The World's Most Valuable Brands,"<http://www.forbes.com/powerful-brands/list/>

Interbrand: A listing of 100 brands by brand value based on the brand's i) competitive strength, ii) role in the purchase decision, and iii) financial performance. To be listed, a brand must be truly global. Top-ranked Apple has an estimated brand value of $98.3 billion, tenth-ranked Toyota $35.3 billion, and last-ranked Gap $3.9 billion. *Interbrand*, "Best Global Brands 2013," <http://www.interbrand.com/en/best-global-brands.
11. Philip Kotler and Kevin Keller, supra at 507.
12. Kantar Media, "Top Ten Advertisers of 2012," http://kantarmediana.com/intelligence/press/us.

11

Price and Market Share Competition

The customer is interested in one thing and that's price, price, price.[1]

In the previous chapter we considered the various options available to the marketer for improving the profitability of products and services already on the market as well as for increasing the likelihood that a new product or services will be profitable. It was proposed that this goal could be achieved by increasing the slope of the demand curve to reduce price sensitivity thereby allowing more pricing discretion. These measures are also designed to prevent price from becoming the dominant marketing strategy variable since direct price competition is known to lead to less than optimal results for most of the competing firms.

These concepts notwithstanding, there are instances where companies find themselves in such a situation either by initiating severe price cuts themselves or being the targets of competitor price cuts. The focus of the present chapter is on competitors and competition especially price and market share competition including no-hold-barred price wars. In addition, the relationship between sales revenue, market share, and profitability will be examined. The chapter continues with special pricing issues as they relate to profitability and concludes with some comments on the gathering of needed marketing intelligence.

11.1   Price as a Competitive Weapon

Severe price competition goes beyond the customary proactive and reactive pricing practices engaged in between competitors where price is just one of the four major marketing strategy variable employed to maintain or increase sales revenue and profits. It also does not concern companies   which have adopted a penetration pricing strategy as a business philosophy and practice such an approach, usually based on a cost or logistics advantage, on a consistent basis. In *severe price competition*, companies aggressively and sporadically use price as a competitive weapon to increase sales revenue and market share at the expense of one or more competitors.

The factors favoring severe price competition include:

* An industry with high fixed and small unit variable costs such as the commercial airline industry.
* The product or service is in the maturity or decline stage of its product life cycle.
* Demand for the product or service is highly elastic meaning that even small price changes have a major impact on the number of units sold.
* The product is frequently purchased and a necessary staple or needed to maintain a certain lifestyle.
* Customers do not perceive the product or service offerings of competitors to be unique or significantly different from each other.
* A low price is not detrimental to sales because of quality concerns.
* Brand loyalty is at a minimum and switching between brands does not involve any risk or extra cost to the buyer.
* The customer rather than a third party is responsible for the entire cost of the product or service.
* Company advertising and sales promotion focus on price to the exclusion of product or service features and benefits.

* In the case of industrial goods, quality and performance are assured by industry or national standards which products must meet for certification before being purchased.

   In such situations, with depressed sales, market share, and profits, marketers have often settled on the price variable as a quick and easy fix knowing that price cuts are easily implemented and, if necessary, reversed while the impact on performance is immediate and significant. More often than not, however, these actions have magnified rather than solved the problem. While a price cut will, in theory, always lead to an increase in sales volume, and where the price elasticity of demand is more than unity, to an increase in sales revenue, total contribution presents a very different picture.

   Table 11-1 shows the profit impact of severe price cuts for unit contribution margins CM_0 of 20%, 50%, and 80% and five price elasticities of demand P.E.D. from 1.0 to 5.0.[2] The table gives the percentage changes in total contribution and profits as a result of three price cuts, namely, 10%, 20%, and 30%. From this listing, it is apparent that major price cuts for products or services with small percentage contribution margins in conjunction with low price elasticities of demand can significantly lower total contribution and profits. Thus, even in the case of a relatively high CM_0 of 50% and a P.E.D. of 2.0, the drop in contribution dollars for the three price cuts amounts to 4%, 16%, and 36%, respectively.

   Steep price cuts cannot only negatively impact the price-setting firm's performance metrics unless its contribution margins and price elasticities of demand prior to the cut are sufficiently high, they can have negative consequences for all the firms in the industry. As Nagle et al have noted: "Price competition is usually a negative-sum game since the more intense price competition is, the more it undermines the value of the market over which one is competing. Price competitors do well, therefore, to forget about what they learned from competing in sports and other positive-sum games, and to try instead to draw lessons from less familiar competitions such as warfare or dueling."[3]

Table 11-1
The Impact of a Price Reduction on
Percentage Total Contribution

P.E.D.	CM_0	Price Reduction		
		10%	20%	30%
1.0	20%	(45.0)	(100.0)	(165.0)
	50%	(12.0)	(28.0)	(48.0)
	80%	(3.8)	(10.0)	(18.8)
2.0	20%	(40.0)	(100.0)	(180.0)
	50%	(4.0)	(16.0)	(36.0)
	80%	5.0	5.0	0.0
3.0	20%	(35.0)	(100.0)	(195.0)
	50%	4.0	(4.0)	(24.0)
	80%	13.8	20.0	18.8
4.0	20%	(30.0)	(100.0)	(210.0)
	50%	12.0	8.0	(12.0)
	80%	22.5	35.0	37.5
5.0	20%	(25.0)	(100.0)	(225.0)
	50%	20.0	20.0	0.0
	80%	31.3	50.0	56.3

Rather than answer a competitor's challenge of a major price cut with a similar one, a more prudent approach would be to carefully examine all the price and non-price options available to the firm before acting. Among the factors to be considered are the size and nature of the price cut and whether it is temporary or permanent, the competitor's relative strength or weakness in terms of competitive advantage, the sales, market share, and profits put at risk by the price cut, and the benefits versus costs of a possible response. In short, because the stakes are high, the best advice that can be given a marketer is not to initiate price competition by deep price cuts, avoid price confrontation where possible, and proceed with caution in responding to a challenge.

11.2 Sales Promotions

Temporary price cuts in form of sales promotions, also known as *price deals*, have become a popular tool in the marketer's kit in lieu of advertising. One can distinguish between general, non-targeted and targeted sales promotions. In non-targeted promotions the product is made available to all buyers while targeted promotions are aimed at more specific audiences. Coupon sales are an example of the latter. Both types are meant to appeal to the more price-sensitive segment of a larger product-market.

11.2.1 General Price Promotions

Sometimes sales promotions are run to quickly sell off excess inventory especially if a new model is ready to replace the model offered for sale. At other times price deals are meant to induce trial of a new product or service. In most cases, however, the motivating factor is to quickly boost sales and/or increase market share. Undoubtedly, promotional pricing creates excitement in the marketplace and focuses buyer attention on the product or service being promoted. These promotions are sure to increase volume market share and, if conditions are right, revenue market share as well. Assuming profitability is also important, the marketer is advised to determine the profit impact of each such promotion. This can be done by inspection of Table 11-1 above or use of one of the methods previously described that allow the marketer to examine the profit impacts of various price change options, namely, in Chapter 5 (Contribution Analysis) or Chapter 7 (Isoprofit Analysis).

For reasons noted above, price promotions involving products with low unit contribution margins in conjunction with low price elasticities of demand, can be problematic. The higher the CM_0 and P.E.D., the better are the chances for favorable results from promotional price cuts. From the Table 11-1 it is also apparent that all contribution dollars are lost where the percentage price cut is equal to or larger than the product's percentage unit contribution margin regardless of the size of the price elasticity of demand. This leads to another pricing rule of thumb:

Pricing Rule of Thumb

Except in unusual circumstances, the total price discount should never exceed the product's unit contribution margin.

An unusual circumstance would be if the firm had an obsolete product or excess inventory which it wanted to sell off in order to recoup its investment or save on future carrying costs. Another example would be if the firm, usually a retailer, wanted to attract customers by selling a product below cost in a practice known as *loss leader pricing*.

Another important consideration concerns the long-term benefits of price promotions. In a well-known paper on the subject, its author found that the resulting benefits are usually as fleeting as the promotion itself. According to this researcher, quoting from an A. C. Nielson publication: "There is overwhelming marketplace evidence that the consumer sales effect is limited to the time period of the promotion itself. A price-off promotion causes sales to rise, but once the promotion stops, they return to their original level."[4] The author, an advertising executive, argued in favor of the long-term superiority of consumer advertising over sales promotions.

Frequent price promotions for the same product or brand are not recommended because these may negatively impact *price credibility* and integrity. It is important that prices not fluctuate too much or too often and be believable. Otherwise, the promotional price will become the customer's new reference price and he or she will not buy until the next deal has come around. At that time the customer will buy in large quantities and stock up to have enough product on hand until the next promotion. This practice of hoarding promotional items is obviously inconsistent with a seller's need for consistent sales revenue and total contribution dollars.

11.2.2 Coupon Sales

A popular type of sales promotion involves *coupons* which entitle a customer to buy a product or service at a discounted price when presented at the cash register during a sale. According to a study by a major consumer products company, over seven percent of household goods by volume were purchased with a coupon.[5] Coupons are an effective segmentation technique because the time and effort required in searching for, clipping, organizing, and redeeming coupons will appeal only to the most price-sensitive segment of a larger product-market while less price-sensitive customers will continue to pay the full price. The marketer's challenge is to get the coupons to preferred target audiences, namely, present users who will be induced to buy more of the product and people who will buy the product for the first time on account of the coupon.

Coupons have several advantages over on-shelf price cuts. The targeting of select customer groups through judicious media selection for coupon placement is one of them. Newspapers, magazines, flyers etc. are all targeted to different audiences and coupons should obviously appear where the target buyers are best reached. Another advantage is that competitors are not as easily alerted to specific coupon deals and therefore less likely to react. Thus, coupons represent a form of stealth price cutting that falls under the radar so to speak. In addition, the product's reference price is not likely to be affected because coupons are less conspicuous than an advertised or on-shelf price reduction. Customers will therefore not permanently associate the coupon price with the product. Finally, with coupon sales there is less opportunity for product hoarding because a coupon is normally good for one item only.

11.3 Price Wars

Price wars among members of an oligopoly are an ever-present danger. Such contests can be ruinous not only to individual firms but to the entire industry as a whole. As Baker et al have noted: "Price wars rarely have any winners—and few survivors are as healthy as they were before the wars broke out. Their destruction is often so severe and long-lasting that the only reliable way to come out ahead is to avoid them altogether."[6] The reason is that the deteriorating price structure during a price war causes sales revenue and profits for the entire industry to shrink while individual firms may be forced into bankruptcy.

11.3.1 Major Historical Conflicts

Price wars often result when the mechanism of price leadership breaks down as was the case in two big contests which involved the ready-to-eat (RTE) breakfast cereal and the commercial airline industries. The breakfast cereal market was highly concentrated and profitable when in 1996 a price war broke out among the industry "big three," namely, Kellogg, General Mills, and Post. At the time, the three firms had a combined volume market share of about 75% with the industry leader Kellogg accounting for 35% followed by General Mills at nearly 25% and Post at 15%. Industry sales were about $8 billion. Kellogg had been consistently raising its prices over the last few years blaming rising costs.

The price war broke out in mid-April 1996 when the Post Cereal Division of Kraft Foods defied the price leader Kellogg by unilaterally slashing prices 20% across the board on all 22 of its brands.[7] Kellogg retaliated with a 19% price cut on selected brands which was followed by a 11% cut by General Mills. Post blamed consumer dissatisfaction with price and value for their action. Most importantly, the company's sales had been declining substantially from the year before leaving them with underutilized plant capacity. Four months into the war, A. C. Nielsen reported a significant shift in market shares—down to 31% for Kellogg, slightly higher at 25% for General Mills, and up two percentage points to 17% for Post. The important point is that the industry as a whole suffered considerable long-term losses due to the depressed prices.

Beginning with the Airline Deregulation Act of 1978, the airline industry has experienced a long history of heavy discounting and fare warfare. In April 1992, the industry leader, American Airlines, instituted "value pricing" to replace the hodge-podge of discounted fares. It involved a simple four-tier fare structure including first-class, regular coach, and 7-day and 21-day advance-purchase economy fares. The new coach fare applied to any flight, any day and any time of day while all four tiers came with price cuts of up to 50%.

The other "big three" carriers, United and Delta, initially followed the American scheme while some smaller ones including Continental, Northwest, and USAir revolted coming out with even steeper cuts. In October, American abandoned "value pricing" after practically all carriers had returned to heavy discounting and a free-for-all had ensued. As industry losses mounted, several of the smaller carriers ended up in bankruptcy. This price war was estimated to have cost the airline industry an amount exceeding the combined profits for the entire industry from its inception.

11.3.2 Preventing and Containing Price Wars

Price leadership is one of the primary means of preventing price wars but, as we saw in the case of the conflicts in the commercial airline and breakfast cereal industries, this mechanism is not always effective. More often than not, the problem is poor communication between the industry leader and its competitors. According to one paper on price warfare, item one on a company's agenda should be to prevent a war before it starts by revealing the firm's strategic intentions.[8] Accordingly, some time before the contemplated price change, the rationale behind it should be made known to the other members of an oligopoly.

Ideally, only the price leader should initiate major pricing moves and that only after testing the waters. By giving advance notice, the other industry members will have time to evaluate the proposal and respond to it. If the reaction is overwhelmingly negative, the price leader should reconsider. This communication, sometimes known as *signaling*, is not illegal if it does not involve direct communication between competitors but rather takes the form of announcements to the general public.

It appears that some of these preliminary activities were not considered in the two cases of price warfare described above but rather the price increases in the case of Kellogg and the deep cuts by American were presented to the other industry members as a fait accompli. The president of American at the time was quoted as saying: "We tried to provide some price leadership, but it didn't work, so we are back to death by a thousand cuts...We are more victims than villains—victims of our dumbest competitors..."[9]

It could be argued, of course, that by unilaterally cutting prices without communicating its intentions in an industry already wracked by heavy fare discounting, American did not provide effective price leadership to prevent the ensuing pricing disaster. To the smaller competitors Americans' actions must have appeared as a way to drive them out of the market. In fact, that is precisely what led financially ailing Continental to sue American in the U.S. federal district court in Galveston, Texas alleging the company was engaged in predatory pricing. That practice is, of course, strictly illegal.

One of the most effective ways to prevent and contain price wars is to refocus competition away from price to such non-price marketing strategy variables as product differentiation and innovation. In the commercial air travel industry, for example, many people have come to view air travel as a commodity in that they perceive little difference in the services offered by the various carriers. This has led to an exclusive focus on the fare price.

Yet there exists no product or service that is not differentiable in some way! Airlines, for example, can and do differentiate themselves by which airports they service, the number of flights to these and their times of day, the number of required stopovers and their lengths, the punctuality of arrivals and departures, the on-board amenities, frequent flyer benefits, and many other factors. The challenge is to implement these unique benefits and effectively communicate these to potential customers so that they will consider these along with the fare price in their choice of airline.

For customers, a price war is, of course, a boon. Is there anyone who does not want to see a significant prices drop especially when price levels are perceived to be too high, the amount of discretionary funds available are small and getting smaller, and competitors are willing to part with their goods and services for ever less money? Probably not. However, the good times rarely outlive the price war. Once the dust has settled, the number of viable competitors is likely to have been reduced and those left standing will soon raise prices to pre-war levels to recoup some of their recently incurred losses.

11.4 Market Share and Profitability

Much price competition is motivated by management's desire to increase sales and market share because of the prevalent belief that large market shares are a prerequisite to long-term profits. There is strong evidence to support this notion. In a major study done in the early 1970s and published in the *Harvard Business Review*, researchers used the data base of the Profit Impact of Market Strategies (PIMS) project of the Marketing Science Institute to conclude that market share is positively related to the rate of return on investment (ROI) earned by a business.[10] These researchers attributed the high rates of return achieved by large-share businesses to three factors, namely, i) economies of scale in procurement, manufacturing, marketing, and other cost components, ii) increased market power which allows firms to bargain more effectively and "administer" prices leading to significantly higher ones, and iii) quality management.

More recently, Dolan and Simon have debunked this "market share mindset" when they noted that, "In one industry after another, the aggressive pursuit of market share has led to overcapacity, price cutting, and profits for nobody. The focus must shift from market share to a broader conception incorporating industry profitability."[11] Nagle et al echoed this sentiment by strongly criticizing the so-called *market share myth* which flaunts market share as the means to competitive success.[12] Before we weigh in on this important issue, let us briefly review what is meant by market share.

11.4.1 Two Market Share Metrics

Market share is an important marketing metric which tells marketers how their product or brand is doing in terms of sales in comparison to the products or brands of competitors. There are actually two ways market share may be computed, namely, *volume market share* based on sales volume (quantity) and *revenue market share* based on sales revenue. Often it is not specified which of the two is being used with the result that market share statistics often lead to faulty interpretations.

In volume market share, sometimes also known as *unit market share*, the firm's unit sales of a particular product, brand, or model are compared to the number of units sold by all competitors of similar products, brands, or models in the entire market served during a particular time frame. *Volume market share* is defined as:

$$\text{VMS } (\%) = \frac{\text{Company Sales (units)}}{\text{Total Market Sales (units)}} \qquad \text{Eq. (11.1)}$$

VMS is popular in the automobile industry to assess the relative popularity of certain brands and models and major newspapers typically list monthly unit sales of these various brands and models together with their market shares. For example, in the month of June General Motors may have had a market share of x% of all passenger cars sold in the United Sates while in the SUV category the company's market share by volume sales may have been y%.

Revenue market share, on the other hand, compares the firm's sales revenue for a product, brand, or model to dollar sales generated by all competitors of identical products, brands, or models in the entire market served during a specific time frame. *Revenue market share* is defined as:

$$\text{RMS } (\%) = \frac{\text{Company Sales (dollars)}}{\text{Total Market Sales (dollars)}} \qquad \text{Eq. (11.2)}$$

As usual, the market share percentages are obtained by multiplying the ratios for VMS and RMS by 100%. For many industries, the denominators of Equations (11-1) and (11.2) are readily obtained from a number of sources including sales data released by individual firms, industry trade associations, and investment houses.

Volume market share cannot be used as a direct indicator of profitability because it can always be raised by simply lowering the price. In fact, VMS can be traded much like corporate stock—it can be "bought" by lowering the price and "sold" by raising it. As the price is lowered to raise the VMS, the price floor, represented by the unit variable cost, is eventually reached and exceeded meaning that there are   little or no contribution dollars generated and operations will become unprofitable. In other words, a high VMS for a product or service does not ensure that it is also profitable.

Unlike volume market share, revenue market share can be an indicator of profitability. Less apparent is   whether the pursuit of market share will necessarily lead to high contribution and profits as has been claimed. As Nagle et al, cited above,   have noted: "A common myth among marketers is that market share is the key to profitability." The myth is the assumption of a *causal* relationship between market share and profitability. "A far more plausible explanation for the correlation," the authors explain, "is that both profitability and market share are caused by the same underlying source of business success: a sustainable competitive advantage in meeting customer needs more effectively or in doing so more efficiently." Furthermore, the authors claim, contrary to another popular myth, profitability improvements *precede* market share increases and not follow it.

11.4.2 Graphical Analysis

Nagel et al's contention that high market share and profitability are both the result of a competitive advantage finds support by examining the relationship between one important source of competitive advantage, a product's unit variable cost, and the optimal prices for sales revenue and contribution maximization. This may be done by use of our now familiar diagram as redrawn in Figure 11-1. As previously shown, on this price response curve P_M-Q_M the optimal price [P] for sales revenue maximization is located at the midpoint of the PRC. Similarly, the optimal price P* for total contribution maximization is found at the midpoint of that portion of the PRC to the right of the unit variable cost VC_0 (the price floor P_F). Clearly, as the VC_0 moves toward zero, P* moves along the PRC toward [P].

The two optimal prices, [P] and P*, meet when the unit variable cost has been reduced to zero. At that point, all sales revenue goes toward total contribution dollars and the two become equal (R = K). Since sales revenue is strongly correlated with the RMS for the product (high sales revenue means high revenue market share), it follows that when unit variable cost is zero, maximum sales revenue, maximum revenue market share, and maximum total contribution occur at the same price point. In other words, by keeping unit variable cost low, the firm can have it all—high sales revenue and revenue market share, and superior profits.

Figure 11-1
The Market Share and Profitability Relationship

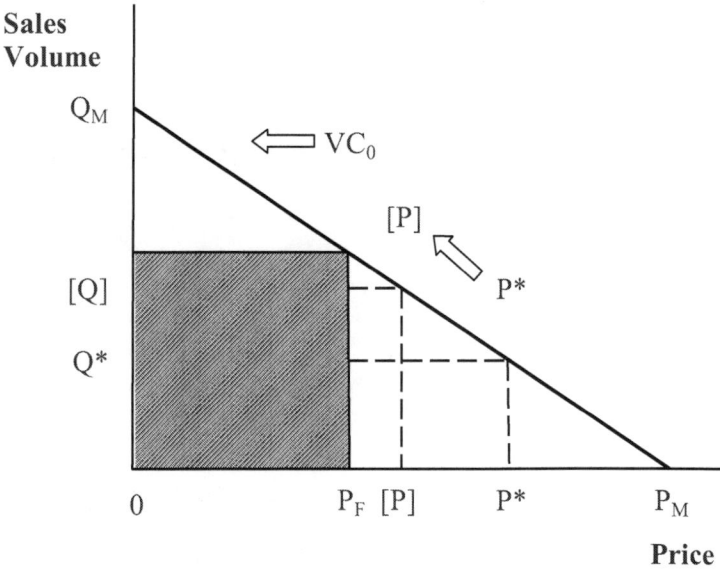

11.5 Pricing Guidelines (II)

Based on Figure 11-1 and the foregoing analysis the following five additional pricing propositions can be stated.

Pricing Proposition 9

In all practical cases, the optimal price for revenue maximization will be different from the optimal price for total contribution and profit maximization so that it is not possible to achieve both sales revenue and profit maximization at the same time.

Pricing Proposition 10

In all practical cases, the optimal price for total contribution and profit maximization is always higher than the optimal price for sales revenue maximization.

Pricing Proposition 11

The optimal prices that will maximize both sales revenue and total contribution (profit) are equal only in the special case where the product's unit variable cost is zero.

Pricing Proposition 12

As a product's unit variable cost decreases toward zero its optimal prices for sales revenue (market share) and contribution (profit) maximization approach each other so that a firm's products with large revenue market shares also tend to be the most profitable.

Pricing Proposition 13

For products and services whose unit variable costs are near zero, maximizing sales revenue will also maximize total contribution and profits.

Obviously, a unit variable cost of zero is an ideal that cannot be fully achieved in practice. What all this means is that firms which can approach this ideal will be able to maximize both profits and market share at the same time without sacrificing one for the other. The above analysis concerned a single product only. Suppose, however, the firm could reduce all of its costs to a minimum, namely, i) its unit variable cost for each of its products, and, ii) its indirect fixed (overhead) cost. The result would be a cost and therefore an important competitive advantage over other firms in its industry. A number of companies are presently in this category with the two most notable ones being Wal-Mart Stores and Toyota Motor. Each enjoys both exceptional revenue market shares and profits in which cost advantages play a major role.

11.6 Profit-Enhancing Measures

In business-to-business and consumer markets, a number of easily implemented techniques are available to improve the bottom line. Four among these involve effectively dealing with the pocket price waterfall, power buyers, ad hoc pricing, and sales force compensation.

11.6.1 Managing the Pocket Price Waterfall

Most every business-to-business sales transaction shows a significant variance between the *list* or *base price* which is the price the seller has set for the particular product or service and the *pocket price*, which is the actual amount of money received by the seller. Separating the two prices is a series of discounts and rebates that result in significant amounts of lost revenue and profit. In a well-known article, Marn and Rosiello of McKinsey & Co. have called this situation of sales revenue cascading down from list price to invoice price to final transaction or pocket price the *pocket price waterfall*.[13] This writer's version of a pocket price waterfall is illustrated in Figure 11-2. In practice, the discount and allowance chain would be longer or shorter depending on the particular circumstances.

The seller in this hypothetical example is a manufacturer of automobile components while the customer is one of its stocking distributors who, in turn, sells the merchandise to auto parts stores. The price of this auto part has been set at $100 which is here called the *base price*. This particular customer is entitled to a 15% ($15.00) distributor discount plus an additional order-size discount of 5% ($5.00) bringing the invoice price to $80.00. In addition, the distributor is allowed several off-invoice discounts and rebates, namely, i) a 3% ($2.40) discount for early payment, ii) a cooperative advertising allowance of 5% ($4.00) for local advertising, iii) a special merchandising discount of 3% ($2.40), and a 1.5% ($1.20) freight allowance. This brings the payable pocket price to $70.00. The total price reduction or *pocket discount* is therefore $30.00 or 30%. Each of these discount and rebate elements represents a *revenue leak*, according to the authors.

Figure 11-2
The Pocket Price Waterfall

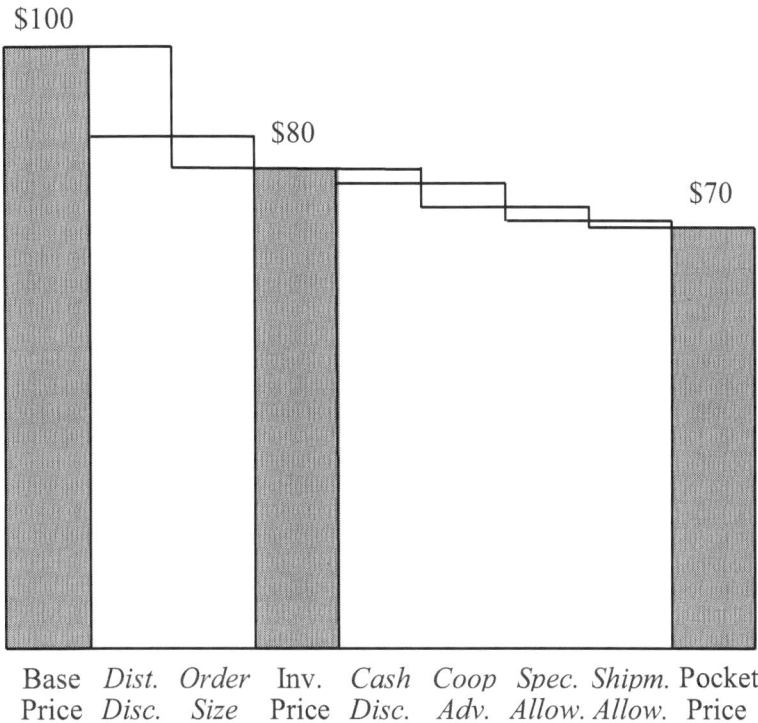

| Base Price | Dist. Disc. | Order Size | Inv. Price | Cash Disc. | Coop Adv. | Spec. Allow. | Shipm. Allow. | Pocket Price |

Typically this auto parts manufacturer would have other customers and channels of distribution with each calling for a different pricing and discount structure. Among these would be original equipment manufacturers (OEMs), and specifically auto companies, as well as other large-volume buyers such as auto parts retail chains. Consequently, this particular part would not have just one pocket price but a whole range of such prices from close to the list price on one end to near the product's unit variable cost on the other. The authors have labeled this range of pocket prices the *pocket price band.* It can be surprisingly and unreasonably large. The authors found companies in diverse industries with pocket price bands ranging from 60% to 500%!

It is these authors' contention, as supported by many actual examples, that actively managing pocket prices and pocket price bands offers a unique opportunity for sales revenue and profit improvements which had hitherto received scant attention from managements. Specifically, they propose systematic transaction price management with the objective of achieving the best net realized price for every order or transaction. In one case, a manufacturer of home appliances, changes in the discount structure to reduce leakage resulted in an increase in the average pocket price levels by 3.5% and a 60% operating profit gain. Some discounts and allowances needed to be repositioned on the discount chain, or reduced or eliminated altogether where they produced no significant benefits. The authors recommend that top managements set quantifiable leakage reduction goals for each element in the pocket price waterfall and monitor the results for each major product line on a quarterly basis.

Furthermore, according to the authors, pocket price should be the only yardstick employed in evaluating products, customers, and individual transactions and that all revenue and profitability calculations should be based on pocket prices. In *Pricing for Profit*, the unit contribution margin CM, expressed either in dollars or percentages, has been a cornerstone of our profitability analyses. Clearly, in computing this metric it is most important that some average pocket price be used and not a list or invoice price. Otherwise the CM will be overstated, i.e., the product will seem more profitable than it is and the computed results wrong and misleading.

11.6.2 Dealing with Power Buyers

Power buyer is a term used by Nagle et al for a firm whose volume purchases give it sufficient leverage to extract the lowest prices and most favorable terms and conditions from its suppliers. One purchase agent at such a power buyer reportedly told one of its suppliers that he expected the supplier to sell him their products at or near cost and make its profit elsewhere. Power buyers are prevalent in highly competitive industries such as the auto industry. According to the authors, "The worst of these [power buyers] was General Motors, which bankrupted most of its suppliers before bankrupting itself."[14] In fact, of the three major American auto companies in the U.S. market only Ford came through the auto industry meltdown of the Great Recession (2007–2009) unscathed while General Motors and Chrysler had to be bailed out by the federal government.

Many mass-merchandisers such as Costco, Home Depot, Lowe's, Target, OfficeMax, Staples, and Wal-Mart fall into this power buyer category as well. Buyers and purchase agents for power buyers tend to be highly sophisticated, skilled, and aggressive and often not above using bully tactics to get their way. Their information resources on competing suppliers and experience in dealing with these make them formidable adversaries. In short, power buyers tend to play hardball and supplier managements must learn to play the same game and not be overly intimidated. Dealing with power buyers calls for special strategies and tactics.

A question any company's management must ask itself is whether to deal with a power buyer in the first place. Unit contribution margins are sure to be low because the power buyer will not allow a firm to capture the full value its products or services represent to this buyer. Consequently, contribution margins tend to be small. This does not mean, of course, that the supplier to a power buyer cannot ever make a profit. It is only more difficult. This point can easily be shown by inspection of the contribution formula given originally by Equation 3.8 of Chapter 3:

$$K = (P - VC) \times Q = CM \times Q \qquad \text{Eq. (11.3)}$$

where K is the total dollar contribution, P the sell price, VC the product's unit variable cost, CM the unit contribution margin, and Q the number of units sold. Clearly, with a low price, the product's unit variable cost must necessarily be small and the quantity high, for significant contributions to fixed cost and profits to be generated.

Successful suppliers to power buyers must consequently enjoy a cost advantage over competitors and have large production capacities. They will have leverage vis-à-vis their power customers in proportion to the uniqueness of their product. Most vulnerable to pricing pressures will be makers of an undifferentiated commodity because the power buyer will have multiple sources of supply. A prime example would be a standardized auto part. A maker of a more differentiated and unique product, on the other hand, would have some leverage while the supplier of a sought-after name brand product would have the most.

Consider, for example, a branded product such as a Braun electric shaver or coffee maker. Braun products are known for style and quality and can command premium prices. Yet they are not only sold at high-end stores but a number of discount chains as well. A firm like Braun would have considerable leverage because the brand adds prestige and luster to the power buyer's product selection and the manufacturer would therefore not be subject to the oppressive tactics that a power buyer might employ with other suppliers. In order to avoid cannibalization of its own products, the company would typically offer special product versions for this price-sensitive segment of the market reserving its premium lines for specialty stores where higher prices and contribution margins are achievable.

Where the firm is being squeezed on price to the extend that margins are disappearing, it is sometimes necessary to consider just walking away from a power buyer. Management should never let itself become so completely dependant on a power buyer's business that the company's survival is at stake if the relationship is broken. If the firm has other and more favorable options for generating revenue and total contribution, it should not hesitate to so inform the power buyer and stand its ground. More often than not, the power customer will accede to the seller's price proposal because it cannot get a better deal elsewhere, despite claims to the contrary, or the cost of switching suppliers will be unacceptably high.

11.6.3 Ad Hoc Pricing

Another means of enhancing profitability is by eliminating *ad hoc* or spur of the moment price decisions in response to price objections from customers. Such   price concessions can significantly erode profit performance especially if it has become routine. In a typical scenario, a buyer is unhappy with a price quotation and calls someone he or she knows at the seller to get a better deal. This may require several calls to ever higher management levels until the right individual is found. The customer's agent is now a hero because of the clout he or she has demonstrated while the seller executive has been able to show clout in being able to overrule lower levels of management. But business transactions should not be about clout and instead about basic economics. While personal relationships are undoubtedly very important in the business world, these should enhance profitability for the firms involved and not undermine it.

The answer to ad hoc pricing is a strong pricing policy that is adhered to throughout the organization. This policy should cover all contingencies including the criteria for price concessions, who may grant them and to whom, by how much a price may be lowered, and what conditions apply. Ideally, only one person in the organization should be authorized to give price concessions and that individual should be the one with overall profit and loss responsibility or a designated representative.

An effective pricing policy will shield all levels of management from outside pricing pressure and uphold the firm's price credibility and integrity so that customers will have no expectation of further price concessions as a result of their lobbying efforts. Most importantly, a pricing policy will help assure that quarterly and yearly sales revenue and profitability goals are met. Where a pricing policy consistently leads to loss of sales revenue and profits, it should obviously be revised and other options considered but ad hoc price concessions should not be among these.

11.6.4 Sales Force Compensation

Where a firm employs a sales force and pays commissions based on sales volume or revenue alone, it would do well to let at least part of each salesperson's commission or bonus take account of the profitability of these sales. Tucker found that "In client companies where commission is paid on contribution, there has been a complete turnabout in profits."[15] As the author noted, if a company pays a flat commission on sales revenue, it serves notice that all sales revenue has the same value. This is clearly not so—sales revenue with a larger total contribution content is obviously more valuable than one with a smaller one. This being the case, why should the reward for high and low-margin sales be the same? Besides not optimizing profits, pushing sales revenue has the added disadvantage of skewing the mix of products sold due to a salesperson's natural inclination to concentrate on products whose sale requires the least amount of time and effort.

A good salesperson does not talk price but value. This means that the employee must be able to communicate value to the customer by convincing him or her that the product offering will meet his or her needs better than a competing brand. For this to happen, salespeople have to understand not only their company's own product offerings and their uses but that of their major competitors as well and, additionally, be fully informed how the product is being used and valued by their customers. In other words, salespeople must be more than order takers and be able to think like their customers and, where possible, put themselves in their place. This takes time and effort which, in turn, should be encouraged by a suitable reward system.

A formula that encourages profit-oriented sales should be fair and equitable and also easy to implement. A number of such formulas can be found in the literature. Nagle et al have proposed one that calculates a *sales credit* based on the difference between the target price and actual price and a profitability factor k or "kicker" that is the reciprocal of the product's percentage contribution margin at the target price:[16]

$$\text{Sales Credit} = [P_T - k \times (P_T - P_A)] \times Q \qquad \text{Eq. (11.4)}$$

where P_T is the target price, P_A the actual price, Q the quantity sold, and $k = 1 / CM_T$ where CM_T is the target contribution margin.

Thus, suppose we have a product priced at $1,000 which is sold at $900 (a 10% discount) and suppose the contribution margin at full price is 20%, then the salesperson would earn a sales credit of

$$\text{Sales Credit} = [\$1,000 - (1 / 0.20) (\$1,000 - \$900)] = \$500$$

for that sale. On the other hand, if the same product was sold at $1,100 (a 10% premium), the sales credit would be:

$$\text{Sales Credit} = [\$1,000 - (1 / 0.20) (\$1,000 - \$1,100)] = \$1,500$$

Another and more direct approach would allow the firm to compute a salesperson's incentive bonus or, in the case of straight commission earnings, the weekly or monthly commissions earned based on the salesperson's sales revenue and total contribution. Thus, for each salesperson and each sale two quantities would be recorded—the actual sales revenue and the total contribution generated by this sale. At the end of the commission period (week or month), the sum total of the salesperson's sales revenue and total contributions would be determined and the following simple formula applied to these totals:[17]

$$\text{Earnings (E)} = (R + w \times K) \times k \qquad \text{Eq. (11.5)}$$

where,
R = Sales revenue (\$)
K = Total contribution (\$)
w = Weighing factor ($0 \le w$)
k = Scaling factor ($0 < k$)

The weighing factor "w" would allow the total contribution to carry more, the same, or less weight than the sales revenue. The scaling factor "k" would allow management to adjust the earnings rate from a small commissions bonus to all-commissions earnings in lieu of a salary. The latter is a common practice in the retail trade.

Example

Peter and Elke are salespeople at Plunkett Home Furnishings. March sales revenue for Peter was \$100,000 with \$25,000 in total contribution dollars while Elke had the same sales revenue but \$50,000 in total contribution. Using weighing and scaling factors of 2.0 and 0.002, respectively, in Equation (11.5) the March bonus dollars earned by the two salespeople would be:

Peter: $E = (\$100,000 + 2.0 \times \$25,000) \times 0.002 = \$300$
Elke: $E = (\$100,000 + 2.0 \times \$50,000) \times 0.002 = \$400$

Thus, Elke would earn \$100 more than Peter in March because of the higher profitability of her sales.

Suppose we wanted to determine March commissions rather than March bonuses using this formula. Raising the scaling factor to 0.025, for example, commissions would be:

Peter: $E = (\$100,000 + 2.0 \times \$25,000) \times 0.025 = \$3,750$
Elke: $E = (\$100,000 + 2.0 \times \$50,000) \times 0.025 = \$5,000$

Elke's earnings would again be higher than Peter's because of the higher total contribution content of her sales. Earned commissions would typically go into each salesperson's individual commissions account from which each would receive a *draw* against commissions of a specific amount each payday.

11.7 Marketing Intelligence

In an adversarial and competitive business environment good and timely information is essential for profitable operations and sometimes even for survival. The collection and evaluation of competitor information especially regarding products and prices is therefore an important business function that should be conducted in a systematic rather than an haphazard manner.

For each major competitor, needed information includes: Company strengths and weaknesses; marketing and pricing goals and strategies; present product and service offerings and associated prices; sales, market shares, and profitability by product; and imminent product and/or price changes. Other vital information concerns technological changes that could pose dangers or opportunities, and shifts and trends in buyer needs and wants.

One of the best sources of reliable marketing intelligence is the firm's own sales force. A company's salespeople are its frontline soldiers and as such among the first to see and hear about a competitor's new products and prices, impending product and/or price changes, quality or delivery problems, and much more. Salespeople should be encouraged to routinely furnish such information on their weekly call reports or in special reports to management.

Loyal customers and members of the firm's distribution chain represent another source of useful information especially if a good working relationship has been cultivated in the past. Trade organizations often collect and publish such statistical data as sales and market shares for the major companies that make up the industry. Much can also be learned at trade shows where competitors come together to showcase their new product offerings. Other sources for competitive information include:

* Statements by company executives
* Company news releases
* Catalogs and price lists
* Product advertisements
* Business newspapers and magazines
* Business sections of daily papers
* Federal and state government statistics
* Annual reports to stockholders
* Financial analysts and stock brokers
* Advertising agencies

Sometimes the same information sources can be used to feed back information to induce competitor conduct favorable to the firm. Care must be taken that it is done in a discrete and lawful manner. What is lawful and not is covered in Chapter 15 of *Pricing for Profit.*

Notes

1. American Airlines spokesman John Hotard as quoted in *USA Today*, 10 July 1992, 1.

2. Table 11-1 is based on the *Profit Impact Formula* given by Equation (14.1) in Chapter 14:

$$\blacktriangle K = \frac{1}{CM_0} \{-\epsilon_0 (\blacktriangle P)^2 + (1 - \epsilon_0 CM_0) \blacktriangle P\}$$

For example, if the product's unit contribution margin before the price change (CM_0) was 20% and the price elasticity of demand at the present price-volume operating point (ϵ_0) was 2.0, a 10% price reduction would cause a 40% reduction in total contribution and profits:

$$\blacktriangle K = 1 / 0.20 \times \{-2.0 (-0.10)^2 + (1 - 2.0 \times 0.20) (-0.10)\} = -0.40$$

3. Thomas Nagle, John Hogan and Joseph Zale, *The Strategy and Tactics of Pricing*, 246.

4. John Philip Jones, "The Double Jeopardy of Sales Promotions," *Harvard Business Review*, September – October 1990, 5.

5. Rafi Mohammed, *The 1% Windfall*, 91

6. Walter Baker, Michael Marn, and Craig Zawada, *The Price Advantage*, 133.

7. George Lazarus, "Price cutting war leaves Kellogg with soggy market share," *Chicago Tribune*, 18 September 1996, B1.

8. Akshay R. Rao, Mark E. Bergen, and Scott Davis, "How to Fight a Price War," *Harvard Business Review on Pricing*, 80.

9. Robert Dolan and Hermann Simon, *Power Pricing*, 98.

10. Robert D. Buzzell, Bradley T. Gale, and Ralph G. M. Sultan, "Market Share—a Key to Profitability," *Harvard Business Review*, January-February 1975, 98,104.

11. Robert Dolan and Hermann Simon, supra at 103.

12. Thomas Nagle, John Hogan, and Joseph Zale, supra at 247-248.

13. Michael V. Marn and Robert L. Rosiello, "Managing Price, Gaining Profit," *Harvard Business Review On Pricing*, 45-73. Also, Walter Baker, Michael Marn, and Craig Zawada, supra at 25-44, 307-325.

14. Thomas Nagle, John Hogan, and Joseph Zale, supra at 108.

15. Spencer Tucker, *Pricing for Higher Profit*, 270.

16. Thomas Nagle, John Hogan, and Joseph Zale, supra at 177.

17. This formula is the author's own contribution to the topic.

CHAPTER

12

Price Optimization

In maturity, when the source of demand is repeat buyers and when competition becomes more stable, one may better gauge the incremental revenue from a price change and discover that a little fine tuning of price can significantly improve profits.[1]

Standard pricing texts do not normally discuss price optimization techniques in any detail although the topic may receive some incidental coverage as noted in Subsection 10.2.2 of Chapter 10 (Marketing and Pricing Dynamics). Delving into this topic could easily lead into a mathematical quagmire with complex mathematical derivations and formulas that may or may not be useful to a marketer for pricing purposes. Nevertheless, most pricing practitioners are much interested in this issue and would like to know what prices they should charge for their diverse products or services in order to best reach their sales revenue, market share, and profit goals.

In this and the following two chapters price optimization is more fully explored. By an optimal price we mean that price that will result in either maximum sales revenue or maximum total contribution and profit for a particular product under the given price-volume and unit variable cost conditions. In prior chapters we have stated some of the conditions that must exist for either to occur and whether a price increase or cut is required to achieve these results. This information was summarized in the pricing rules of Table 8-1 in Chapter 8 (Pricing Strategies). However, this prior material did not enlighten us as to how much a price must change to achieve optimal results. We are now in a position to develop a set of simple techniques and formulas by which this may be achieved using readily available data. In other words, these chapters are about the "fine tuning" of established prices. Chapters 13 and 14 focus specifically on sales revenue and total contribution maximization, respectively.

12.1 Price Optimization and the P.E.D.

The key to effective price optimization is the point price elasticity of demand which is simply the percentage quantity change resulting from a percentage price change. Equation (6.3) of Chapter 6 (Market Demand) defines this quantity as:

$$\varepsilon = - \frac{\Delta Q}{\Delta P} \frac{P}{Q} \qquad \text{Eq. (12.1)}$$

where ΔQ is the quantity change (units) and ΔP the price change (dollars), respectively. The minus sign was introduced to ensure that the P.E.D. is always a positive number. Since Equation (6.3) was too cumbersome to manipulate mathematically, with Equation (6.4) we introduced the following simplified expression:

$$\varepsilon = - \frac{\blacktriangle Q}{\blacktriangle P} \qquad \text{Eq. (12.2)}$$

where $\blacktriangle P$ is the percentage price change and $\blacktriangle Q$ the percentage quantity change. More specifically, if the subscripts 0 and 1 represent the variables before and after a price change, respectively, one has:

$$\blacktriangle Q = \frac{Q_1 - Q_0}{Q_0} \qquad \text{Eq. (12.3)}$$

and $$\blacktriangle P = \frac{P_1 - P_0}{P_0}$$ Eq. (12.4)

The P.E.D. plays such a crucial role in price optimization because it is the nexus between factors inside the firm such as product cost and profit margins and outside such as buyer perceptions and market demand for the product. It essentially represents the aggregate assessment of many buyers and potential buyers regarding their relative needs and wants to possess the product and their value perception of it in relation to all competing products on the market. This evaluation is reflected in the buyers' relative sensitivities to the product's price and specifically in the product's P.E.D. at any given operating point (P_0, Q_0) on the product's demand curve. Furthermore, as mentioned before, the P.E.D. represents a useful surrogate for a demand schedule or curve which is almost never available.

The price elasticity of demand is not without problems. While not quite as difficult to come by as a demand schedule or curve, it too requires some effort and care to determine. The various techniques available for estimating the price elasticity of demand before a contemplated price change were previously covered in Section 6.4 of Chapter 6 (Market Demand).

A more fundamental problem with the P.E.D. was pointed out by Tucker and later writers.[2] This is the fact that the elasticity factor is not linear in any amount or direction. As Tucker noted, in some cases a 5 percent price increase can cut volume by 30 percent but a similar price cut may raise volume by only 8 percent. However, Tucker's scenario is undoubtedly an extreme case. That the P.E.D. is not linear should not be surprising since the demand curve is, as the name implies, a curve. In estimating the P.E.D. we use a linear approximation to it which necessarily departs from the true curve.

To effectively deal with this nonlinearity issue, only small (incremental) price increments should be considered. In fact, price adjustments should, as a rule of thumb, not exceed about 25% percent of the original price in either direction. Results from sales revenue and total contribution computations for larger price changes are highly suspect and should be used only to establish trends, and general rules and guidelines as we have done in previous chapters.

12.2 Price Optimization Methods

In this chapter we consider five methods and techniques for determining optimal prices for maximum sales revenue and total contribution each of which has its unique advantages and disadvantages. Much of this material is new to the literature and presented in *Pricing for Profit* for the first time.

12.2.1 Pricing Rules of Thumb

Application of the pricing rules of thumb given in Chapter 6 and Chapter 7 and summarized in Table 8-1 of Chapter 8 is the simplest and quickest way to determine the direction of required price changes to achieve maximum sales revenue or total contribution and profit. Restated for convenience these are

i) For sales revenue maximization:
Lower the price if the product's P.E.D. is larger than 1.0, *hold* it if it equal to 1.0, and *raise* it if it is less than 1.0.

ii) For total contribution and profit maximization:
Lower the price if the product's P.E.D. is larger than $1 / CM_0$, *hold* it if it is equal to $1 / CM_0$, and *raise* it if it is less than $1 / CM_0$.

These decision rules, derived from standard microeconomic theory, do not give the magnitudes of the required price changes.

12.2.2 Linear Demand or Price Response Curve

Where a linear demand or price response curve can be drawn from the available price-volume data, the optimal prices for sales revenue or total contribution and profit maximization can be obtained in two ways:

i) By Inspection

Referring to Figure 10-1 of Chapter 10 (Marketing and Pricing Dynamics) and Appendix I. ("Formula Derivations A. Optimal Prices on Price Response Curve"), the optimal price for sales revenue maximization is one-half of the product's maximum (reservation) price. For total contribution and profit maximization, the optimal price lies midway between the product's unit variable cost and the maximum (reservation) price. Specifically, it is one-half the sum of the reservation price and the unit variable cost.

ii) By Formula

This more formal procedure requires that the equation of the linear demand or price response curve be determined. For a linear demand curve, for example, it will take the form $P = a - (a / b) Q$ where "a" is the vertical (price) axis intercept, "b" the horizontal (quantity) axis intercept, "a / b" the line's slope, and "P" and "Q" the y-axis and x-axis labels, respectively. Using this equation, the expressions for sales revenue R and total contribution K can be derived which will both have the shape of a parabola. The first derivative of each expression yields a second equation which gives its slope. Since at the apex of a parabola this slope is zero, one need only set this second equation equal to zero to obtain the price and quantity points where R and K reach their maximum values.

12.2.3 Incremental Search

In what may be called the *incremental search technique*, use is made of Equation (12.2) above and the standard incremental relationships to construct a table of sales revenue and total contribution. For obtaining the optimal price for sales revenue maximization [P], four steps are required for each point on the sales revenue curve:

i) $P_1 = P_0 (1 + \blacktriangle P)$
ii) $\blacktriangle Q = - \epsilon_0 \blacktriangle P$
iii) $Q_1 = Q_0 (1 + \blacktriangle Q)$
iv) $R_1 = P_1 Q_1$

For obtaining the optimal price for contribution maximization P*, two more steps are added:

v) $V_1 = VC_0 \; Q_1$
vi) $K_1 = R_1 - V_1$

In practice, small price increments such as 1%, 3%, or 5% are chosen and a series of computations made using steps i) through vi) and tabulated. This table will identify the price points at which sales revenue and total contribution are maximized.

12.2.4 Graphical

In this approach the formulas for sales revenue and total contribution are developed and then plotted on graph paper or the incremental technique described above is extended to the entire range of prices and plotted. From these curves the price optima for sales revenue [P] and total contribution P* may simply be read off. This technique requires the most effort but has the advantage of displaying all the price-quantity options for the entire price range from zero to the reservation (maximum) price.

12.2.5 Optimization Formulas

In Chapters 13 and 14 and the associated Appendices special formulas are developed by which optimal price changes may be computed directly knowing just three parameter values, namely, the price-volume point prior to the contemplated price change (P_0, Q_0), the price elasticity of demand at that point $\mathcal{E}_0$, and the product's original unit contribution margin CM_0 (%). These formulas for the required percentage price [▲P] and quantity [▲Q] changes for sales revenue maximization and required percentage price ▲P* and quantity ▲Q* changes for total contribution maximization are, respectively:

$$[\blacktriangle P] = \frac{1 - \mathcal{E}_0}{2\,\mathcal{E}_0} \qquad \text{Eq. (12.5)}$$

$$[\blacktriangle Q] = \frac{\mathcal{E}_0 - 1}{2} \qquad \text{Eq. (12.6)}$$

$$\blacktriangle P^* = \frac{1 - \mathcal{E}_0\, CM_0}{2\,\mathcal{E}_0} \qquad \text{Eq. (12.7)}$$

$$\blacktriangle Q^* = \frac{\mathcal{C}_0 \, CM_0 - 1}{2} \qquad \text{Eq. (12.8)}$$

As usual, the right-hand sides of the four equations are to be multiplied by 100% to obtain the actual percentages while CM_0 is the percentage contribution margin in decimal form.

12.3 Application

The following example will demonstrate use of these five techniques.

Illustrative Example: Wein♦Glas Ltd.

Claudia Chianti has been operating a small import business from her home for the past two years. Her customers are wine aficionados who highly value her selection of wine glasses, decanters, cork screws, bottle storage racks, and similar items. One of her products is a set of stemware which costs her, inclusive of freight and import duties, a total of $50 and which she sells on the Internet for $100 plus shipping. Her monthly sales are 50 sets. Three months ago, Claudia charged just $80 for the set and shipped 100 sets a month. Then, at a trade show she heard that most mail order businesses use a simple rule of thumb by which a product's sell price should be at least double its cost. After her return, she raised her prices accordingly. While this price increase was just 25%, Claudia was surprised to find her sales volume plummet by 50%. She now wonders whether she did the right thing.

To obtain some clarification Claudia went to see her friend Rosalind Riesling who teaches Marketing at nearby Champaign Community College. On hearing about the results of the recent price change, Rosalind determined that this product's P.E.D. was 2.0 (50% / 25%) meaning that demand for it was highly elastic. Rosalind told Claudia that when she raised her price, many customers presumably decided it was too steep for them after finding a less costly substitute elsewhere. Rosalind then proceeded to show her friend how to determine the optimal prices for sales revenue and contribution maximization for her stemware product.

Rosalind established these initial conditions for Claudia's product:

$$P_0 = \$80 \quad Q_0 = 100 \quad P_1 = \$100 \quad Q_1 = 50 \quad VC_0 = \$50$$

From this she obtained the following basic information:

$\blacktriangle P = (\$100 - \$80) / \$80 = \$20 / \$80 = 0.25$ or 25%

$\blacktriangle Q = (50 - 100) / 100 = -0.50$ or -50%

$\varepsilon_0 = \blacktriangle Q / \blacktriangle P = 50\% / 25\% = 2.0$

$CM_0 = (\$80 - \$50) / \$80 = 0.375$ or 37.5%

12.3.1 Pricing Rules of Thumb Solution

In our example, the CM_0 is 0.375 and its reciprocal is 2.67. Since the actual P.E.D. (2.0) is less than this required P.E.D. (2.7), the price needs to be raised to maximize total contribution and profit. As previously mentioned, our pricing rule of thumb can only tell us the direction but not the amount of the required price change.

12.3.2 Linear Demand Curve Solution

This illustrative example is one of the rare cases where a linear demand curve (or, alternatively, a price response curve) may be constructed from the available data. Rosalind decided to draw a traditional liner demand curve for Claudia's stemware by labeling the vertical axis "Price" and the horizontal axis "Quantity," entering the two known price-volume points, and connecting these as shown in Figure 12-1 (solid line). She then extended this line in both directions (broken lines) to obtain the price and volume intercepts which are seen to be $120 and 300 units, respectively.

i) By Inspection

On Figure 12-1 Rosalind noticed that at the midpoint of the product's linear demand curve the price was $60. Similarly, she found that one-half of the sum of the reservation price ($120) and the product's unit variable cost ($50) came to $85. These, Rosalind told Claudia, were her optimal prices for sales revenue and total contribution maximization, respectively.

Figure 12-1
Linear Demand Curve for Wein♦Glas Ltd.

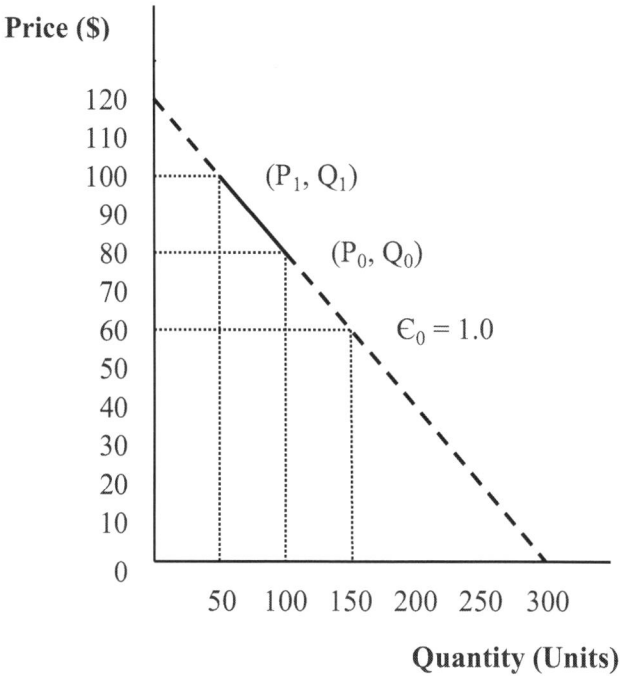

Price ($)

(graph showing linear demand curve with points (P_1, Q_1) at price 100, (P_0, Q_0) at price 80, and $\epsilon_0 = 1.0$ at price 60; Price axis marked 0, 10, 20, 30, 40, 50, 60, 70, 80, 90, 100, 110, 120; Quantity axis marked 50, 100, 150, 200, 250, 300)

Quantity (Units)

ii) By Formula

Rosalind continued her analysis by finding the equation for this linear demand curve. Using the two axes intercepts and slope of Figure 12-1, the equation for the linear demand curve is:

$$P = 120 - (120 / 300) Q = 120 - 0.40 Q$$

The sales revenue function is therefore:

$$R = P Q = 120 Q - 0.40 Q^2$$

Differentiating R w.r.t. Q and setting the result equal to zero yields the optimal quantity for sales revenue maximization [Q]:

$$R' = 120 - 0.80 Q = 0$$

$[Q] = 150$

The optimal price and maximum sales revenue are therefore:

$$[P] = 120 - (0.40)(150) = \$60$$

$$[R] = [P] [Q] = (\$60)(150) = \$9,000$$

Following the same procedure, Rosalind now obtained the optimal quantity Q* and price P* for total contribution maximization, and the maximum total contribution K*:

$$K = (P - VC_0) Q = (120 - 0.40 Q - 50) Q = 70 Q - 0.40 Q^2$$

$$K' = 70 - 0.80 Q = 0$$

$$Q* = 87.5$$

$$P* = 120 - (0.40) (87.5) = \$85$$

$$K* = (P* - VC_0) Q* = (\$85 - \$50)(87.5) = \$3,063$$

Thus, Rosalind explained, a price cut to $60 would have resulted in a 12.5% sales revenue increase while a price increase to $85 would have caused a contribution increase but of just 2.1%.

12.3.3 Incremental Search Solution

Since Rosalind already knew the optimal prices [P] and P*, she could narrow her search to just a few price points and decided to confine the price range of her search from $50 to $100 with price increments of $\blacktriangle P = \pm 0.05$ or $\pm 5\%$. Starting with the price-volume operating point prior to the price change, she computed a second one following the six steps given above and letting $\blacktriangle P = -0.05$:

$$P = \$80 (1 - 0.05) = \$76$$
$$\blacktriangle Q = -2.0 (-0.05) = 0.10$$
$$Q = 100 (1 + 0.10) = 110$$
$$R = (\$76)(110) = \$8,360$$
$$V = (\$50) (110) = \$5,500$$
$$K = \$8,360 - \$5,500 = \$2,860$$

Rosalind computed a third point by letting $\blacktriangle P = -0.10$ and continued incrementing until she arrived at $52 when she reversed direction by letting $\blacktriangle P = + 0.05$ and so on. From her tabulation as shown, Rosalind was able to determine that the maximum sales revenue was achieved at a price of $[P] = \$60$ with a sales revenue of $9,000 while the maximum total contribution occurred near $P^* = \$84$ for a total contribution of about $3,060.

$\blacktriangle P$	P ($)	$\blacktriangle Q$	Q	R ($)	V ($)	K ($)
0	80.00	0	100.0	8,000	5,000	3000
-0.05	76.00	0.10	110.0	8,360	5,500	2,860
-0.10	72.00	0.20	120.0	8,640	6,000	2,640
-0.15	68.00	0.30	130.0	8,840	6,500	2,340
-0.20	64.00	0.40	140.0	8,960	7,000	1,960
-0.25	60.00	0.50	150.0	9,000	7,500	1,500
-0.30	56.00	0.60	160.0	8,960	8,000	960
-0.35	52.00	0.70	170.0	8,840	8,500	340
0.05	84.00	-0.10	90.0	7,560	4,500	3,060
0.10	88.00	-0.20	80.0	7,040	4,000	3,040
0.15	92.00	-0.30	70.0	6,440	3,500	2,940

The values for maximum sales revenue agree with the two previous results while those for maximum total contribution are slightly off because the 5% price increments used were a little too large.

12.3.4 Graphical Solution

To show Claudia the complete array of pricing options with the associated sales volumes Q, sales revenues R, and total contributions K, Rosalind decided to plot all three curves in the price range from zero to the reservation price of P of $120. Using the PRC format, she placed P on the horizontal axis and Q, R and K on the vertical axis. The equation for this PRC was found to be:

$$Q = 300 - 2.5 \, P$$

The expression for sales revenue was therefore:

$$R = P \, Q = -2.5 \, P^2 + 300 \, P$$

Similarly, the total contribution now became:

$$K = (P - 50) \, (300 - 2.5 \, P)$$
$$K = -2.5 \, P^2 + 425 \, P - 15,000$$

Figure 12-2
Sales & Total Contribution for Wein♦Glas Ltd.

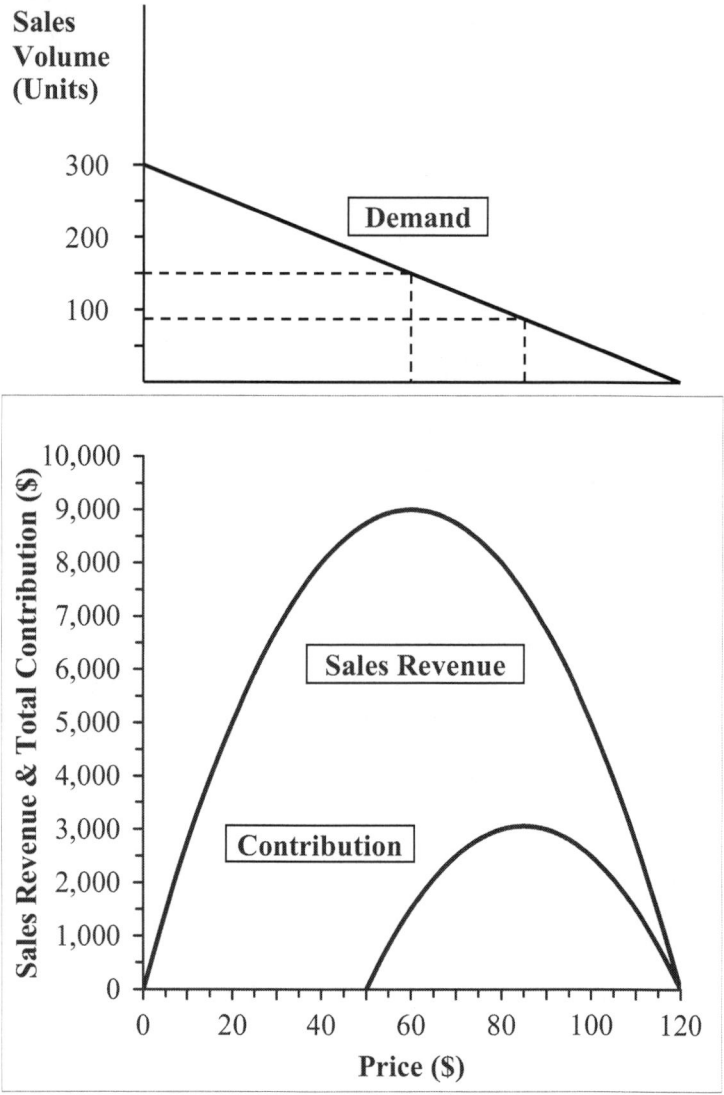

These three expressions are plotted in Figure 12-2. Sales revenue and total contribution are again seen to peak at $60 and $85, respectively. As Rosalind expected, no contribution dollars were generated at and below a price of $50 because that is the product's unit variable cost. As we learned earlier, no contribution dollars are earned at or below that cost which we have labeled a product's price floor. The two lower curves also demonstrate the important fact that even small price variances from the optimal prices can severely impact sales revenue and total contribution. According to Rosalind, in a real-life situation the two curves would not be as perfectly symmetrical as shown but more skewed to one side or the other. That is because the demand curve was assumed to be perfectly linear which it would normally not be.

12.3.5 Formula Solution

The price adjustment formulas given by Equations (12.5) through (12.8) present the most direct and accurate means of determining the desired information on the optimal prices and maximum sales revenue and total contribution. Using the given data, Rosalind computed these values for revenue maximization:

$$[\blacktriangle P] = (1 - 2.0) / (2 \times 2.0) = -0.25 = -25\%$$

$$[P] = (1.0 - 0.25)\,(\$80) = \$60$$

$$[\blacktriangle Q] = (2.0 - 1) / 2 = 0.50 = 50\%$$

$$[Q] = (1 + 0.50)(100) = 150$$

$$[R] = (\$60)(150) = \$9,000$$

For contribution maximization, Rosalind made these calculations:

$$\blacktriangle P^* = (1 - 2.0 \times 0.375) / (2 \times 2.0) = 0.0625 = 6.25\%$$

$$P^* = (1 + 0.0625)(\$80) = \$85$$

$$\blacktriangle Q^* = (2.0 \times 0.375 - 1) / 2 = -0.125 = -12.5\%$$

$$Q^* = (1 - 0.125)(100) = 87.5$$

$$K^* = (\$85 - \$50)(87.5) = \$3,063$$

These formula results were identical to those found by the three previous techniques but here Rosalind arrived at the solution directly using only the product's P.E.D. and unit contribution margin.

12.3.6 Recommendation

Rosalind recommended to her friend Claudia that she reduce her price for this stemware set from the present $100.00 to $84.95 even though the contribution increase was only minimal. This would be a return to close to her original price of $80.00 and bring back at least some of her lost customers. Per Rosalind, since she was operating out of her home and her overhead cost was minimal, this contribution of a little over $3,000 would be close to her monthly profit as well. Rosalind also suggested to Claudia that she search for and offer more unique and differentiated products for which substitutes were not as readily available. She might even invent some exotic names for her different sets which would enhance their uniqueness and appeal. According to Rosalind, such products would be less price sensitive (have steeper demand curves) allowing Claudia to charge higher prices and achieve larger margins and profits.

Notes

1. Thomas Nagle, John Hogan, and Joseph Zale, *The Strategy and Tactics of Pricing*, 152.

2. Spencer Tucker, *Pricing for Higher Profit*, 13.

CHAPTER

13

Pricing for Maximum Sales Revenue

Growth which fails to fulfill its promise of profitability can spell disaster and has in fact brought ruin to many a company whose managers were guided by the mistaken belief that growth was its own reward.[1]

Not every firm sets prices for its products and services to maximize contribution and profits. Many business managers focus on sales and market share goals instead believing that being a strong force in the market will eventually lead to price leadership and increased profitability. For other firms, such as those with high indirect fixed and small unit incremental costs, as found in public transportation and other industries, it is more common and meaningful to talk about revenues rather than profits. The more tickets a public transportation company sells the more contribution dollars it generates to cover continuing operating expenses.

This chapter will show pricing practitioners and marketers how to compute sell prices that lead to maximum sales revenue and revenue market share. First the necessary formulas to make these computations are introduced. The formula derivations are not included in this chapter but the interested and mathematically inclined reader may peruse these in Appendix I. (See "Formula Derivations B. Sales Revenue Maximization"). Next a reference chart is presented which the busy marketer can use to look up the needed information without having to use the formulas. An illustrative example is worked out to show how this optimization procedure may be applied. The chapter concludes with some useful observations and a pricing rule.

13.1 The Sales Revenue Maximizer Formulas

The twelve formulas presented are based on Equation (3.3) of Chapter 3 whereby sales revenue R is the product of the net sell price P and the quantity Q sold at that price:

$$R = P \, Q$$

If one lets the subscripts 0 and 1 designate the parameters before and after an incremental price change, respectively, and Δ the dollar change resulting from such a price change, one obtains:

$$\Delta R = R_1 - R_0 = P_1 \, Q_1 - P_0 \, Q_0$$

13.1.1 The Revenue Impact Formula (RIF)

An important price optimization formula developed in the Appendix allows the pricer to compute the percentage change in sales revenue $\blacktriangle R$ as a result of a percentage change in the sell price $\blacktriangle P$ given the price elasticity of demand ε_0 at the present price-volume operating point (P_0, Q_0):

$$\blacktriangle R = -\varepsilon_0 \, (\blacktriangle P)^2 + (1 - \varepsilon_0) \, \blacktriangle P \qquad \text{Eq.(13.1)}$$

Because the expression gives the impact of a price change on sales revenue, one may call it the *revenue impact formula* or RIF.

If one places $\blacktriangle P$ on the x (horizontal) axis and $\blacktriangle R$ on the y (vertical) axis, and plots Equation (13.1), the result is a parabola which rises from zero to a maximum value at $[\blacktriangle P]$, the optimal price change for sales revenue maximization, and drops back to zero.

13.1.2 The Sales Revenue After a Percentage Price Change

Since the price after the optimal price change equals the original price plus the incremental price change given by Eq. (13.1), one has:

$$R_1 = R_0 (1 + \blacktriangle R)$$

$$R_1 = R_0 \{ - \epsilon_0 (\blacktriangle P)^2 + (1 - \epsilon_0) \blacktriangle P + 1 \} \quad \text{Eq. (13.2)}$$

This expression too is a parabola.

13.1.3 The Optimal Percentage Price Change

From the RIF of Equation (13.1), the optimal percentage price change to achieve maximum sales revenue can be shown to be:

$$[\blacktriangle P] = \frac{1 - \epsilon_0}{2 \epsilon_0} \quad \text{Eq (13.3)}$$

It is interesting to note that the optimum incremental price change for sales revenue maximization depends on only one quantity, namely, the product's price elasticity of demand. Nothing else matters.

13.1.4 The Optimal Condition

Conditions are optimal when no price change is required to achieve maximum sales revenue. Microeconomic theory informs us that for this to happen, the price elasticity of demand at the present price-volume operating point must be 1.0:[2]

$$\epsilon_0 = [\epsilon] = 1.0 \quad \text{Eq. (13.4)}$$

This is precisely the result obtained when one sets Equation (13.3) for the optimal percentage price change equal to zero. We also know (see Table 8-1 of Chapter 8) that if the P.E.D. is less than 1.0, the price must be raised for sales revenue maximization, lowered if it is larger than 1.0, and held if it is equal to 1.0. Equation (13.3) lets the marketer compute the exact amounts of such required price changes.

13.1.5 The Price Range for Positive Revenue Changes

By setting Equation (13.1) equal to zero and finding the two price points at which the parabola described by this equation crosses the x ($\blacktriangle P$) axis, one obtains:

$$\blacktriangle P = 0; \quad \frac{1 - \epsilon_0}{\epsilon_0} \quad \text{Eq. (13.5)}$$

Hence, the curve crosses the x-axis at 0 and a point which is twice the optimal price change given by Equation (13.3). The favorable price range therefore extends from $\blacktriangle P = 0$ to $\blacktriangle P = 2 \times [\blacktriangle P]$.

13.1.6 The Optimal Price

The optimal price is simply the original price P_0 plus the optimal percentage price change as given by Eq. (13.3):

$$[P] = P_0 (1 + [\blacktriangle P])$$

$$[P] = \frac{P_0}{2\,\mathcal{E}_0} (\mathcal{E}_0 + 1) \qquad \text{Eq. (13.6)}$$

The optimal price is thus dependant on only the present price P_0 and the P.E.D. at that price.

13.1.7 The Sales Revenue Price Range

The range of prices over which sales revenue can be generated under the given conditions extends from zero to twice the optimal price $[P]$ as given by Equation (13.6):

$$0 < P_1 < \frac{P_0 (\mathcal{E}_0 + 1)}{\mathcal{E}_0} \qquad \text{Eq. (13.7)}$$

Below and above this price range no sales revenue is generated.

13.1.8 The Optimal Percentage Quantity Change

The optimal percentage quantity change follows directly from the definition of the P.E.D. and Equation (13.3):

$$[\blacktriangle Q] = - \mathcal{E}_0 [\blacktriangle P]$$

$$[\blacktriangle Q] = \frac{\mathcal{E}_0 - 1}{2} \qquad \text{Eq. (13.8)}$$

13.1.9 The Optimal Quantity

The optimal quantity is the original quantity Q_0 plus the percentage quantity change as given by Eq. (13.8):

$$[Q] = Q_0 (1 + [\blacktriangle Q])$$

$$[Q] = \frac{Q_0}{2} (\epsilon_0 + 1) \qquad \text{Eq. (13.9)}$$

13.1.10 The Optimal Sales Revenue Change

Based on the above optimal price and volume changes, the optimal percentage sales revenue change can be shown to be:

$$[\blacktriangle R] = \epsilon_0 [\blacktriangle P]^2 \qquad \text{Eq. (13.10)}$$

This expression together with that for $[\blacktriangle P]$ of Equation (13.3) are the two key formulas for sales revenue maximization.

13.1.11 The Maximum Sales Revenue

The product of the optimal price, Equation (13.6), and optimal quantity, Equation (13.9), yields the maximum sales revenue achievable under the given conditions:

$$[R] = [P] [Q]$$

$$[R] = \frac{R_0}{4 \epsilon_0} (\epsilon_0 + 1)^2 \qquad \text{Eq. (13.11)}$$

13.1.12 The Optimal Unit Contribution Margin

The optimal price change results in a new unit contribution margin:

$$[CM] = \frac{[P] - VC_0}{[P]} \qquad \text{Eq. (13.12)}$$

where $[P]$ is the optimal price given by Equation (13.6).

13.2 Application

The following illustrative example will show how the above formulas may be used to analyze and solve a sales revenue pricing problem either mathematically or graphically or both.

Illustrative Example: Humperdinck's Party Supplies

Humperdinck's is a distributor of supplies commonly used by business firms, churches, clubs, and other organizations for their occasional parties, picnics, and other festivities. The company is owned and operated by Engelbert Humperdinck who decided to start his own business after an unprofitable venture writing children's operas back in the Old Country. Engelbert buys his supplies such as paper plates, towels, utensils, napkins, and decorative items in bulk and repackages these to fill individual orders.

One of the most popular of Humperdinck's packages, called PartyTime-3, sells for \$25 and costs him \$10. Sales average about 200 per month. Engelbert wants to grow his business and is willing to cut his price by as much as 20% which he estimates will raise demand by about a third (35%). Unfortunately, he has no clue as to how a 10% or 20% price reduction would affect his sales revenue. Would dollar sales increase or decrease and by how much?

13.2.1 Formula Solution

Using the twelve formulas in the sequence presented, one obtains these results.

i) Suppose, the PartyTime-3 price was reduced by 10%, what would be the impact on sales revenue? Since the P.E.D. is estimated to be 1.75 (35% / 20%), one has from Equation (13.1):

$$\blacktriangle R = -1.75 \, (-0.10)^2 + (1 - 1.75)(-0.10) = 0.0575$$

Thus, a 10% price reduction would increase monthly sales revenue by about 6%.

ii) The monthly sales revenue after the 10% price reduction would be:

$$R_1 = R_0 \, (1 + \blacktriangle R) = \$5.000 \, (1 + 0.0575) = \$5,287.50$$

The same result is obtained more directly from Equation (13.2):

$$R_1 = \$5,000 \, \{ -1.75 \, (-0.10)^2 + (1 - 1.75)(-0.10) + 1 \} = \$5,287.50$$

iii) The optimal percentage price change is found from Equation (13.3):

$$[\blacktriangle P] = (1 - 1.75) / (2)(1.75) = -0.2143$$

Thus, the optimal price change is a price reduction of 21.4%. This is very close to the price adjustment Engelbert had planned.

iv) Since the P.E.D. is 1.75 and therefore more than 1.0, by our pricing rule of thumb a price reduction is called for. This was shown above to amount to 21.4%.

v) The range of percentage price changes that will add to sales revenue extends from 0 to 2 × (− 0.2143) or from 0 to a price reduction of 42.9%. This means that the favorable price range extends from the present $25 down to $14.30 ($25 × 0.571).

vi) The optimal price for the PartyTime-3 package is:

$$[P] = P_0 (1 + [\blacktriangle P] = \$25 (1 - 0.2143) = \$19.64$$

The same result may be obtained more directly from Equation (13.6):

$$[P] = \$25 (1.75 + 1) / (2)(1.75) = \$19.64$$

vii) Under the given conditions, sales revenue will be generated only in the price range given by Equation (13.7):

$$0 < P_1 < \$25 (1.75 + 1) / 1.75$$
$$0 < P_1 < \$39.3$$

viii) From Equation (13.8), the optimal percentage quantity change is:

$$[\blacktriangle Q] = (1.75 - 1) / 2 = 0.375$$

Thus the 21.4% price reduction will cause a sales volume increase of 37.5%.

ix) The optimal quantity is therefore:

$$[Q] = Q_0 (1 + \blacktriangle Q) = 200 (1 + 0.375) = 275$$

The same result may be obtained more directly from Equation (13.9):

$$[Q] = 200 (1.75 + 1) / 2 = 275$$

x) The optimal sales revenue change is by Equation (13.10):

$$[\blacktriangle R] = (1.75)(-0.2143)^2 = 0.0804$$

Thus, the optimal sales revenue increase is about 8%.

xi) The maximum sales revenue after the optimal price change will be:

$$[R] = R_0(1 + [\blacktriangle R]) = \$5,000(1 + 0.0804) = \$5,402$$

The same result is obtained more directly from Equation (13.11):

$$[R] = \$5,000(1 + 1.75)^2 / (4)(1.75) = \$5,402$$

xii) The unit contribution margin after the optimal price change is found from Equation (13.12):

$$[CM] = (\$19.64 - \$10.00) / \$19.64 = 0.491$$

Hence, the price reduction would reduce the unit contribution margin from the present 60% to about 49%.

12.2.2 Graphical Solution

One may also arrive at these results using a graphical approach. Thus, if one inserts the PartyTime-3 parameter values in Equation (13.2) for the sales revenue after a price change one obtains:

$$R_1 = \$5,000\{-1.75(\blacktriangle P)^2 - 0.75 \blacktriangle P + 1\}$$

Rather than plot R_1 as a function of $\blacktriangle P$, it is more useful to plot R_1 as a function of P_1 by selecting values of P_1 and computing $\blacktriangle P$:

$$\blacktriangle P = (P_1 - P_0) / P_0 = (P_1 - \$25) / \$25$$

Thus if $P_1 = \$5$, for example, one has $\blacktriangle P = (\$5 - \$25) / \$25 = -0.80$ resulting in a sales revenue of $R_1 = \$2,400$.

Figure 13-1 shows the completed graph of sales revenue versus price. It may be noted that the curve peaks at a price of about $20, the optimal price [P], and a monthly sales revenue of $5,400. These values match the prior results obtained by formula.

Figure 13-1
Sales Revenue for PartyTime-3

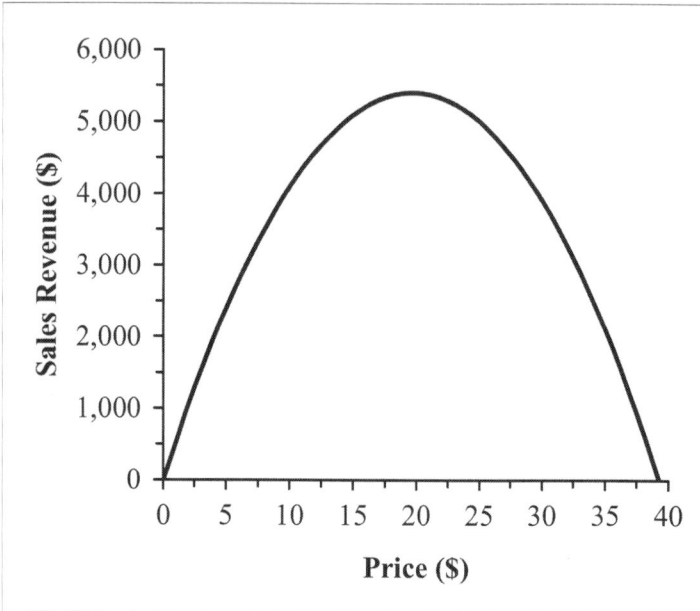

12.2.3 Conclusion

Engelbert was correct in assuming that his PartyTime-3 package was overpriced since his goal was to maximize sales revenue. A price reduction from $25 to about $20 would give him a nearly 40% increase in sales volume but only a modest 8% increase in sales revenue from $5,000 to $5,400 per month. This is the best he can hope to do given the present conditions of price, incremental cost, and price elasticity of demand. PartyTime-3 suffers from the fact that it is a largely undifferentiated commodity-type product with only its name giving it some uniqueness.

The interested reader will find another example of sales revenue maximization in Appendix II. In that hypothetical case study it is shown how a revised fare structure in a public transportation system can substantially increase operating revenue.

13.3 Reference Table

Using diverse formulas to obtain the desired information can seem like a tedious chore and marketers and pricers would obviously prefer to look it up in a table or graph. This was done in previous chapters of *Pricing for Profit* and the practice is continued here. Figure 13.2 is a graphical representation of Equation (13.3) for the optimal percentage price change for sales revenue maximization. As

Figure 13-2
Optimal Percentage Price Change for Revenue Maximization

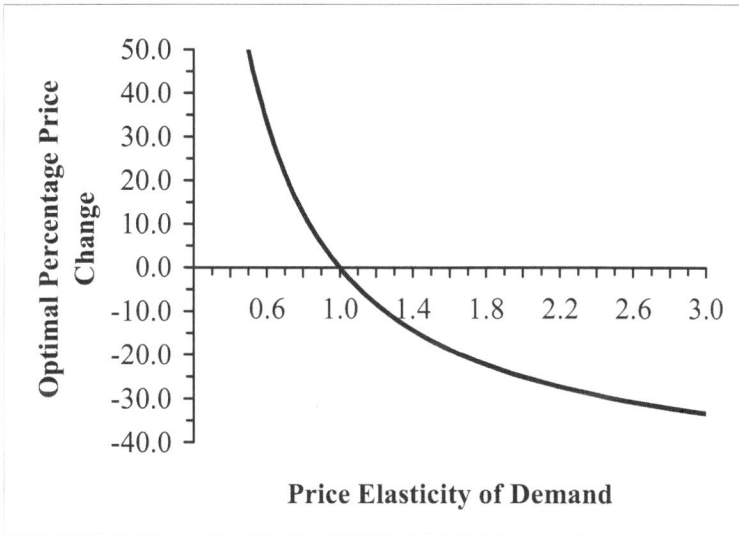

expected, the curve crosses the horizontal (P.E.D) axis at 1.0 (unitary elasticity), i.e., at the optimal price elasticity [ε]. At this P.E.D. no price change is required, i.e., it is the point of maximum achievable sales revenue. As the graph clearly shows, price elasticities below this point ($\varepsilon_0 < 1.0$) require a price increase, while P.E.D.s in the elastic range ($\varepsilon_0 > 1.0$) call for a price reduction.

Table 13-1 is a listing of the two most important parameters, namely, the optimal percentage price and maximum percentage sales revenue changes. These computations are based on Equations (13.3) and (13.10), respectively. The table allows a fast and easy means of solving common pricing problems associated with revenue maximization. Most of the other parameter values for which the formulas were given above, such as optimum price, optimum quantity change, optimum quantity, and maximum sales revenue, are derived from these two tabulations without much further effort.

Taking the Humperdinck's example above, we note from Table 13-1 that for a P.E.D of 1.75 the optimal percentage price and maximum sales revenue changes are −21.4% and 8.0%, respectively. From this, the other parameter values are derived in the usual manner:

$$[P] = P_0 (1 + [\blacktriangle P]) = \$25.00 (1 - 0.214) = \$19.65$$

$$[\blacktriangle Q] = - \epsilon_0 [\blacktriangle P] = - (1.75) (- 0.214) = 37.5\%$$

$$[Q] = Q_0 (1 + [\blacktriangle Q]) = 200 (1 + 0.375) = 275$$

$$[R] = R_0 (1 + [\blacktriangle R]) = \$5,000 (1 + 0.080) = \$5,400$$

These values agree with the formula results obtained previously.

13.4 Pricing Guidelines

The above formulas and Figures 13-1 and 13-2 lead to three additional pricing propositions and a pricing rule.

Pricing Proposition 14

For any product or service there exists one and only one optimal sell price for revenue maximization and all price points below or above this optimal price will result in less than maximum sales revenue for that product or service.

Pricing Proposition 15

The optimal price change for sales revenue maximization depends on only one parameter, namely, the product's price elasticity of demand.

Pricing Proposition 16

The larger the deviation from the optimal price for sales revenue maximization, the greater will be the rate of sales revenue decline so that if the sell price is below the optimal level and is further reduced or is above the optimal level and is further increased, the adverse effects on sales revenue will be multiplied.

Price Optimization Rule 1: Sales Revenue Maximization

Where the pricing objective is to maximize sales revenue for a given product or service and its price elasticity of demand ϵ_0 does not equal 1.0 (unitary elasticity) an incremental price adjustment in the amount of

$$[\blacktriangle P] = \frac{1 - \epsilon_0}{2\,\epsilon_0} \times 100\%$$

is required.

Notes

1. André Gabor, *Pricing*, 30-31.
2. J. P. Gould and C. E. Ferguson, *Microeconomic Theory*, 111.

Table 13-1
Price Optimization for Maximum Sales Revenue

P.E.D. (ϵ_0)	Optimal Price Change (%)	Maximum Revenue Change (%)	P.E.D. (ϵ_0)	Optimal Price Change (%)	Maximum Revenue Change (%)
0.30	117.0	41.1	1.70	(20.6)	7.2
0.35	92.9	30.2	1.75	(21.4)	8.0
0.40	75.0	22.5	1.80	(22.2)	8.9
0.45	61.1	16.8	1.85	(23.0)	9.8
0.50	50.0	12.5	1.90	(23.7)	10.7
0.55	40.9	9.2	1.95	(24.4)	11.6
0.60	33.3	6.7	2.00	(25.0)	12.5
0.65	26.9	3.6	2.05	(25.6)	13.4
0.70	21.4	3.2	2.10	(26.2)	14.4
0.75	16.7	2.1	2.15	(26.7)	15.4
0.80	12.5	1.3	2.20	(27.3)	16.4
0.85	8.8	0.7	2.25	(27.8)	17.4
0.90	5.6	0.3	2.30	(28.3)	18.4
0.95	2.6	0.1	2.35	(28.7)	19.4
1.00	0.0	0.0	2.40	(29.2)	20.4
1.05	(2.4)	0.1	2.45	(29.6)	21.5
1.10	(4.5)	0.2	2.50	(30.0)	22.5
1.15	(7.1)	0.6	2.55	(30.4)	23.6
1.20	(8.3)	0.8	2.60	(30.8)	24.6
1.25	(10.0)	1.3	2.65	(31.1)	25.7
1.30	(11.5)	1.7	2.70	(31.5)	26.8
1.35	(13.0)	2.3	2.75	(31.8)	27.8
1.40	(14.3)	2.9	2.80	(32.1)	28.9
1.45	(15.5)	3.5	2.85	(32.5)	30.0
1.50	(16.7)	4.2	2.90	(32.8)	31.1
1.55	(17.7)	4.9	2.95	(33.1)	32.2
1.60	(18.8)	5.6	3.00	(33.3)	33.3
1.65	(19.7)	6.4	3.50	(35.7)	44.6

CHAPTER

14

Pricing for Maximum Profit

There is always a price that maximizes profit. A price which is too high is as bad as a price which is too low.[1]

Profit maximization is the ultimate goal of most firms for diverse reasons even though they may focus more on sales revenue, market share, or some other marketing or financial objective in the short term. Managers are consequently vitally interested in selling their products and services at the most profitable prices. This chapter provides the market-based formulas and pricing rules by which a marketer can ensure that the contribution generated by each of the firm's products and services is maximized.

In this chapter's presentation of the formulas we shall follow the exact sequence as that used in the previous chapter on sales revenue maximization so that the reader may note the similarities and differences between the two sets. As before, the bare formulas are listed while their derivation has been relegated to Appendix I. (See "Formula Derivations C. Profit Maximization"). An illustrative example is worked out to show application of all formulas. Next follow some general observations regarding profit maximization and a pricing rule. The chapter ends with an examination of the relationship between sales volume and profitability and another pricing rule of thumb. The interested reader will find a hypothetical case study from the restaurant industry further illustrating use of this optimization technique in Appendix II.

14.1 The Profit Maximizer Formulas

The sixteen formulas appearing below start with the basic profit equations, namely, Equations (3.1) and (3.5) of Chapter 3 whereby profit is the difference between sales revenue and total cost:

$$I = R - C$$

$$I = (P - VC) Q - F$$

where,
I = Profit (\$)
R = Sales revenue (\$)
C = Total cost (\$)
P = Sell price (\$)
VC = Unit variable cost (\$)
Q = Quantity (units)
F = Total indirect fixed cost (\$)

If one can assume that the incremental price change is sufficiently small so that VC and F do not change with the price change and if one lets the subscripts 0 and 1 designate the parameters before and after such a price change, respectively, and lets Δ designate the dollar change resulting from this price change, one obtains for this *special case* with $VC_1 = VC_0$ and $F_1 = F_0$:

$$\Delta I = \Delta K = (P_1 - VC_0) Q_1 - (P_0 - VC_0) Q_0$$

Four more formulas are derived in the Appendix to cover the *general case* for which these two cost restrictions do not apply.

14.1.1 The Contribution (Profit) Impact Formula (PIF)

Of considerable interest to a marketer is the impact of an incremental percentage price change in a product or service on its total contribution and profit. A formula allowing this computation makes use of two familiar quantities, namely, the percentage unit contribution margin CM_0 and the price elasticity of demand ϵ_0 at the present price-volume operating point (P_0, Q_0):

$$\blacktriangle K = \frac{1}{CM_0} \{- \varepsilon_0 (\blacktriangle P)^2 + (1 - \varepsilon_0 CM_0) \blacktriangle P\} \qquad \text{Eq. (14.1)}$$

As usual, the symbol $\blacktriangle$ stands for a percentage change expressed as a decimal. Equation (14.1) may properly be called the *profit impact formula* or PIF and will be so referred to in this book.

14.1.2 The Contribution After a Percentage Price Change

The above formula may be extended to allow computation of the new total contribution after the incremental price change:

$$K_1 = R_0 \{- \varepsilon_0 (\blacktriangle P)^2 + \qquad\qquad \text{Eq. (14.2)}$$
$$(1 - \varepsilon_0 CM_0) \blacktriangle P + CM_0\}$$

14.1.3 The Optimal Percentage Price Change

From the PIF of Equation (14.1), it can readily be shown that the optimal percentage price change to achieve maximum contribution and profit can be found using this expression:

$$\blacktriangle P^* = \frac{1 - \varepsilon_0 CM_0}{2 \varepsilon_0} \qquad \text{Eq (14.3)}$$

Thus, the optimal incremental price change for profit maximization is a function of both the price elasticity of demand and the unit contribution margin prior to the price change.

14.1.4 The Optimal Condition

Conditions are optimal when no price change is required to achieve maximum contribution and profit. If one sets Eq. (14.3) equal to zero ($\blacktriangle P^* = 0$), this occurs when the P.E.D. equals the reciprocal of the unit contribution margin:

$$\varepsilon^* = \frac{1}{CM_0} \qquad \text{Eq. (14.4)}$$

The quantity ε^* is the optimal P.E.D. for profit maximization.[2] This formula is, of course, already familiar as Equation (7.13) of Chapter 7 on Isoprofit Analysis. Table 8-1 of Chapter 8 tells the marketer in which direction prices must be adjusted if this condition is not met. Here we go a significant step further and in Equation (14.3) give her or him a formula by which the exact amount of the necessary incremental price change may be computed.

14.1.5 The Price Range for Positive Contribution Changes

Almost as important as the optimal price for maximum total contribution is knowing the range of prices that will add to total contribution. This information may be obtained by setting the PIF of Equation (14.1) equal to zero to find its roots, i.e., the two points at which the percentage total contribution change $\blacktriangle K$ equals zero. This occurs when:

$$\blacktriangle P = 0; \quad \frac{1- \mathcal{E}_0\ CM_0}{\mathcal{E}_0} \qquad \text{Eq. (14.5)}$$

Comparing the second root of Equation (14.5) with Equation (14.3), it is seen to be twice the optimal percentage price change for contribution maximization. Hence the price range for positive contribution changes extends from $\blacktriangle P = 0$ to $\blacktriangle P = 2 \times \blacktriangle P^*$.

14.1.6 The Optimal Price

The optimal price is the original price P_0 plus the optimal incremental price change as given by Eq. (14.3):

$$P^* = \frac{P_0}{2\ \mathcal{E}_0} \{1 + \mathcal{E}_0\ (2 - CM_0)\} \qquad \text{Eq. (14.6)}$$

14.1.7 The Total Contribution Price Range

Sales revenue can generate total contribution only within a limited price range under the given conditions. This range is:

$$VC_0 < P_1 < \frac{P_0\ (\mathcal{E}_0 + 1)}{\mathcal{E}_0} \qquad \text{Eq.(14.7)}$$

The lower price limit is the unit variable cost VC_0 since no contribution can be generated below this price point. The upper limit is identical to the sales revenue price range of Equation (13.7).

14.1.8 The Optimal Percentage Quantity Change

From the defining relationship between the P.E.D., price, and quantity one obtains from Equation (14.3):

$$\blacktriangle Q^* = \frac{\mathcal{E}_0\, CM_0 - 1}{2} \qquad \text{Eq. (14.8)}$$

14.1.9 The Optimal Quantity

The optimal quantity is the original quantity Q_0 plus the optimal incremental quantity change as given by Eq. (14.8):

$$Q^* = \frac{Q_0}{2}\,(\mathcal{E}_0\, CM_0 + 1) \qquad \text{Eq. (14.9)}$$

14.1.10 The Optimal Total Contribution Change

The change in total contribution as a result of an optimal price change is found by inserting the optimal price change $\blacktriangle P^*$ of Equation (14.3) into Equation (14.1):

$$\blacktriangle K^* = \frac{\mathcal{E}_0}{CM_0}\,(\blacktriangle P^*)^2 \qquad \text{Eq. (14.10)}$$

This formula relates, in compact form, the optimal percentage contribution change, the initial P.E.D., the initial unit contribution margin, and the optimal percentage price change.

14.1.11 The Maximum Total Contribution

The maximum total contribution is the original contribution K_0 plus the optimal contribution change as given by Eq. (14.10):

$$K^* = \frac{R_0}{4\,\mathcal{E}_0}\,(\mathcal{E}_0\, CM_0 + 1)^2 \qquad \text{Eq. (14.11)}$$

14.1.12 The Optimal Unit Contribution Margin

After the optimal price change, the unit contribution margin is given by:

$$CM^* = \frac{P^* - CV_0}{P^*} \qquad \text{Eq. (14.12)}$$

where the optimal price P^* is given by Equation (14.6).

14.1.13 The Optimal Sales Revenue

The marketer will also want to know the sales revenue after an optimal price change for profit maximization. This information may be obtained by inserting the optimal price change $\blacktriangle P^*$ into Equation (13.2) of Chapter 13 (Sales Revenue Maximization):

$$R^* = \frac{R_0}{4\,\mathcal{E}_0}\{1 + \mathcal{E}_0{}^2\, CM_0\,(2 - CM_0) + 2\,\mathcal{E}_0\} \qquad \text{Eq. (14.13)}$$

14.1.14 The Optimal Price Elasticity of Demand

The optimal price and optimal P.E.D. are related by Equation (14.4) for the optimal condition:

$$\mathcal{E}^* = \frac{P^*}{P^* - VC_0} \qquad \text{Eq.(14.14)}$$

Inserting Equation (14.6) into Equation (14.14) results in this expression for the optimal P.E.D. for contribution maximization:

$$\mathcal{E}^* = \frac{P_0 + \mathcal{E}_0\,(P_0 + VC_0)}{P_0 + \mathcal{E}_0\,(P_0 - VC_0)} \qquad \text{Eq. (14.15)}$$

According to this formula, the optimal price elasticity of demand for profit maximization is either 1.0 or larger than 1.0 and can never be less than 1.0 ($\mathcal{E}^* \geq 1.0$). In other words, the optimum price for profit maximization must always lie on the elastic portion of the product's demand curve.

14.1.15 A Comparison of Optimal Prices

In a practical case where the unit variable cost is not zero, the marketer will want to know how far apart the optimal prices for total contribution P* and sales revenue maximization [P] are. If one takes the difference between these optimal prices as given by Equation (14.6) above and Equation (13.6) of Chapter 13 one obtains:

$$\Delta P = P^* - [P]$$

$$\Delta P = \frac{P_0}{2}(1 - CM_0) \qquad\qquad \text{Eq. (14.16)}$$

Clearly, as the percentage unit contribution margin CM_0 increases, the price difference between the two optimal prices gets smaller so that when $CM_0 = 1.0$ (100%) and $VC_0 = 0$, the price difference is zero.

14.2 Application

The above sixteen formulas will now be applied to an illustrative example to show how these may be used to solve a profit maximization problem both mathematically and graphically.

Illustrative Example: Droneco Ltd. (II)

For this demonstration, we return to Droneco which was introduced in Chapter 9 (Market Oriented Pricing) as a manufacturer of small surveillance drones for governmental and private use. One of the company's most popular models is the Firebird-7 which is being successfully used on the West Coast for spotting and monitoring wildfires. Once the drone has spotted such a fire, it hovers over it and sends back photographic images as well as real-time data including the fire's exact position, its intensity, the area covered, its speed and direction, and endangered structures in the fire's path.

The average net price of the Firebird-7 is $12,000 while the unit variable cost is $8,400 giving it a unit contribution margin of $3,600 (30.0%). Monthly sales are 10 vehicles for a sales revenue of $120,000 and total contribution of $36,000. The marketing manager has estimated that a 10% price increase will reduce sales volume by only 15% (P.E.D. of 1.5). Management would like to make an incremental price change for this model to maximize income.

In solving this pricing problem, we shall follow the sequence of formulas given above and then apply the familiar graphical technique using just Equations (13.2) and (14.2) for sales revenue and total contribution, respectively, to plot the two functions.

14.2.1 Formula Solution

The above sixteen formula will be applied in the exact sequence given.

i) Suppose, the Firebird-7 price was increased by 10%, what would be the impact on total contribution. By the PIF of Equation (14.1) one obtains:

$$\blacktriangle K = 1 / 0.30 \{- 1.5 (0.10)^2 + (1 - 1.5 \times 0.30) (0.10)\} = 0.133$$

Thus, a 10% price increase would raise monthly total contribution by 13.3%.

ii) The monthly total contribution after the price change would simply be the contribution prior to the price change plus the added contribution from the price change:

$$K_1 = K_0 (1 + \blacktriangle K) = \$36,000 (1 + 0.1333) = \$40,800$$

The same result is obtained directly from Equation (14.2):

$$K_1 = \$120,000 \{- 1.5 (0.10)^2 + (1 - 1.5 \times 0.30) 0.10 + 0.30\}$$
$$K_1 = \$40,800$$

iii) The optimal percentage price change is found from Equation (14.3):

$$\blacktriangle P^* = (1 - 1.5 \times 0.30) / (2 \times 1.5) = 0.1833$$

The optimal incremental price adjustment for profit maximization is therefore a price increase of 18.3%

iv) By Equation (14.4) the optimal P.E.D. requiring no price change is $\mathcal{E}^* = 1 / CM_0 = 1 / 0.30 = 3.33$. Since the estimated P.E.D. in the present case is $\mathcal{E}_0 = 1.50$ so that $\mathcal{E}_0 < \mathcal{E}^*$, by the pricing rule of thumb given in Table 8-1 of Chapter 8, the price should be raised. This was indeed found to be the case above.

v) From Equation (14.5), the end points for positive contribution changes are:

$$\blacktriangle P = 0 \text{ and } \blacktriangle P = (1 - 1.5 \times 0.30) / 1.5 = 0.367$$

Thus, the price range for positive total contribution changes extends from \$12,000 to \$16,400 (\$12,000 × 1.367).

vi) The optimal price is the original price plus the incremental price increase for profit maximization:

$$P^* = \$12,000 \ (1 + 0.1833) = \$14,200$$

The same result may also be obtained directly from Equation (14.6):

$$P^* = \$12,000 \ \{1 + 1.5 \ (2 - 0.30)\} / (2 \times 1.5) \ = \$14,200$$

vii) The range of prices for which sales revenue generates total contribution is given by Equation (14.7):

$$\$8,400 < P_1 < \ \$12,000 \ (1.5 + 1) / 1.5$$
$$\$8,400 < P_1 < \$20,000$$

viii) The optimal percentage quantity change is obtained from Equation (14.8):

$$\blacktriangle Q^* = (1.5 \times 0.30 - 1) / 2 = -0.275$$

Thus, the 18.3% price increase comes at the expense of a 27.5% drop in sales volume.

ix) The optimal quantity sold is the original quantity plus the incremental quantity change due to the price change:

$$Q^* = 10 \ (1 - 0.275) = 7.25$$

One can obtain the same result by use of Equation (14.9):

$$Q^* = (10 / 2) \ (1.5 \times 0.30 + 1) = \ 7.25$$

x) The optimal total contribution change may be computed from Equation (14.10):

▲K* = 1.5 (0.1833)^2 / 0.30 = 0.168

Thus, the 18.3% price increase results in a 16.8% profit increase.

xi) The maximum total contribution is the original contribution plus the added total contribution from the price increase:

K* = $36,000 (1 + 0.168) = $42,050

Using Equation (14.11) the same result is obtained directly:

K* = $120,000 / 6.0 {(1.5 × 0.30 + 1)^2} = $42,050

xii) Equation (14.12) gives the optimal unit contribution margin:

CM* = ($14,200 − $8,400) / $14,200 = 0.408

Hence, the price increase resulted in a substantial contribution margin increase from 30.0% to 40.8%.

xiii) The optimal sales revenue is by Equation (14.13):

R* = $120,000 / 6.0 {1 + (1.5)^2(0.30) (2 − 0.30) + 3.0} = $103,000

This represents a sales revenue reduction of about 14%.

xiv) The optimal P.E.D. after the optimal price change is found by Equation (14.14):

€* = $14,200 / ($14,200 − $8,400) = 2.45

This result may be verified using Equation (14.15):

€* = {$12,000 + 1.5 ($12,000 + $8,400)} / {$12,000 + 1.5 ($12,000 − $8,400)} = 2.45

This represents a P.E.D. increase of over 63% pushing the new price-volume operating point further into the elastic region.

xv) The price difference between the optimal prices for total contribution maximization P* and sales revenue maximization [P] is given by Equation (14.16):

Δ P = $12,000 (1 − 0.30) / 2 = $4,200

This is as expected because by Equation (13.6) of Chapter 13, the optimal price for sales revenue maximization is:

$$[P] = \$12,000\,(1.5 + 1) / (2 \times 1.5) = \$10,000$$

This is \$4,200 less than the optimal price for total contribution computed in item vi) above.

Figure 14-1
Sales Revenue & Total Contribution for Firebird-7

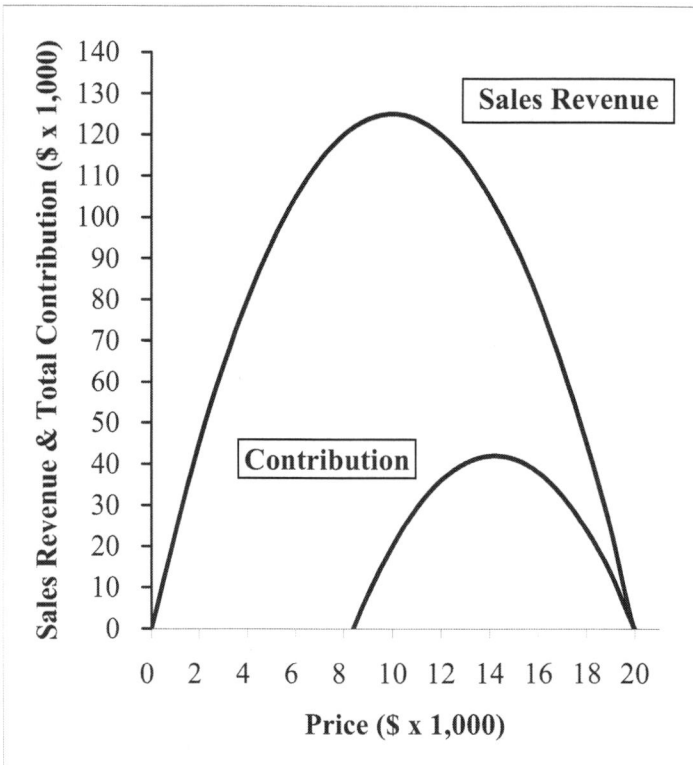

14.2.2 Graphical Solution

To plot the graph for total contribution, we apply Equation (14.2) using the given parameter values:

$$K_1 = \$120,000 \{ - 1.5 \, (\blacktriangle P)^2 + 0.55 \, \blacktriangle P + 0.30 \}$$

The sales revenue curve may be plotted using Equation (13.2) of Chapter 13 and the given parameter values:

$$R_1 = \$120,000 \{ - 1.5 \, (\blacktriangle P)^2 - 0.5 \, \blacktriangle P + 1 \}$$

As was done in the previous chapter, rather than plot sales revenue R_1 and total contribution K_1 as a function of price change $\blacktriangle P$, we plot the two curves using price P_1 in lieu of $\blacktriangle P$ on the horizontal axis. Selecting values of P_1, one can convert to $\blacktriangle P$ by use of the expression $\blacktriangle P = (P_1 - P_0) / P_0$ with $P_0 = \$12,000$.

The two curves are shown in Figure 14-1. Looking at the contribution curve, it may be noted that total contribution for the Firebird-7 reaches a maximum of $42,000 when the price is $14,200. The sales revenue at that point is seen to be about $103,000. Total contribution is positive within the price range of $8,4000 to $20,000 the lower limit being the unit variable cost VC_0 below which no contribution is generated. The optimal price for profit maximization is found exactly at the midpoint of this price range. These results agree with those obtained by formula. The sales curve of Figure 14-1 tells us that sales revenue peaks at a price of $10,000 which represents a 16.7% price reduction. This is, of course, of interest only if sales revenue maximization were management's goal.

14.2.3 Conclusion

Our analysis has shown that the Firebird-7 surveillance drone is under-priced in view of the goal of maximum total contribution and profit. The price requires an upward adjustment of about 18% to $14,200 which will result in a total contribution and profit improvement of about 17% to $42,050. With the adjusted price, the monthly sales volume will decline from 10 to 7 units and the sales revenue from $120,000 to $103,000.

Considering the new and higher Firebird-7 prices the question arises whether the other Droneco models now require repricing in order to keep a logical sequence in price and value as has been proposed. (See the Weber-Fechner Effect discussed in Section 9.2 of Chapter 9). Not necessarily. To the extent that other models are designed for and marketed to product-market segments other than wildfire surveillance, they will face completely different demand curves and price elasticities of demand and should therefore be priced accordingly. Only models serving the same product-market segment need to be priced so as to reflect value differences.

14.3 Reference Tables

The marketer's required computational efforts are significantly reduced by use of reference tables. Before we get to these, inspection of Figure 14-2 is instructive. It is a representation of Equation (14.3) for computing optimal price changes using unit contribution margins of 20%, 50%, and 80%.

Figure 14-2
Optimal Percentage Price Change for Profit

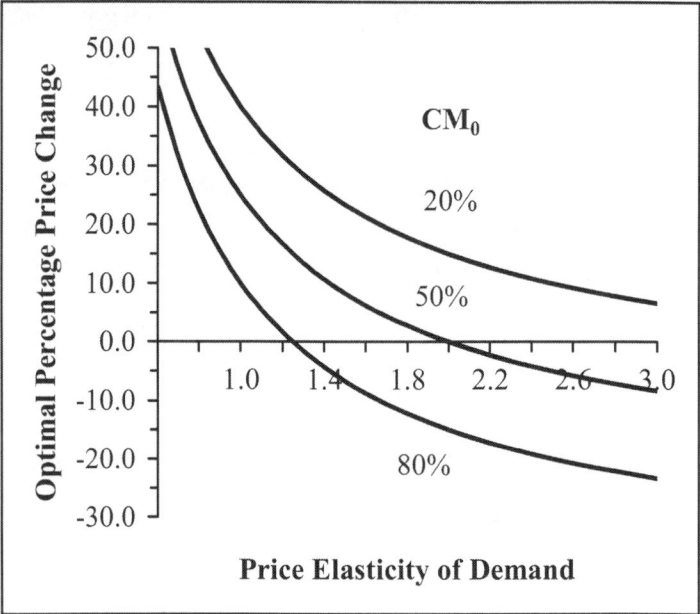

As one might expect, the curves for 80% and 50% cross the horizontal x-axis where the optimal price change is zero. This occurs at price elasticities of demand of 1.3 and 2.0, respectively, which are the optimal P.E.D.s (ε^*) for these two percentage contribution margins. The curve for a 20% contribution margin never crosses the horizontal axis because the optimal P.E.D. for this contribution margin is 5.0 and off the scale.

Of the sixteen formulas presented in Section 14.1 the two most useful ones are Equation (14.3) for the optimal percentage price change $\blacktriangle P^*$ and Equation (14.10) for the maximum percentage contribution change $\blacktriangle K^*$. These two formulas were used to compute the values of Tables 14-1 and 4-2 for the optimal percentage price change and the maximum percentage total contribution change, respectively, for unit contribution margins CM_0 ranging from 5% to 100% and P.E.D.s from 0.5 to 3.0, respectively. In the tables, O.P.C. and M.C.C. stand for *optimal price change* and *maximum contribution change*, respectively. Both are expressed in percent obtained in the usual manner by multiplying the result of the formula computations by 100%.

From these tabulations, the optimum sell price P^* and maximum total contribution K^* and other important parameters are readily obtained. Using Droneco as an example, from Tables 14-1(a) and 14-2(a) we find that for a P.E.D. of 1.50 and a CM_0 of 30.0%, the optimal percentage price change $\blacktriangle P^*$ and optimal percentage contribution change $\blacktriangle K^*$ are 18.3% and 16.8%, respectively. The optimum price and maximum total contribution are therefore:

$$P^* = P_0 (1 + \blacktriangle P^*) = \$12,000 (1 + 0.183) = \$14,196$$
$$K^* = K_0 (1 + \blacktriangle K^*) = \$36,000 (1 + 0.168) = \$42,048$$

14.4 Pricing Guidelines (IV)

The above analyses may be summarized in a number of additional pricing propositions and a second pricing rule.

Pricing Proposition 17

For any product or service there exists one and only one optimal sell price for total contribution and profit maximization and all price points below or above this optimal price will result in less than maximum total contribution and profit for that product or service.

Pricing Proposition 18

The optimal price change for total contribution and profit maximization depends on only two parameters, namely, the product's unit contribution margin and its price elasticity of demand at the price-volume operating point (P_0, Q_0) prior to the price change.

Pricing Proposition 19

The larger the deviation from the optimal price for total contribution and profit maximization, the greater will be the rate of decline in total contribution and profit so that if the sell price is below the optimal level and is further reduced or is above the optimal level and is further increased, the negative effects will be multiplied.

Pricing Proposition 20

Since the optimal price elasticity of demand for total contribution and profit maximization will always be larger than one $(\epsilon^* > 1.0)$, the optimal price must always lie in the elastic range of the demand curve except for the special case where the product's unit variable cost is zero when it lies at unitary elasticity $(\epsilon^* = 1.0)$.

Pricing Proposition 21

With changes in price, sales revenue and total contribution may move in the same or opposite directions (increase or decrease) depending on whether the price moves are toward or away from the optimal prices so that increasing sales revenue will not ensure increasing total contribution and profit but may, in fact, reduce these.

Pricing Proposition 22

Because each product has a unique optimal price for total contribution and profit maximization and it is usually not feasible to determine and implement optimal prices for large numbers of products, most products in multi-product firms will be either underpriced or overpriced.

Price Optimization Rule 2: Contribution and Profit Maximization

Where the pricing objective is to maximize total contribution and profit for a given product or service and its price elasticity of demand ϵ_0 does not equal $1 / CM_0$, an incremental price adjustment in the amount of

$$\blacktriangle P^* = \frac{1 - \epsilon_0 \, CM_0}{2 \, \epsilon_0} \times 100\%$$

is required.

14.5 Multi-Product Price Optimization

In this and the two previous chapters of *Pricing for Profit*, we have been concerned with optimizing the price of just one product or service at a time. What is to be done when companies offer a multitude of products or services as is the norm in most industries? This is the question Baker, Marn, and Zawada of McKinsey & Co. asked themselves.[3] They found that in most companies price changes are cost or margin driven and the resulting price increases are implemented either across-the-board or by product category. As the authors noted, this approach unfortunately misses the "unique 'DNA' of individual products." As an answer, they developed an approach that uses all available information to "develop *multiple indicators* of the *relative risk* of raising prices." Their three-step approach was successfully implemented at an office products distributor with 100,000 individual SKU numbers.

The three steps are:

i) Analytically estimate your price position versus the market: This first step involves checking to see how the item compares with other category items in terms of volume changes (up or down), size of margins, and volume changes after previous price increases. For example, if a pen showed higher volume growth than other pens, this would indicate that it was in a "value-advantaged position" pointing to a price increase. Similarly, if a pen's margin was lower than average, it was underpriced.

ii) Analytically estimate relative price sensitivity: In this step the question to be answered is, "Of all the products, which are the ones that carry the least amount of risk if prices are increased or reduced?" Several indicators are employed to assess customer price sensitivity including the item's order frequency, its absolute price level, and whether the product has a competitive advantage.

iii) Differentially increase or decrease price by SKU based on risk. This step combines the two previous ones and results in a decision matrix in which the horizontal axis represents the current price relative to a market benchmark price (below, within range, high) and the vertical axis a price risk score (low to high). Thus, at the extreme corners of the matrix, for example, where the item's current price was below the benchmark price and the price risk score was low, a large price increase would be called for. If the current price was above the benchmark price and the price risk score was high, the price should be reduced.

This approach is obviously an improvement over price change techniques based on cost changes. A shortcoming is that it does not tell the pricer by how much the item price should be changed to reach an optimal level. However, there is no reason why the optimal pricing technique developed in the present chapter of *Pricing for Profit* could not be incorporated in these authors' method. Specifically, the P.E.D. information developed in their 3-step approach could be used with *Price Optimization Rule 2* (see Section 14.4 above) and the process automated to routinely develop an optimal price for each and every product and SKU number. This would allow the firm to maximize its total contribution dollars and profits across its entire product line.

14.6 Sales Volume Versus Contribution

The business sections of major dailies and other media often report on the quarterly financial results of major companies. Sales revenue and net income changes are obviously of much interest especially to investors in these firms. Sometimes the news is good with hefty increases in both revenue and earnings. Most often it is less favorable with either revenue or income increasing while the other is declining. The question often asked is whether these movements in sales and income can serve as a clue about the firms' price levels and, more specifically, whether this information is sufficient to tell management whether or not its prices need adjustment and, if so, in which direction. The answer is yes but only if one considers the relationship between sales volume (quantity sold) and total contribution or profit. That between sales revenue and earnings is too complex and intractable for a first-order analysis.

Figure 14-3 shows two typical total contribution curves labeled K which are seen to closely resemble the ones shown in Figure 12-2 of Chapter 12 and Figure 14-1 of the present chapter.

Figure 14-3
Total Contribution and Quantity Changes vs. Price

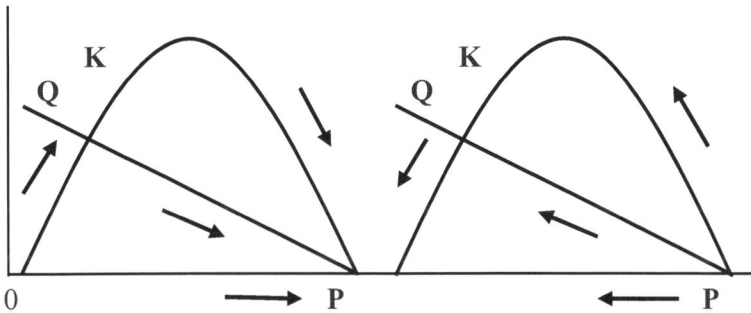

Also shown and labeled Q are the linear price response curves showing the number of units sold at each price level during a given time period. In the left-hand graph, the movement of K is in the clockwise direction, as indicated by the two arrows, and the right-hand graph by movement in the counterclockwise direction also shown by two arrows. One can identity four pricing situations:

i) In the left-hand graph, as contribution K increases toward the maximum value (reached when the price P is at P*), sales volume Q is seen to decrease. By the law of demand, a quantity reduction is accompanied by a price increase. Since the movement to a higher value of K is favorable, the direction of the price change is also favorable, i.e., a further price increase is called for.

ii) In the left-hand graph, after contribution K has peaked and is declining, sales volume Q continues to drop while the price P is increasing. Since the reduction in K is unfavorable, its decline must be reversed by decreasing the price P and increasing quantity Q.

iii) In the right-hand graph, as contribution K is increasing so is sales volume Q. An increasing sales volume means a reduction in price P. Since an increasing K is favorable, the price movement is favorable also and the price should continue to be reduced.

iv) In the right-hand graph, after contribution has peaked, sales volume Q continues to increase while the price drops. Since the reduction in K is unfavorable, the situation must be reversed and the price increased with a consequent reduction in sales volume Q.

This analysis leads to a final pricing proposition and rule of thumb. An example follows to illustrate their use.

Pricing Proposition 23

When over an interval of time, and price being the only variable, total contribution and sales volume for a given product change (increase or decrease) in the same direction, a price reduction leads to higher contribution dollars while if they change in opposite directions, higher contribution dollars are generated with a price increase.

Pricing Rule of Thumb

To increase contribution and profit for a given product, service or line of products or services, lower or raise prices depending on whether sales volumes (quantities sold) and total contributions change in the same or opposite directions—

i) lower prices if the changes are in the same direction, and
ii) raise prices if the changes are in opposite directions.

Illustrative Example: West Valley Auto Sales

West Valley Auto Sales markets the automobiles of one of the top three American makes and has been very profitable over the years. The firm tracks monthly sales by brand name and model type along with the total contribution dollars earned. General manager

Kate Windsor has recently noticed a disturbing trend over the past three months for one of their most popular models. While the number of cars sold has been on the rise each month, the profitability of these sales has been significantly declining. She is at a loss to explain the situation because there have been no formal price changes or special promotions for that brand nor was anything else undertaken that could have caused the trend.

Analyzing the problem, Kate realized that it could have resulted from any number of factors but that the pricing option was most likely the key especially since her sales force has considerable discretion in setting individual prices. The West Valley scenario fits situation iv) described above of increasing quantity sales Q and declining total contribution K, i.e., the optimal price level for contribution maximization has been passed and prices are declining when they should be rising. In line with the pricing rule of thumb given above, Kate has now decided to enlist her salespeople in a concerted effort to halt the suspected price erosion and stabilize prices by issuing new guidelines on available price discretion. In addition, she is considering an upward price adjustment as well after she has completed her price-sensitivity analysis.

14.7 Concluding Comments

Price optimization offers the marketer an alternative to isoprofit analysis (see Chapter 7) for analyzing price changes with the goal of improving contribution and profits. There are differences and similarities between the two techniques and the marketer may come to prefer one over the other or use the two in combination. With isoprofit (also equal-profit, or break-even) analysis, the marketer asks, "Will a price change of x percent be profitable?" With price optimization the question is, "What price must we charge to maximize profit?"

Both techniques depend on knowing two quantities, namely, the unit contribution margin and the price elasticity of demand. In price optimization use of the P.E.D. is explicit because it enters directly into the formulas. In isoprofit analysis the requirement to know the P.E.D. is implicit because the marketer must estimate by what percentage sales volume will change as a result of the contemplated percentage price change. Knowing this ratio is, of course, equivalent to knowing the P.E.D..

Clearly then, having good and valid estimates of these two quantities, namely, the P.E.D. and the unit contribution margin is crucially important in evaluating price change options for any product or service and by any method the marketer may choose. It will be incumbent on the marketer's cost accounting department to arrive at accurate values for the average unit variable cost VC_0, the average net sell price P_0, and the average unit contribution margin CM_0 for the particular product or service. The marketer, on the other hand, must become very knowledgeable about the price sensitivity of his or products and services, i.e., how incremental price changes will affect the quantities sold so as to be able to develop accurate estimates for the P.E.D. (ε_0).

Notes

1. Robert Dolan and Hermann Simon, *Power Pricing*, 28.

2. It is easy to demonstrate that the optimal condition for profit maximization as given by Equation (14.4) is the equivalent of the formula

$$MR = P - \frac{P}{\epsilon}$$

found in many economic texts. See, for example, J. P. Gould and C. E. Ferguson, *Microeconomic Theory*, 112, and Ross Eckert and Richard Leftwich, *The Price System and Resource Allocation*, 356. Since economic theory holds that at the optimal price for profit maximization, marginal revenue equals marginal cost (MR = MC) and since marginal cost can be approximated by the unit variable cost (MC = VC), replacing MR with VC in the above equation and transposing terms one obtains:

$$\epsilon = \frac{P}{P - VC} = \frac{1}{CM\,(\%)} \quad QED$$

3. Walter Baker, Michael Martin, and Craig Zawada, *The Price Advantage*, 207-212.

Table 14-1(a)
Optimal Percentage Price Changes for Total Contribution (Profit) Maximization

CM₀ (%)	Price Elasticity of Demand (€₀)												
	0.5	0.6	0.7	0.8	0.9	1.0	1.1	1.2	1.3	1.4	1.5	1.6	1.7
5	97.5	80.8	68.9	60.0	53.1	47.5	43.0	39.2	36.0	33.2	30.8	28.8	26.9
10	95.0	78.3	66.4	57.5	50.6	45.0	40.5	36.7	33.5	30.7	28.3	26.3	24.4
15	92.5	75.8	63.9	55.0	48.1	42.5	38.0	34.2	31.0	28.2	25.8	23.8	21.9
20	90.0	73.3	61.4	52.5	45.6	40.0	35.5	31.7	28.5	25.7	23.3	21.3	19.4
25	87.5	70.8	58.9	50.0	43.1	37.5	33.0	29.2	26.0	23.2	20.8	18.8	16.9
30	85.0	68.3	56.4	47.5	40.6	35.0	30.5	26.7	23.5	20.7	18.3	16.3	14.4
35	82.5	65.8	53.9	45.0	38.1	32.5	28.0	24.2	21.0	18.2	15.8	13.8	11.9
40	80.0	63.3	51.4	42.5	35.6	30.0	25.5	21.7	18.5	15.7	13.3	11.3	9.4
45	77.5	60.8	48.9	40.0	33.1	27.5	23.0	19.2	16.0	13.2	10.8	8.8	6.9
50	75.0	58.3	46.4	37.5	30.6	25.0	20.5	16.7	13.5	10.7	8.3	6.3	4.4
55	72.5	55.8	43.9	35.0	28.1	22.5	18.0	14.2	11.0	8.2	5.8	3.8	1.9
60	70.0	53.3	41.4	32.5	25.6	20.0	15.5	11.7	8.5	5.7	3.3	0.0	(0.6)
65	67.5	50.8	38.9	30.0	23.1	17.5	13.0	9.2	6.0	3.2	0.8	(1.3)	(3.1)
70	65.0	48.3	36.4	27.5	20.6	15.0	10.5	6.7	3.5	0.7	(1.7)	(3.8)	(5.6)
75	62.5	45.8	33.9	25.0	18.1	12.5	8.0	4.2	1.0	(1.8)	(4.2)	(6.3)	(8.1)
80	60.0	43.3	31.4	22.5	15.6	10.0	5.5	1.7	(1.5)	(4.3)	(6.7)	(8.8)	(10.6)
85	57.5	40.8	28.9	20.0	13.1	7.5	3.0	(0.8)	(4.0)	(6.8)	(9.2)	(11.3)	(13.1)
90	55.0	38.3	26.4	17.5	10.6	5.0	0.5	(3.3)	(6.5)	(9.3)	(11.7)	(13.8)	(15.6)
95	52.5	35.8	23.9	15.0	8.1	2.5	(2.0)	(5.8)	(9.0)	(11.8)	(14.2)	(16.3)	(18.1)
100	50.0	33.3	21.4	12.5	5.6	0.0	(4.6)	(8.3)	(11.5)	(14.3)	(16.7)	(18.8)	(20.6)

Table 14-1(b)
Optimal Percentage Price Changes for Total Contribution (Profit) Maximization

CM_0 (%)	Price Elasticity of Demand ($€_0$)												
	1.8	1.9	2.0	2.1	2.2	2.3	2.4	2.5	2.6	2.7	2.8	2.9	3.0
5	25.3	23.8	22.5	21.3	20.2	19.2	18.3	17.5	16.7	16.0	15.4	14.7	14.2
10	22.8	21.3	20.0	18.8	17.7	16.7	15.8	15.0	14.2	13.5	12.9	12.2	11.7
15	20.3	18.8	17.5	16.3	15.2	14.2	13.3	12.5	11.7	11.0	10.4	9.7	9.2
20	17.8	16.3	15.0	13.8	12.7	11.7	10.8	10.0	9.2	8.5	7.9	7.2	6.7
25	15.3	13.8	12.5	11.3	10.2	9.2	8.3	7.5	6.7	6.0	5.4	4.7	4.2
30	12.8	11.3	10.0	8.8	7.7	6.7	5.8	5.0	4.2	3.5	2.9	2.2	1.7
35	10.3	8.8	7.5	6.3	5.2	4.2	3.3	2.5	1.7	1.0	0.4	(0.3)	(0.8)
40	7.8	6.3	5.0	3.8	2.7	1.7	0.8	0.0	(0.8)	(1.5)	(2.1)	(2.8)	(3.3)
45	5.3	3.8	2.5	1.3	0.2	(0.8)	(1.7)	(2.5)	(3.3)	(4.0)	(4.6)	(5.3)	(5.8)
50	2.8	1.3	0.0	(1.2)	(2.3)	(3.3)	(4.2)	(5.0)	(5.8)	(6.5)	(7.1)	(7.8)	(8.3)
55	0.3	(1.2)	(2.5)	(3.7)	(4.8)	(5.8)	(6.7)	(7.5)	(8.3)	(9.0)	(9.6)	(10.3)	(10.8)
60	(2.2)	(3.7)	(5.0)	(6.2)	(7.3)	(8.3)	(9.2)	(10.0)	(10.8)	(11.5)	(12.1)	(12.8)	(13.3)
65	(4.7)	(6.2)	(7.5)	(8.7)	(9.8)	(10.8)	(11.7)	(12.5)	(13.3)	(14.0)	(14.6)	(15.3)	(15.8)
70	(7.2)	(8.7)	(10.0)	(11.2)	(12.3)	(13.3)	(14.2)	(15.0)	(15.8)	(16.5)	(17.1)	(17.8)	(18.3)
75	(9.7)	(11.2)	(12.5)	(13.7)	(14.8)	(15.8)	(16.7)	(17.5)	(18.3)	(19.0)	(19.6)	(20.3)	(20.8)
80	(12.2)	(13.7)	(15.0)	(16.2)	(17.3)	(18.3)	(19.2)	(20.0)	(20.8)	(21.5)	(22.1)	(22.8)	(23.3)
85	(14.7)	(16.2)	(17.5)	(18.7)	(19.8)	(20.8)	(21.7)	(22.5)	(23.3)	(24.0)	(24.6)	(25.3)	(25.8)
90	(17.2)	(18.7)	(20.0)	(21.2)	(22.3)	(23.3)	(24.2)	(25.0)	(25.8)	(26.5)	(27.1)	(27.8)	(28.3)
95	(19.7)	(21.2)	(22.5)	(23.7)	(24.8)	(25.8)	(26.7)	(27.5)	(28.3)	(29.0)	(29.6)	(30.3)	(30.8)
100	(22.2)	(23.7)	(25.0)	(26.2)	(27.3)	(28.3)	(29.2)	(30.0)	(30.8)	(31.5)	(32.1)	(32.8)	(33.3)

Table 14-2(a)
Optimal Percentage Contribution Changes for Total Contribution (Profit) Maximization

CM$_0$ (%)	Price Elasticity of Demand (e_0)												
	0.5	0.6	0.7	0.8	0.9	1.0	1.1	1.2	1.3	1.4	1.5	1.6	1.7
5	951	784	665	576	507	451	406	368	336	309	285	265	246
10	451	368	309	265	230	203	180	161	146	132	120	110	101
15	285	230	191	161	139	120	106	93.4	83.1	74.3	66.7	60.2	54.4
20	203	161	132	110	93.4	80.0	69.1	60.2	52.6	46.3	40.8	36.1	32.0
25	153	120	97.2	80.0	66.7	56.3	47.8	40.8	35.0	30.2	26.0	22.5	18.3
30	120	93	74.3	60.2	49.4	40.8	34.0	28.5	23.8	20.0	16.8	14.1	11.8
35	97.2	74.3	58.2	46.3	37.2	30.2	24.6	20.0	16.3	13.3	10.7	8.6	6.9
40	80.0	60.2	46.3	36.1	28.5	22.5	17.8	14.1	11.1	8.6	6.7	5.1	3.8
45	66.7	49.3	37.2	28.4	21.9	16.8	12.9	9.8	7.4	5.4	3.9	2.7	1.8
50	56.3	40.8	30.2	22.5	16.8	12.5	9.2	6.7	4.7	3.2	2.1	1.3	0.7
55	47.8	34.0	24.6	17.8	12.9	9.2	6.4	4.4	2.8	1.7	0.9	0.4	0.1
60	40.8	28.4	20.0	14.1	9.8	6.7	4.4	2.7	1.6	0.8	0.3	0.0	0.0
65	35.0	23.8	16.3	11.1	7.4	4.7	2.8	1.6	0.7	0.2	0.0	0.0	0.2
70	30.2	20.0	13.3	8.7	5.4	3.2	1.7	0.8	0.2	0.0	0.1	0.3	0.8
75	26.0	16.8	10.7	6.7	3.9	2.1	0.9	0.3	0.0	0.1	0.3	0.8	1.5
80	22.5	14.1	8.6	5.1	2.7	1.3	0.4	0.0	0.0	0.3	0.8	1.5	2.4
85	19.4	11.8	6.9	3.8	1.8	0.7	0.1	0.0	0.2	0.8	1.5	2.4	3.4
90	15.1	9.8	5.4	2.7	1.1	0.3	0.0	0.1	0.6	1.3	2.3	3.4	4.6
95	14.5	8.1	4.2	1.9	0.6	0.1	0.0	0.4	1.1	2.0	3.2	4.4	5.9
100	12.5	6.7	3.2	1.3	0.3	0.0	0.2	0.8	1.7	2.9	4.2	5.6	7.2

Table 14-2(b)
Optimal Percentage Contribution Changes for Total Contribution (Profit) Maximization

CM₀ (%)	Price Elasticity of Demand (ϵ_0)												
	1.8	1.9	2.0	2.1	2.2	2.3	2.4	2.5	2.6	2.7	2.8	2.9	3.0
5	230	216	203	191	180	170	161	153	146	139	132	126	120
10	93.4	86.4	80.0	74.3	69.2	64.5	60.1	56.3	52.6	49.4	46.3	43.4	40.9
15	49.4	44.9	40.8	37.2	34.0	31.1	28.4	26.0	23.8	21.9	20.0	18.3	16.8
20	28.5	25.3	22.5	20.0	17.8	15.9	14.1	12.5	11.1	9.8	8.6	7.6	6.7
25	16.8	14.5	12.5	10.7	9.2	7.9	6.7	5.6	4.7	3.9	3.2	2.5	2.1
30	9.8	8.1	6.7	5.4	4.4	3.5	2.7	2.1	1.6	1.1	0.8	0.5	0.3
35	5.4	4.2	3.2	2.4	1.7	1.2	0.8	0.4	0.2	0.1	0.0	0.0	0.1
40	2.7	1.9	1.3	0.8	0.4	0.2	0.0	0.0	0.0	0.1	0.3	0.6	0.8
45	1.1	0.6	0.3	0.2	0.0	0.0	0.1	0.3	0.6	1.0	1.3	1.8	2.3
50	0.3	0.1	0.0	0.1	0.2	0.5	0.8	1.3	1.7	2.3	2.9	3.5	4.2
55	0.0	0.0	0.2	0.5	0.9	1.4	1.9	2.6	3.2	4.0	4.7	5.6	6.4
60	0.1	0.4	0.8	1.3	1.9	2.6	3.4	4.2	5.0	5.9	6.9	7.9	8.9
65	0.6	1.1	1.7	2.4	3.2	4.1	5.0	6.0	7.0	8.1	9.2	10.4	11.6
70	1.3	2.0	2.9	3.8	4.7	5.8	6.9	8.0	9.2	10.5	11.8	13.1	14.4
75	2.3	3.2	4.2	5.2	6.4	7.6	8.9	10.2	11.6	13.0	14.4	15.9	17.4
80	3.4	4.4	5.6	6.9	8.2	9.6	11.0	12.5	14.0	15.6	17.2	18.8	20.4
85	4.6	5.9	7.2	8.6	10.1	11.7	13.3	14.9	16.6	18.3	20.0	21.8	23.5
90	5.9	7.4	8.9	10.5	12.1	13.8	15.6	17.4	19.2	21.0	22.9	24.8	26.8
95	7.4	9.0	10.7	12.4	14.2	16.1	18.0	19.9	21.9	23.9	25.9	28.0	30.0
100	8.9	10.7	12.5	14.4	16.4	18.4	20.4	22.5	24.6	26.8	28.9	31.1	33.3

CHAPTER
15

Pricing and the Law

Antitrust laws in general, and the Sherman Act in particular, are the Magna Carta of free enterprise. They are as important to the preservation of economic freedom and our free enterprise system as the Bill of Rights is to the protection of our fundamental personal freedoms.[1]

Laws and regulations, both federal and state, have a major impact on business conduct especially in the domain of pricing. The reason is obvious. Anticompetitive pricing practices can do substantial harm to a free enterprise system which presupposes prices set by market forces and not by monopolies and cartels or agreements among rival firms to reduce or eliminate competition.

It is important for the marketer to know what the boundaries of legal conduct are since ignorance of the law can lead to losses on two fronts. On one hand, managers may become too conservative and risk-averse in their pricing practices and find in cost-plus or a similar pricing scheme a safe heaven. They thereby forego the significant sales and profit opportunities that can result from market oriented pricing. On the other hand, as a result of not knowing the law a firm and its managers may engage in conduct which is proscribed and suffer the often costly consequences. Some of these are chronicled in Section 15.1 below.

The law is complex and ever changing in response to new legislation and especially court decisions as judges continue to apply existing law to new cases and sometimes reinterpret the law resulting in legal precedents. Legal advise is beyond the scope of *Pricing for Profit* and this chapter can therefore not serve as a substitute for sound, up-to-date legal counsel from attorneys knowledgeable in business and especially antitrust law. Rather, this brief presentation is meant merely to set forth and discuss the major legal issues. It is to alert the marketer to areas of conduct that may be unlawful so that in cases of uncertainty legal counsel may be sought in a timely manner.

This chapter begins with some prominent cases reported in the media on past cases and ongoing litigation related to price and pricing. Various business practices, both lawful and unlawful, and how they are impacted by the law are covered next. This includes price fixing, predatory pricing, resale price maintenance, price discrimination, conscious parallelism, and price signaling. To afford the reader a better understanding of the rules of law and the underlying issues, the actual court cases out of which these arose are discussed. Since antitrust laws are not unique to the United States, the chapter also includes an overview of applicable European laws. It concludes with some ethical issues relating to pricing that should be of concern to both managers and the general public.

15.1 A Sampling of Antitrust Cases in the Media

When firms and their managements run afoul of the law the penalties incurred can be severe including large fines and even imprisonment for guilty executives and managers. Many cases are settled without a formal trial as a result of plea bargaining while still others are dropped for lack of sufficient evidence. A small sampling of antitrust cases reported in the print media in recent years follows.

* Vitamin price fixing draws record $755 million in fines
Chicago Tribune, May 21, 1999, 3.
Synopsis: Two companies, Hoffman-LaRoche of Switzerland and BASF of Germany entered a plea deal with the Justice department

agreeing to pay $750 million in fines. The firms were accused of price-fixing and bid-rigging in the vitamin industry which caused American consumers to pay inflated prices.

* Prison for ADM execs
Chicago Tribune, July 10, 1999, 1.
Synopsis: Two senior executives from Archer Daniels Midland Co. were convicted on charges of conspiring with Japanese and Korean firms to fix the world-wide price of the livestock feed additive lysine. Each received a two year prison sentence and was fined $350,000.

* U.S. Will Not Pursue Price-Fixing Case Against Mercedes-Benz Dealers
The New York Times, December 25, 2003, C1.
Synopsis: The Department of Justice had charged Mercedes-Benz dealers from New York, New Jersey, and Connecticut of having fixed prices at secret dealer meetings. The case was initiated by a disgruntled Mercedes dealer who was dropped after unauthorized discounting. The Justice Department decided not to prosecute.

* 4 Agree to Jail Sentences in Chip Price-Fixing Case
The New York Times, December 3, 2004, C3.
Synopsis: Four marketing and sales executives from Infineon Technologies (three German and one American) entered a plea deal with the Justice Department. They had been accused of conspiring with competitors to fix prices in computer memories.

* Visa and MasterCard Settle Lawsuit but Merchants Aren't Celebrating
The New York Times, August 9, 2012, B6.
Synopsis: In a civil suit brought by 7 million retail merchants Visa and MasterCard agreed to a $7.3 billion settlement. The two credit card companies were accused of colluding, separately, with banks to eliminate competition and increase their transactions fees.

* U.S. Now Paints Apple as 'Ringmaster' in Its Lawsuit on E-Book Price-Fixing
The New York Times, May 15, 2013, B1.

Synopsis: The Justice Department charged Apple and five publishers (Hachette, HarperCollins, Macmillan, Penguin, and Simon & Schuster) with conspiring to fix e-book prices at a level above the standard $9.99 charged by Amazon. The publishers agreed to settle the charges leaving Apple the only defendant.

* Companies Admit They Fixed Prices of Car Parts
The New York Times, September 27, 2013, B1.
Synopsis: Nine Japanese automotive suppliers including Hitachi Automotive and Mitsubishi Electric agreed to plead guilty to criminal conspiracy charges and pay more than $740 million in fines. Over 25 million cars sold in the U.S. were affected by the illegal conduct.

As may be noted, all the above news items involved price-fixing charges but not all antitrust cases are, of course, of that nature. Price fixing typically results in the biggest penalties and such cases are therefore the most newsworthy.

15.2 Antitrust Enforcement

The antitrust laws of the United States are enforced by the Antitrust Division of the Department of Justice (DOJ) and the Federal Trade Commission (FTC). The Justice Department has authority over the Sherman Act, the primary federal law to combat antitrust violations, and is empowered to bring both civil and criminal actions while the FTC is confined to civil actions only. Both the DOJ and the FTC have jurisdiction over the Robinson-Patman Act which deals with price discrimination. The antitrust laws also allow private civil actions by any person who is injured in his business or property. Relief can take the form of an injunction forbidding the unlawful conduct or damages equal to three times the economic damage actually incurred known as "treble damages." In addition, each state has its own antitrust laws which generally follow federal law.

15.3 Monopolies and Monopolizing

The Sherman Act dates to 1890 and was the country's first antitrust statute. It was enacted to ensure competition in the marketplace and to prevent the establishment of monopolies and cartels with power to restrict output, increase prices, and earn monopoly profits at the expense of consumers. The statute was meant to codify English and American common law precedents in the area of restraints of trade. The authors of the statute realized that its the open-ended provisions could not stand on their own and encouraged the courts to examine the question of illegal versus legal conduct on a case-by-case basis. Indeed, the case literature of Supreme Court and Court of Appeals decisions is quite voluminous.

15.3.1 The Sherman Act

The first two section of the Sherman Act are reproduced following the *Notes* at the end of this chapter. A brief summary in non-legal language follows.

i) According to Section 1, any agreement or conspiracy made in restraint of trade or commerce among the States or with foreign nations is declared a felony and anyone guilty of making such an agreement or entering into a conspiracy is subject to punishment by a fine in the case of a corporation and a fine and/or imprisonment in the case of an individual at the discretion of the court.

ii) According to Section 2, any person who monopolizes or attempts to monopolize or conspires with another person to restrain any part of the trade or commerce among the States or with foreign countries is deemed guilty of a felony punishable by a fine and/or imprisonment at the discretion of the court.

It is important to note that there must be a contract or agreement between two or more parties for the conduct to be illegal. This means that for a guilty verdict the fact finder must determine that such an agreement did in fact exist. Specifically, unilateral action by a seller is not unlawful according to the statute.

15.3.2 The Stare Decisis Doctrine

Stare decisis is an important component of English and American common law. It means "to stand on decided cases" and requires judges to follow precedent. Cases decided by the Supreme Court become the law of the land and all lower courts are bound by its rulings. Most cases do not reach the Supreme Court. Some cases tried in a federal district court are appealed to the Court of Appeals for the circuit with jurisdiction in that area of the country. The decision of the Circuit Court then becomes part of the case law for that jurisdiction. Even the Supreme Court decides cases on the basis of stare decisis but has the option of overturning a previous ruling. When the Court overturned its prior decision in *Dr. Miles* (see Section 15.6 below) it stated: *We have overruled our precedents when subsequent cases have undermined their doctrinal underpinnings.* Clearly, the law is continuously evolving which makes it important to keep up-to-date.

15.3.3 Standing and Antitrust Injury

Not explicitly in the statute and judicially created is the requirement of *antitrust injury* which means that the plaintiff must plead and proof to have suffered injury as a direct result of the unlawful conduct of the defendant. According to the *Brunswick Doctrine* in a private damage action for treble damages: *Plaintiffs must prove antitrust injury, which is to say injury of the type the antitrust laws were intended to prevent and that flow from that which makes defendants' acts unlawful. The injury should reflect the anticompetitive effect either of the violation or of the anticompetitive acts made possible by the violation.*[2] Antitrust injury is also closely related to the judicial concept of *standing*, i.e., whether a plaintiff can bring a case claiming antitrust violation in a federal court. Generally, without antitrust injury a plaintiff will have no standing to sue.

15.3.4 Judicial Antitrust Standards

The courts have set two standards in evaluating anticompetitive conduct. Some conduct is *per se* (in itself) illegal while other conduct falls under the *rule of reason*. Where an activity is blatantly anticompetitive it is considered per se illegal and courts are not required to make further inquiries whether the activity is reasonable or not. Under the rule of reason standard the trial court makes more factual inquiries to determine whether the challenged conduct is unreasonably anticompetitive and thereby illegal. As stated in one court opinion: *As its name suggests, the rule of reason requires the factfinder to decide whether under all the circumstances of the case the restrictive practice imposes an unreasonable restraint on competition.*[3] Regarding the usage trend of the two standards, antitrust authors Sullivan and Harrison have observed that "the per se rule of illegality is applied less and less frequently."[4]

15.3.5 Monopoly and Market Power

Section 2 of the Sherman Act makes monopolizing or attempting to monopolize any portion of the trade among the States a felony. This has led courts to look into the concept of market power. What is market power? In the *DuPont de Nemours* case the Supreme Court has defined monopoly power thus: *A party has monopoly power if it has, over 'any part of the trade or commerce among the several States,' a power of controlling prices or unreasonably restricting competition....Monopoly power is the power to control prices or exclude competition.*"[5] Courts have used a quantitative measure known as the *Lerner Index* (named for economist Abba Lerner) to assess market power:

$$L = (P - C) / P \qquad \text{Eq. (15.1)}$$

where L is the Lerner Index, P is the firm's profit maximizing price and C ist the marginal cost at the profit maximizing output."[6] The larger the Lerner Index, the greater is the firm's market power.

The reader will recall from Equation (14.14) of Chapter 14 that a product's optimal price P*, optimal price elasticity of demand ε* at that price, and unit variable cost VC_0 are related by:

$$\varepsilon^* = P^* / (P^* - VC_0) \qquad \text{Eq. (15.2)}$$

If in Equation (15.1), we let P = P*, and C = VC_0, and invert both sides of Equation (15.2), one obtains:

$$L = 1 / \varepsilon^* = (P^* - VC_0) / P^* = CM^* \qquad \text{Eq. (15.3)}$$

In words, the Lerner Index is directly proportional to the optimal contribution margin CM* and inversely proportional to the optimal price elasticity of demand. Thus, the higher the CM* and the smaller the optimal P.E.D., the greater will be the market power for that product. Products with inelastic demand ($\varepsilon < 1.0$) and high unit profit margins are, of course, characteristic of a monopoly.

15.4 Horizontal Price Fixing

The courts distinguish between *horizontal* and *vertical* restraints of trade. Horizontal restraints generally involves collusion among entities at the same organizational level such as between competing companies. Vertical restraints exist if the illegal agreement is among entities at different organizational levels such as between a manufacturer and a retailer. Agreement among competitors to fix prices, divide territories and markets, or restrict output are examples of horizontal restraints.

15.4.1 Per Se Rule Application

As previously noted, horizontal price fixing is the most egregious of antitrust offenses and the most severely punished. It is a *per se* offense meaning that the only question facing the trial court is whether there is sufficient evidence of an agreement. This principle was established in the *Trenton Potteries* case in which twenty-three companies and twenty individuals were convicted of fixing prices in vitreous pottery.[7] Incidentally, *joint ventures* among competitors are exempt from the per se rule and are scrutinized under the rule of reason since these can both restrain and benefit competition. It should come as no surprise that express, signed agreements between competitors are rarely found but that is not much of a shield. An early Supreme Court ruling held that an express agreement was not necessary to establish a Section 1 violation but that an agreement could be inferred from circumstantial evidence.[8]

15.4.2 The Temptation to Fix Prices

Two individuals associated with the Harvard Business School have identified several industry and company characteristics that are conducive to price-fixing schemes. For the industry, these include i) overcapacity, ii) undifferentiated products, iii) contact with competitors, and iv) large, price-sensitive customers. Company characteristics include i) a collusion culture, ii) high rewards for profits, iii) decentralized pricing decisions, iv) widespread trade association participation, v) reactive rather than proactive legal staff, and vi) loose ethics rules. It goes without saying that where these conditions exist special company efforts are required to move from the "danger zone" to the "safety zone."[9]

For their findings, the authors studied the folding-carton industry that was rocked by a price-fixing scandal in the mid-1970s. This industry was the very antithesis of the collusion prone oligopoly since it consisted of 450 box-making companies the largest of which had a market share of less than ten percent. Subsequently, several firms entered into a price-fixing conspiracy enabling them to control seventy percent of annual industry sales of $1.5 billion. Some twenty-two companies and forty-eight executives were prosecuted and convicted of antitrust violations with fifteen sent to prison and fined while the others were put on probation and fined. After the criminal convictions, there followed forty-five civil suits for money damages filed by customers who were overcharged.

15.4.3 Common Sense Advise (1)

While most executives and managers would never contemplate entering a price-fixing conspiracy with competitors, they may still be in danger of inadvertently being drawn into one. The first rule is therefore never to discuss pricing or prices with a competitor or exchange price information with one or more competitors! Needless to say, ample opportunities exist for personal contacts with competitors at stateside and overseas trade shows and fairs, trade organization meetings, and conferences. During lunches, dinners, parties, and other get-togethers pricing and prices are likely to come up. At that point any prudent manager should ask to be excused and leave. It is the safest way to remain free of even a suggestion of impropriety.

15.5 Market and Customer Allocation

Rather than fixing prices for products and services, firms have at times engaged in *market allocation* schemes whereby each competitor is granted a given percentage of the total market, or each is given a certain territory in which the others will not compete, or else customers are divided up among the competitors. These are horizontal restraints of trade and, not surprisingly, the courts have made these *per se* illegal. In the *Topco* case, the Supreme Court reversed the trial court and, quoting from a previous case, stated: *The Court has reiterated time and time again that 'horizontal territorial limitations...are naked restraints of trade with no purpose except stifling of competition.'*[10] Topco was a grocery chain whose independent member firms agreed to sell Topco product only within their assigned territories. On remand, the trial court permitted Topco to designate areas of "primary responsibility" for each member and for reasonable compensation where one member sold in another's primary area.

15.6 Resale Price Maintenance (RPM)

Companies are much interested in the prices their products are sold for at the retail level. For image reasons, luxury goods manufacturers may wish to establish minimum prices at which their products may be purchased or they may want to do business with certain select retailers only. Other firms may want to set maximum resale prices. These are vertical restraints of trade, i.e., they involve *vertical price-fixing*, and are referred to as resale price maintenance (RPM). The question is, In light of the antitrust laws, is RPM legal?

15.6.1 The Colgate Doctrine

According to the *Colgate Doctrine*, resale price maintenance is legal as long as there is no agreement between the manufacturer and the distributor, retailer or any other distribution channel member.[11] The Sherman Act encompasses only contracts and agreements. As the Court in *Colgate* eloquently stated: *In the absence of any purpose to create or maintain a monopoly, the Act does not restrict the long recognized right of trader or manufacturer engaged in an entirely private business, feely to exercise his own independent discretion as to parties with whom he will deal; and, of course, he may announce in advance the circumstances under which he will refuse to sell....* In other words, the seller may unilaterally declare the price his product is to be sold for and the terms of sale and refuse to make further sales to a dealer who does not adhere to the manufacturer's pricing policy and other terms.

15.6.2 The Case Law

The next question is whether an *agreement* between a supplier and his distribution channel members can be legal. The answer was given in a 1911 Supreme Court decision in *Dr. Miles* in which the defendant wanted to set *minimum* retail prices for its products.[12] The Court held that such practices violate the Sherman Act and are *per se* illegal. In *Albrecht*, the Court reaffirmed an earlier decision concerning the legality of *maximum* retail prices.[13] The Court held that agreements to fix maximum prices *no less than those to fix minimum prices, cripple the freedom of traders and thereby restrain their ability to sell in accordance with their own judgment.* In 1997, the Court overturned *Albrecht* and in *Khan* held that *maximum* price-fixing schemes should be analyzed by the rule of reason rather than per se because they are often procompetitive.[14]

Finally, in 2007 the Supreme Court overturned *Dr. Miles* in *Leegin* holding: *For these reasons the Court's decision in Dr. Miles...is now overruled. Vertical price restraints are to be judged according to the rule of reason.*[15] In *Leegin*, a disgruntled shoe retailer brought suit against a manufacturer claiming violation of the antitrust laws by entering into vertical agreements with its retailers and setting *minimum* resale prices. When the store sold below the minimum suggested retail prices, Leegin discontinued selling to it. The trial court had ruled for the plaintiff and the Appellate Court, relying on *stare decisis*, applied the per se rule and affirmed.

It is important to note that *Leegin* leaves the ruling in *Colgate* undisturbed since that case did not involve an agreement but unilateral action by the seller which is legal. In summary, setting minimum, exact, or maximum resale prices is subject to the rule of reason standard. Some lawmakers, State and federal, are reportedly strongly opposed to the *Leegin* opinion and it may not be the last word on the subject of minimum resale price maintenance but for now it is the law.

15.6.3 Common Sense Advise (2)

Leegin notwithstanding, the safest course of action with the smallest risk of potential lawsuits under the rule of reason standard is to continue to be guided by the Colgate Doctrine. This means that a supplier should not discuss prices or pricing nor make agreements, verbal or written, with members of its distribution channel but instead to unilaterally announce prices along with maximum allowable discounts and such other terms of sale as seem appropriate. Prices and instructions can always be updated as market conditions change along with the option of dropping any channel member who does not comply with the seller's pricing policy. Knowing that noncompliance can result in not getting further shipments of the supplier's goods is normally sufficient to ensure compliance especially in the case of branded goods that are much in demand.

15.7 Predatory Pricing

A firm is said to engage in *predatory pricing* if it prices a product or products below cost to drive competitors from the market so that it may afterwards charge higher prices and recoup its losses while earning monopoly profits. Such conduct would seem to be anticompetitive and courts have, although reluctantly, agreed to hear complaints based on predatory pricing theories. The courts are necessarily conflicted because the antitrust laws are meant to guard the public from inflated prices due to collusion among competitors while predatory prices are the result of competitor rivalries that bring down prices which is in line with the intent of the antitrust laws.

15.7.1 Subsidizing Theory

One early legal theory advanced by plaintiffs was that their competitor was subsidizing below-cost prices in their market with profits from higher prices charged in another. That was the major argument made by *Zenith Radio* when it accused Japanese television manufacturer Matsushita Electric of conspiring with others to under-price their television sets in the U.S. while charging higher prices in Japan.[16] The Supreme Court affirmed a summary judgment against the plaintiff because its conspiracy theory did not seem plausible. As

Sullivan and Harrison noted: "Today, the notion that a predator uses one market to subsidize another has been abandoned."[17]

15.7.2 The Areeda-Turner Test

To assist the courts in assessing whether a price is to be considered predatory or not, Professors P. Areeda and D. Turner proposed a test which has since come to be known by their names. According to the *Areeda-Turner Test* prices below reasonable anticipated short-run marginal costs should be considered predatory. Because marginal cost is difficult to compute, this quantity has been replaced by average variable cost so that the revised test is: A price at or above anticipated average variable cost (AVC) should be presumed lawful while a price below this cost should conclusively be presumed unlawful.[18]

Based on previous material in *Pricing for Profit*, this test makes perfect sense. Thus, the quantity "average variable cost" in the Areeda-Turner Test is what we have herein called the "unit variable cost" (VC). We know that a price at or below this cost will generate zero or negative contribution dollars and we have consequently labeled it the *price floor*. Under ordinary circumstances, it would be foolish to sell below that price because each additional sale would lead to a unit contribution loss equal to the difference between the sell price and the unit variable cost $(P - VC)$ and a total loss of $(P - VC) \times Q$ where Q is the quantity sold and $P < VC$.

15.7.3 A New Standard

The most important decision on this topic has come with *Brooke Group* in which the Supreme Court set down a definitive standard to be met by plaintiffs to prevail in a case of predatory pricing.[19] The cigarette industry, a highly concentrated oligopoly, is known for its occasional price skirmishes and wars and *Brooke Group* was an outgrowth of such a battle. In its lawsuit Ligget alleged that its rival Brown & Williamson was selling its cigarettes to wholesalers below cost in order to force Ligget to raise its generic cigarette prices to levels closer to those of its branded ones.

In its analysis of the case, the Court combined provisions in the Section 2 of the Sherman Act and the Robinson-Patman Act (see Section 15.9 below) to announce a new standard. In order to prevail the plaintiff must show that the defendant had i) charged prices "below an appropriate measure" of its costs, and there existed ii) either a reasonable prospect or a dangerous probability it would recoup its investment in below cost prices. Using this standard, the Court held for the defendant. Clearly, with this heavy burden of proof, the Court set the bar sufficiently high to make it difficult, although not impossible, for a plaintiff to prevail in a predatory pricing action.

15.8 Conscious Parallelism and Price Signaling

In Sections 8.3 and 8.4 of Chapter 8 we discussed oligopolies and leadership pricing, respectively, and stated that oligopolies tend to be very *interdependent* and that engaging in *leadership pricing* is one way they attempt to prevent direct price competition and possible price wars. It was also pointed out that an effective price leader gives the price followers advance public notice of its intention to make a major price change so that they will not be taken by surprise and react in a negative way. In legal parlance acting in concert with other members of an oligopoly is known as *conscious parallelism* and announcing a price change as *price signaling*. Clearly, these activities could be termed tacit collusion and the question is whether they are legal under the antitrust laws. Generally speaking, the courts have treated oligopolistic conduct with kid gloves presuming it to be a natural component of doing business in a free market economy.

15.8.1 Conscious Parallelism

Conscious parallelism is legal with an important caveat. Thus, in *Theatre Enterprises* the Court held: *The mere existence of an oligopolistic market structure in which a small group of manufacturers engage in consciously parallel pricing of an identical product does not violate the antitrust laws.*[20] Since the conduct of the defendants (certain movie producers and distributors) stemmed from independent action rather an agreement, tacit or express, the Court affirmed judgment for the defendants who had been sued for treble damages and an injunction under § 4 and § 16 of the Clayton Act.

The outcome can be different when an agreement can be inferred from the existence of a number of "plus factors."[21] These were present in *Interstate Circuit*, and included i) defendant's conduct constituted a radical departure from prior practice, ii) defendant was aware that its co-defendants had been solicited to act similarly, iii) defendant had been invited to participate, iv) defendants had a substantial profit motive for concerted action, v) defendant actually participated in the scheme of uniform conduct, and vi) compliance by all defendants was necessary to make the scheme profitable to any one. The bottom line is that conscious parallelism is not illegal provided no agreement exists or can be inferred from certain plus factors. These plus factors, it should be noted, are not present in conventional leadership pricing.

15.8.2 Price Signaling

The practice of giving advance public notice of a price change, which may facilitate tacit price collusion among oligopolies, may be presumed legal based on a case brought by the FTC against *DuPont* and Ethyl, the country's two leading producers of lead antiknock gasoline additives.[22] In its complaint, the FTC alleged "unfair methods of competition" and "unfair acts and practices" in violation of Section 5 of the FTC Act. The complaint alleged that the defendants had, among several other supposedly illegal practices, i) used a 30-day price change advance notice clause in all contracts, and ii) had given advance price change notices to the press thereby facilitating price coordination throughout the country.

The FTC entered a cease and desist order which defendants appealed to the Second Circuit. In a strongly worded opinion this court rejected the FTC's analysis, vacated its order, and put forth the following rule of law: *Before business conduct in an oligopolistic industry may be labeled "unfair" within the meaning of § 5 a minimum standard demands that, absent a tacit agreement, at least some indicia of oppressiveness must exist such as (1) evidence of anticompetitive intent or purpose on the part of the producer charged, or (2) the absence of an independent legitimate business reason for its conduct.* Specifically, the Court held that *The mere existence of an oligopolistic market structure in which a small group of manufacturers engage in consciously parallel pricing of an identical product does not violate the antitrust laws.*

In the *ATP* case, the DOJ alleged in a civil complaint that the Airline Tariff Publishing Company (ATPCO) and eight airlines had violated Section 1 of the Sherman Act by using the ATPCO fare dissemination system to fix prices and raise fares.[23] ATPCO is owned by the carriers to disseminate fare and seat information provided by each airline among all the carriers and four computer reservation systems (CRSs). The latter, in turn, provide flight information to travel agents. Since the instant communication inherent in the system allowed rapid and continuous fare changes, including subsequent modification or withdrawal of announced ones, the carriers were virtually working together. The Department obtained an injunction that allowed the carriers to continue to use the ATP system but with several important restrictions. Because there was no trial, no definitive ruling resulted from the case.

15.9 Price Discrimination

As we saw in Section 10.2 (Chapter 10), one of the accepted marketing practices for maximizing sales revenue or profits of products is to customize prices to accommodate different customer groups with different value perceptions. In target segments with high price sensitivity, the marketer will typically charge less than in ones where demand is inelastic and customers are able and willing to pay more. Usually these products are very similar and can be produced and marketed with no or little cost differences. The question is, Is price discrimination, while profitable, also legal? Price discrimination is illegal only if certain stringent conditions exist and none of the available defenses are met.

Price discrimination in the marketplace is made unlawful by § 2(a)-(f) of the Robinson-Patman Act (the "Act") which amends § 2 of the Clayton Act. This Act has seen less enforcement activity at the federal level in recent years possibly because it seems to run counter to conventional antitrust legislation which seeks to protect the consumer. Robinson-Patman was enacted in 1936 to protect small independent retailers from encroachment by chain stores which were able to extract price concessions from producers as a result of their greater buying power. As Sullivan and Harrison have noted: "A great deal of controversy has focused on the Robinson-Patman Act in recent years. The Act prohibits price and other forms of discriminations. This Depression era Act was passed principally to protect competitors. Arguments based on economic theory suggest that it may actually cause prices to increase and output to decrease. Consequently, the Act is viewed by many as misguided in the context of modern antitrust theory." [24]

Due to the fact that price discrimination is impacted by not only the Robinson-Patman Act but also the Sherman and Clayton acts and that these were written with different antitrust goals in mind, the case law in this area of antitrust litigation is unusually complex. The important Supreme Court cases are typically appeals from decisions that originated with actions brought by the FTC. We begin by stating the elements that make for a prima facie case of price discrimination under the Act and continue with the available defenses. The interested reader will find Sections 1.(a) and 1(b) of the Act reproduced following the *Notes* at the end of this chapter.

15.9.1 Elements of a Prima Facie Case

For a *prima facie* case of illegal price discrimination under the Robinson-Patman Act five elements must be present and proved:

i) Interstate Commerce: Congress is authorized to regulate commerce among the States by Section 8 of Article I of the Constitution and therefore the antitrust laws, including the Robinson Patman Act, require that the sales take place in interstate commermerce. The courts have used the terms "stream of commerce" or "flow of commerce" in describing sales under these provisions.

ii) Two Prices and Two Sales: By a 1974 Supreme Court decision in *Gulf Oil*, there must have been at least two reasonably contemporaneous sales to different purchasers and at least one of these must have crossed state lines.[25] For intrastate price discrimination, state laws apply. The courts have also held that non-sale transactions such as mere offers of sale, consignments, or lease agreements are not covered by the Act.

iii) Price Discrimination: In an important 1960 decision in *Anheuser-Busch*, the Supreme Court ruled that price discrimination means merely a price difference.[26] Without this ruling, price discrimination would be difficult to litigate since it would require weighing the economics in each case. While the term price discrimination is still used, the question to be asked is, Did the seller charge different buyers different prices?

Because the Act contains no express reference to *functional discounts* this topic has been the subject of much litigation including the *Morton Salt* (1948), *Texaco* (1990), and *Smith Wholesale* (2007) cases.[27] A functional discount is a means by which a seller reimburses its distribution chain for services rendered (holding inventory, servicing retailers, advertising etc.) with the most "upstream" members of the chain (distributors, wholesalers) receiving the largest discounts. In *Morton Salt*, the producers of table salt had offered substantial discounts to customers that bought salt in greater than carload lots. The FTC found Morton guilty of price discrimination. The Court of Appeals reversed and the Supreme Court reversed again. The company had argued that the discounts were available to all. The Court found that since only five companies qualified for the largest discount, functionally they were not.

The Court in *Morton Salt* also held that *a legitimate functional discount that constitutes a reasonable reimbursement for the purchasers' actual marketing functions does not violate the Act*. In *Texaco*, Hasbrouck and a group of gasoline station owners who were Texaco customers sued after the company gave two distributors substantial discounts making it impossible for the retailers to compete with the distributors' own stations. The Court found that the services performed by the distributors were insubstantial and did not merit the large discounts. The plaintiffs were awarded treble damages for their competitive injuries. In *Smith Wholesale*, the plaintiffs, distributors of Phillip Morris cigarettes to retail outlets, alleged that the cigarette company's discount schedule, which was based on the percentage of their total cigarette sales that were of the defendant's brand, was discriminatory and unlawful under the Act. The Court of Appeals found no violation and affirmed the district court's summary judgment for the defendant holding *that if concessions are available equally and functionally to all customers there is no violation.*

iv) Commodities of "Like Grade and Quality": The commodities language is interpreted to mean tangible goods and to exclude all types of services. The leading case regarding the "like grade and quality" requirement is the *Borden Co.* litigation in which the FTC found Borden, a milk producer, to be in violation of the Act because it charged different prices for its branded and private label evaporated milk even though the two were chemically identical. On appeal, the circuit court set aside the FTC ruling holding that the branded and private label milk were different products. The Supreme Court reversed holding that a public preference for a name brand for which it was willing to pay a higher price did not establish that the two products were different. The Court suggested the lower court consider the cost justification and competitive injury provisions of the Act. On remand, the circuit court allowed Borden's price differential after finding that it caused no substantial competitive injury.[28]

v) Injury to Competition: The Act requires a showing that the effect of such price discrimination "may be substantially to lessen competition." In *primary-line* price discrimination the injury is to a competitor of the price discriminator (usually in the form of lost sales and profits) while in *secondary-line* injury the seller's disfavored customer may sue the price discriminating seller if it suffers injury competing with the favored customer. *Utah Pie* is the foremost primary-line discrimination case. The petitioner, a local producer of frozen desert pies, alleged that certain large national competitors had entered the Utah market charging lower prices than elsewhere resulting in a substantial loss in petitioner's market share. The jury sided with the petitioner, the Court of Appeals reversed, and, in a controversial decision, the Supreme Court reversed again finding for the petitioner and awarding treble damages.[29] The Court held that there was sufficient evidence by which the jury could find competitive injury. As to secondary-line price discrimination, the *Morton Salt* case cited above dealt with that situation.

15.9.2 Defenses

The Act makes three defenses available to rebut a prima facie case of price discrimination.

i) ***Cost Justification***: A price discriminator may escape liability by showing, according to § 2(a) of the Act, that price differentials *make only due allowance for differences in the cost of manufacture, sale, or delivery*. The cost defense was successfully used at the trial level in an earlier *Borden* case in which the government alleged the company had discriminated in milk prices to independent grocery stores and grocery store chains.[30] On appeal, the Supreme Court reversed because of the defendant's faulty methodology in arriving at costs. As we have seen earlier in *Pricing for Profit* (see Chapter 2), computing a unit total costs requires the equitable allocation of total fixed costs among the products. That is rarely successful making a meaningful cost versus price comparison nearly impossible. As Sullivan and Harrison have noted "The [cost] defense, for the most part, has not been of great value to defendants."[31]

ii) ***Meeting Competition***: Section 2(b) of the Act allows rebuttal of the prima facie case by showing that the lower price *was made in good faith to meet an equally low price of a competitor*. This defense is available only in primary-line cases and is applicable to either retain old customers or gain new ones. The defense allows meeting but not beating a competitor's price. Unlike the cost justification defense, this defense is very effective and has been successfully raised by many defendants. The *good faith* standard was annunciated in a 1945 case and reaffirmed in *U.S. Gypsum* where the Court held that the price discriminating seller must *show the existence of facts which would lead a reasonable and prudent person to believe that the granting of a lower price would in fact meet the equally low price of a competitor.*[32] This rule requires no interseller exchange of price information to verify a competitor's price. In fact, in *Container Corp.* the Court made the exchange of price information a violation of the Sherman Act.[33] Here, the defendants had exchanged information on the last prices charged. or quoted. In reversing the district court, which had dismissed the complaint, the Court held that *price is too critical, too sensitive a control to allow it to be used even in an informal manner to restrain competition.*

iii) Changing Conditions: This defense in *response to changing conditions* allows the anticompetitive sale of goods that are perishable and about to spoil, or have become obsolete and been discontinued, or offered to clear out inventory because the seller is going out of business.

15.10 Concluding Comments

In this short presentation, we have dealt with only the most important areas of antitrust law that would be of interest to managers. Areas of the law that were not covered include antitrust exemptions and immunities concerning State actions, political activity (Noerr-Pennington), regulated industries, agricultural cooperatives, newspapers, professional sports, and unions. In addition, there exists a large body of statutory and case law dealing with mergers. Mergers among competitors raise antitrust issues because of the potential for the merged firms to monopolize their respective industries giving them an incentive to raise prices and extract monopoly profits.

Because antitrust law is complex and business activity is equally so, managers are cautioned to be ever vigilant to avoid engaging in any activities proscribed by law. Private suits especially should be cause for concern because of the provision of Section 4(a) of the Clayton Act which allows any person who has suffered injury to his business or property as a result of an antirust law violation to recover treble damages plus the cost of suit. Aside from good legal counsel, either inside or on retainer, certain antitrust guidelines periodically published by the Department of Justice and the Federal Trade Commission can assist managers in this effort.

15.11 European Union Antitrust Law

Multinational companies must satisfy the legal requirement of more than one jurisdiction which, in the case of firms with operations in both the United States and the European Union (EU), means that they are subject to both American and European antitrust laws. In the EU, antitrust laws are enforced by the European Commission (EC) and, specifically, the Directorate General for Competition. The EC is the executive arm of the EU and is located in Brussels, Belgium. Its decisions can be appealed to the General Court and from there to the European Court of Justice (ECJ). The ECJ hears cases involving questions of law only. The EU antitrust law is contained in Articles 101 and 102 of the Treaty on the Functioning of the European Union. As is the case in the U.S. where each state has its own laws to deal with intrastate antitrust issues, each member country of the EU has its own laws and enforcement agencies to deal with antitrust violations for goods sold within its borders.

Article 101: This article prohibits all agreements and concerted practices which may affect trade between member states and which have as their object or effect the prevention, restriction, or distortion of competition within the European Union including horizontal (price-fixing or market sharing) and vertical agreements. The EC can levy fines of up to ten percent of a company's annual world-wide sales on conviction. It is also empowered to grant total immunity to a firm that is the first to submit actionable evidence of wrongful conduct. Private suits for damages based on EC decisions can be brought in the courts of member countries.

Article 102: Article 102 prohibits firms from holding a dominant position in a market and abusing that position. In assessing dominance, the EC analyzes the relevant product-market and the firm's market share. The relevant product-market is made up of all products/services which customers consider to be substitutes in terms of their characteristics, prices, and intended use. Market share is considered a strong indicator in assessing dominance—the higher a company's market share and the longer the time it has been held, the more dominant it is. If market share lies below forty percent, dominance is not considered likely.

European antitrust law has been strongly influenced by American law which has a longer history but there are major differences in the substantive law due to the different objectives of the U.S. and EU antitrust laws. Furthermore, because of the different systems of law there are also procedural differences. The American system is based on the *common law* of England in which case law (sometimes called judge-made law) is a major component. European law, known as the *civil law* has its origin in the Corpus Juris Civilis of ancient Rome and adjudication is based on the codified law with less reliance on case law. It is therefore important for American businesses with European operations to seek legal counsel from attorneys knowledgeable in EU antitrust law and procedure and not to rely solely on advise obtained from domestic counsel.

15.12 Ethics in Pricing

A pricing practice may be profitable and it may be legal but that does not mean that it is also ethical. Ethics involves moral values and standards and on many issues people in business will disagree on what is acceptable and not. This section of *Pricing for Profit* is not intended to offer guidelines or judgments but merely to point out that ethics is part of pricing just as the law is part of it. Undoubtedly, there are people who would even consider perceived value pricing wrongful and unethical because, unlike cost-plus pricing, it seems to set no limit to profits and corporate greed. This author would strongly disagree with that notion.

To begin with, there is nothing unethical in pricing ones goods and services to make a profit. That is the whole purpose of business in a free market economy. As we know, a firm in order to exist and survive it must be profitable or at least break even. Clearly then, if a firm's objective is to make a profit, it might as well seek to maximize it. In fact, in the absence of unregulated monopoly power, a firm cannot earn one dollar more in profits than its customers are willing to allow it to earn. That is why profits increase with rising prices until an optimal price point is reached and then decline again to zero. It is only logical for marketers to price at this optimal level dictated by market forces and customer demand.

While pricing for profit cannot be classified as unethical per se, there are occasions where the practice becomes patently or borderline so. This can happen in industries in which prices are not free to move but are controlled by unregulated entities determined to extract monopoly profits from a captive customer base with few options. The healthcare industry is often cited as a prime example. Thus, hospital out-patients have been billed thousands of dollars for the most minor of emergency room procedures. Pharmaceutical companies have earned exorbitant profits on life saving drugs whose development was funded by government subsides. Some drug companies with expiring patents have been known to pay off generic producers to delay marketing a generic replacement drug so that they can continue earning outsized profits. The list goes on and on.

Fortunately, most unethical practices eventually become known and the media and social networks can be expected to spread the word. In the most egregious cases new regulations and laws are eventually enacted to protect the public. More often though, unethical pricing just earns the offending business very bad publicity creating sufficient ill will to impact the bottom line. It almost goes without saying but pricing that is both lawful and ethical will in the long run also be the most profitable.

Notes

1. *United States vs. Topco Associates, Inc.*, 405 U.S. 596 (1972).

2. *Brunswick Corp. v. Pueblo Bowl-O-Mat, Inc.*, 429 U.S. 477 (1977).

3. *Arizona v. Maricopa County Medical Society*, 457 U.S. 332 (1982).

4. E. Thomas Sullivan and Jeffrey Harrison, *Antitrust And Its Economic Implications*, 129.

5. *United States v. E. I. DuPont de Nemours & Co.*, 351 U.S. 377 (1956).

6. E. Thomas Sullivan and Jeffrey Harrison, supra at 23-24.

7. *United States v. Trenton Potteries Co.*, 273 U.S. 392 (1927).

8. *United States v. A. Schrader's Son, Inc.*, 252 U.S. 85 (1919).

9. Jeffrey Sonnenfeld and Paul R. Lawrence, "Why Do Companies Succumb to Price Fixing?" *Harvard Business Review*, July-August 1978, 9.

10. *United States v. Topco Associates*, Inc., supra.

11. *United States v. Colgate & Company*, 250 U.S. 300 (1919).

12. *Dr. Miles Medical Co. v. Park & Sons*, 220 U.S. 373 (1911).

13. *Albrecht v. The Herald Co.*, 390 U.S. 145 (1968).

14. *State Oil v. Khan*, 522 U.S. 3 (1997).

15. *Leegin Creative Leather Products v. PKS, Inc.*, 551 U.S. 877 (2007).

16. *Matsushita Electric Industry Co. v. Zenith Radio Corp.*, 475 U.S. 574 (1986).

17. E. Thomas Sullivan and Jeffrey Harrison, supra at 287.

18. E. Thomas Sullivan and Jeffrey Harrison, supra at 290-292.

19. *Brooke Group Ltd. v. Brown & Williamson Tobacco Co.*, 509 U.S. 209 (1993).

20. *Theatre Enterprises v. Paramount Film Distributing Corp.*, 346 U.S. 537 (1954).

21. *Interstate Circuit, Inc. v. United States*, 306 U.S. 208 (1939); also, E. Thomas Sullivan and Jeffrey Harrison, supra at 166-167.

22. *E. I. DuPont de Nemours & Co. v. Federal Trade Commission*, 729 F.2d 128 (2nd Circuit, 1984); also, E. Thomas Sullivan and Jeffrey Harrison, supra at 175.

23. *United States v. Airline Tariff Publishing Co et al.*, Civil Action No. 92 2854 SSH (1993).

24. E. Thomas Sullivan and Jeffrey Harrison, supra at 361.

25. *Gulf Oil Corp. v. Copp Paving Co.*, 419 U.S. 186 (1974).

26. *FTC v. Anheuser -Busch, Inc.*, 363 U.S. 536 (1960).

27. *FTC v. Morton Salt Co.*, 334 U.S. 37 (1948); *Texaco, Inc. v. Hasbrouck*, 496 U.S. 543 (1990); and *Smith Wholesale Co. v. Phillip Morris USA, Inc.*, 477 F.3d 854 (6th Circuit 2007).

28. *FTC v. Borden Co.*, 383 U.S. 637 (1966).

29. *Utah Pie Co. v. Continental Baking Co.*, 386 U.S. 685 (1967).

30. *U.S. v. Borden Co.*, 370 U.S. 460 (1962)

31. E. Thomas Sullivan and Jeffrey Harrison, supra at 380.

32. *United States v. United States Gypsum Co.*, 438 U.S. 422 (1978).

33. *United States v. Container Corp. of America*, 393 U.S. 333 (1969).

Excepts From the Sherman and Robinson-Patman Acts

The Sherman Act [15 U.S.C. § 1-7]

Section 1: Every contract, combination in the form of trust or otherwise, or conspiracy, in restraint of trade or commerce among the several States, or with foreign nations, is declared to be illegal. Every person who shall make any contract or engage in any combination or conspiracy hereby declared to be illegal shall be deemed guilty of a felony, and, on conviction thereof, shall be punished by fine not exceeding $10,000,000 if a corporation, or, if any other person, $350,000, or by imprisonment not exceeding three years, or by both said punishments, in the discretion of the court.

Section 2: Every person who shall monopolize, or attempt to monopolize, or combine or conspire with any other person or persons, to monopolize any part of the trade or commerce among the several States, or with foreign nations, shall be deemed guilty of a felony, and, on conviction thereof, shall be punished by fine not exceeding $10,000,000 if a corporation, or, if any other person, $350,000, or by imprisonment not exceeding three years, or by both said punishments, in the discretion of the court.

The Robinson-Patman Act [15 U.S.C. § 13]

Section 1 (a): It shall be unlawful for any person engaged in commerce, in the course of such commerce, either directly or indirectly, to discriminate in price between different purchasers of commodities of like grade and quality, where either or any of the purchases involved in such discrimination are in commerce, where such commodities are sold for use, consumption, or resale within the United States or any Territory thereof or the District of Columbia or any insular possession or other place under the jurisdiction of the United States, and where the effect of such discrimination may be substantially to lessen competition or tend to create a monopoly in any line of commerce, or to injure, destroy, or prevent competition with any person who either grants or knowingly receives the benefit of such discrimination, or with customers of either of them: *Provided*, That nothing herein contained shall prevent differentials which make only due allowance for differences in the cost of manufacture, sale, or delivery resulting from the differing methods or quantities in which such commodities are to such purchasers sold or delivered: *Provided, however*, That the Federal Trade Commission may, after due investigation and hearing to all interested parties, fix and establish quantity limits, and revise the same as it finds necessary, as to particular commodities or classes of commodities, where it finds that available purchasers in greater quantities are so few as to render differentials on account thereof unjustly discriminatory or promotive of monopoly in any line of commerce; and the foregoing shall then not be construed to permit differentials based on differences in quantities greater than those so fixed and established: *And provided further*, That nothing herein contained shall prevent persons engaged in selling goods, wares, or merchandise in commerce from selecting their own customers in bona fide transactions and not in restraint of trade: *And provided further*, That nothing herein contained shall prevent price changes from time to time where in response to changing conditions affecting the market for or the marketability of the goods concerned, such as but not limited to actual or imminent deterioration of perishable goods, obsolescence of seasonal goods, distress sales under court process, or sales in good faith in discontinuance of business in the goods concerned.

Section 1 (b):   Upon proof being made, at any hearing on a complaint under this section, that there has been discrimination in price or services or facilities furnished, the burden of rebutting the prima facie case thus made by showing justification shall be upon the person charged with a violation of this section, and unless justification shall be affirmatively shown, the Commission is authorized to issue an order terminating the discrimination: *Provided, however*, That nothing herein contained shall prevent a seller rebutting the pima facie case thus made by showing that his lower price or the furnishing of services or facilities to any purchaser or purchasers was made in good faith to meet an equally low price of a competitor, or the services or facilities furnished by a competitor.

Bibliography

Baker, Walter L., Michael V. Marn, and Craig C. Zawada. *The Price Advantage*. 2nd ed. Hoboken, NJ: John Wiley & Sons, 2010.

Dean, Joel. "Pricing Policies for New Products." *Harvard Business Review on Pricing*. Boston: Harvard Business School Publishing, 2008: 101-131.

Dolan, Robert J., and Hermann Simon. *Power Pricing: How Managing Price Transforms the Bottom Line*. New York: The Free Press, 1996.

Eckert, Ross D., and Richard H. Leftwich. *The Price System and Resource Allocation*. 10th ed. Chicago: The Dryden Press, 1988.

Eiteman, Wilford J. *Price Determination in Oligopolistic and Monopolistic Situations*. (Michigan Business Reports No. 33). Ann Arbor: The University of Michigan, 1960.

Gabor, André. *Pricing: Concepts and Methods for Effective Marketing*. 2nd ed. Hants, UK: Gower Publishing Co., 1988.

Gould, J. P., and C. E. Ferguson. *Microeconomic Theory*. 5th ed. Homewood, IL: Richard D. Irwin, Inc., 1980.

Kotler, Philip. *Marketing Management: Analysis, Planning, and Control*. 2nd ed. Englewood Cliffs, NJ: Prentice-Hall, Inc., 1972.

Kotler, Philip and Kevin L. Keller. *Marketing Management*. 13th ed. Upper Saddle River, NJ: Pearson Education, Inc., 2009.

Levitt, Theodore. *The Marketing Mode: Pathways to Corporate Growth*. New York: McGraw-Hill Book Company, 1969.

Marn, Michael V., and Robert L. Rosiello. "Managing Price, Gaining Profit." *Harvard Business Review on Pricing*. Boston: Harvard Business School Publishing Corp., 2008: 45-73.

Mohammed, Rafi. *The 1% Windfall: How Successful Companies Use Price to Profit and Grow*. New York: HarperCollins Publishers, 2010.

Monroe, Kent B. *Pricing: Making Profitable Decisions*. 2nd ed. New York: McGraw-Hill Publishing Co., 1990.

Morris, Michael H., and Gene Morris. *Market Oriented Pricing: Strategies for Management*. Lincolnwood, IL: NTC Business Books, 1992.

Nagle, Thomas T. and Reed K. Holden. *The Strategy and Tactics of Pricing: A Guide to Profitable Decision Making.* 3rd ed. Upper Saddle River, NJ: Pearson Education, Inc., 2002.

Nagle, Thomas T., John E. Hogan, and Joseph Zale. *The Strategy and Tactics of Pricing: A Guide to Growing More Profitably.* 5th ed. Upper Saddle River, NJ: Pearson Education, Inc., 2011.

Rao, Akshay R., Mark E. Bergen, and Scott Davis. "How to Fight a Price War." *Harvard Business Review on Pricing.* Boston: Harvard Business School Publishing Corp., 2008: 75-100.

Stiving, Mark. *Impact Pricing: Your Blueprint for Driving Profits.* Madison, WI: Entrepreneur Press, 2011.

Sullivan, E. Thomas, and Jeffrey L. Harrison. *Understanding Antitrust and Its Economic Implications.* 5th ed. Newark, NJ: Mathew Bender & Co., 2009.

Tucker, Spencer A. *Pricing for Higher Profit: Criteria, Methods, Applications.* New York: McGraw-Hill Co., 1966.

Appendix I. Formula Derivations

A. Optimal Prices on Price Response Curve

1. Optimal Price for Sales Revenue Maximization

The linear price response curve of Figure 10-1 of Chapter 10 has the equation:

$$Q = Q_M - (Q_M / P_M) P$$

Sales revenue is therefore:

$$R = P Q$$

$$R = - \frac{Q_M}{P_M} P^2 + Q_M P$$

This expression for sales revenue R versus price P has the shape of a parabola. The optimal price [P] at which R reaches a maximum is found by taking the first derivative of R w.r.t. P and setting the result equal to zero:

$$R' = - \frac{2 Q_M}{P_M} P + Q_M = 0$$

$$[P] = \frac{P_M}{2} \qquad QED \qquad \text{Eq. (A.1)}$$

In words, the optimal price for sales revenue maximization is one-half the maximum (reservation) price P_M. This means that [P] lies at the midpoint of the PRC where the price elasticity of demand is equal to one $(\mathcal{E} = 1.0)$.

2. Optimal Price for Total Contribution Maximization

Total contribution is the difference between sales revenue and total variable cost:

$$K = R - V = R - VC_0 Q$$

Since,

$$R = - \frac{Q_M}{P_M} P^2 + Q_M P$$

and
$$Q = Q_M - \frac{Q_M}{P_M} P$$

$$K = - \frac{Q_M}{P_M} P^2 + \frac{Q_M (P_M + VC_0)}{P_M} P - VC_0 \, Q_M$$

This equation for total contribution too has the shape of a parabola. It can be differentiated with respect to P and the result set equal to zero to obtain the optimal price P* that will maximize total contribution:

$$K' = - \frac{2 \, Q_M}{P_M} P + \frac{Q_M (P_M + VC_0)}{P_M} = 0$$

$$P^* = \frac{P_M + VC_0}{2} \qquad\qquad \text{QED} \qquad\qquad (A.2)$$

In words, the optimal price for contribution maximization is one-half the sum of the maximum (reservation) price and the product's unit variable cost. Thus, P* is located at the midpoint of that section of the PRC between the unit variable cost VC_0 and the reservation price P_M.

Appendix I. Formula Derivations

B. Sales Revenue Maximization

1. The Revenue Impact Formula (RIF)

The sales revenue prior to and after an incremental price change is, respectively:

$$R_0 = P_0 Q_0$$
$$R_1 = P_1 Q_1$$

where R, P, and Q are the sales revenue, price, and quantity, respectively. Let Δ stand for an incremental dollar change and $\blacktriangle$ for an incremental percentage change (expressed as a decimal), then:

$$\Delta R = R_1 - R_0$$
$$\Delta R = P_1 Q_1 - P_0 Q_0$$

$$\text{Let} \quad P_1 = P_0 (1 + \blacktriangle P)$$
$$Q_1 = Q_0 (1 + \blacktriangle Q)$$

$$\Delta R = R_0 P_0 (1 + \blacktriangle P)(1 + \blacktriangle Q) - R_0$$
$$\Delta R = R_0 \blacktriangle P + R_0 \blacktriangle Q_0 + R_0 \blacktriangle P_0 \blacktriangle Q$$

$$\text{Let} \quad \blacktriangle Q = - \mathcal{E}_0 \blacktriangle P$$

$$\Delta R = R_0 \blacktriangle P - R_0 \mathcal{E}_0 \blacktriangle P - R_0 \mathcal{E}_0 (\blacktriangle P)^2$$
$$\Delta R = R_0 \{ - \mathcal{E}_0 (\blacktriangle P)^2 + (1 - \mathcal{E}_0) \blacktriangle P \}$$
$$\blacktriangle R = - \mathcal{E}_0 (\blacktriangle P)^2 + (1 - \mathcal{E}_0) \blacktriangle P \qquad \text{Eq. (B.1)}$$

Equation (B.1) gives the percentage revenue change resulting from a percentage price change and will be referred to as the *revenue impact formula*. If one plots the RIF on x-y coordinates with $\blacktriangle P$ on the x (horizontal) axis and $\blacktriangle R$ on the y (vertical) axis, it takes the shape of a parabola rising from zero to a maximum value at $[\blacktriangle P]$, the optimal $\blacktriangle P$, and returning to zero.

2. The Sales Revenue After an Incremental Price Change

$$\text{Let} \quad R_1 = R_0 (1 + \blacktriangle R)$$

Inserting Equation (B.1):

$$R_1 = R_0 \{ - \mathcal{E}_0 (\blacktriangle P)^2 + (1 - \mathcal{E}_0) \blacktriangle P + 1 \} \qquad \text{Eq. (B.2)}$$

This equation too is a parabola.

3. The Optimal Percentage Price Change

Taking the first derivative of Eq. (B.1) and setting the result equal to zero yields the percentage price change for revenue maximization:

$$\blacktriangle R' = -2\,\epsilon_0\,\blacktriangle P + 1 - \epsilon_0 = 0$$

$$[\blacktriangle P] = \frac{1 - \epsilon_0}{2\,\epsilon_0} \qquad\qquad \text{Eq. (B.3)}$$

4. The Optimal Condition

When the required price change for revenue maximization is zero, the price elasticity of demand is from Equation (B.3):

$$[\blacktriangle P] = \frac{1 - \epsilon_0}{2\,\epsilon_0} = 0$$

$$[\epsilon] = 1.0 \qquad\qquad \text{Eq. (B.4)}$$

where $[\epsilon]$ is the optimal price elasticity of demand for maximum sales revenue.

5. The Price Range for Positive Sales Revenue Changes

By setting Equation (B.1) equal to 0, one obtains the two points on the x ($\blacktriangle P$) axis at which the percentage sales revenue change is zero:

$$\blacktriangle R = -\epsilon_0\,(\blacktriangle P)^2 + (1 - \epsilon_0)\,\blacktriangle P = 0$$

$$\blacktriangle P = 0; \quad \frac{1 - \epsilon_0}{\epsilon_0} \qquad\qquad \text{Eq. (B.5)}$$

As may be noted, the second point is just twice the optimal percentage price change given by Equation (B.3). Hence the price range for positive sales revenue changes extends from $\blacktriangle P = 0$ to $\blacktriangle P = 2 \times [\blacktriangle P]$.

6. The Optimal Price

$$\text{Let} \qquad P_1 = P_0\,(1 + \blacktriangle P)$$

Inserting Equation (B.3):

$$[P] = P_0\,(1 + \frac{1 - \epsilon_0}{2\epsilon_0})$$

$$[P] = \frac{P_0}{2\,€_0}\,(€_0 + 1) \qquad\qquad \text{Eq. (B.6)}$$

7. The Sales Revenue Price Range

As noted before, the typical sales revenue curve R_1 is a parabola that rises from zero to a maximum at the optimal price [P] and returns to zero. (See, for example, Figure 12-2 in Chapter 12). Since this curve is symmetrical, the price at which it returns to zero is simply twice the optimal price [P]. The sales revenue price range is therefore from Equation (B.6):

$$0 < P_1 < \frac{P_0\,(€_0 + 1)}{€_0} \qquad\qquad \text{Eq. (B.7)}$$

Below and above this price range sales revenue is zero.

8. The Optimal Percentage Quantity Change

$$\text{Let}\quad \blacktriangle Q = -\,€_0\,\blacktriangle P$$

$$[\blacktriangle Q] = -\,€_0\,[\blacktriangle P]$$

Inserting Equation (B.3):

$$[\blacktriangle Q] = \frac{€_0 - 1}{2} \qquad\qquad \text{Eq. (B.8)}$$

9. The Optimal Quantity

$$\text{Let}\quad Q_1 = Q_0\,(1 + \blacktriangle Q)$$

Inserting Equation (B.8):

$$[Q] = Q_0\,(1 + \frac{€_0 - 1}{2})$$

$$[Q] = \frac{Q_0}{2}\,(€_0 + 1) \qquad\qquad \text{Eq. (B.9)}$$

10. The Optimal Sales Revenue Change

From Equation (B.1):

$$\blacktriangle R = -\,€_0\,(\blacktriangle P)^2 + (1 - €_0)\,\blacktriangle P$$

From Equation (B.3):

$$1 - \varepsilon_0 = 2\,\varepsilon_0\,[\blacktriangle P]$$

$$[\blacktriangle R] = -\varepsilon_0\,[\blacktriangle P]^2 + 2\,\varepsilon_0\,[\blacktriangle\ P]^2$$

$$[\blacktriangle R] = \varepsilon_0\,[\blacktriangle P]^2 \qquad\qquad \text{Eq. (B.10)}$$

11. The Maximum Sales Revenue

From Equations (B.6) and (B.9):

$$[R] = [P]\,[Q]$$

$$[R] = \frac{R_0}{4\,\varepsilon_0}\,(\varepsilon_0 + 1)(\varepsilon_0 + 1)$$

$$[R] = \frac{R_0}{4\,\varepsilon_0}\,(\varepsilon_0 + 1)^2 \qquad\qquad \text{Eq. (B.11)}$$

12. The Optimal Unit Contribution Margin

After the optimal price change, the unit contribution margin in percent is:

$$[CM] = \frac{[P] - VC_0}{[P]} \qquad\qquad \text{Eq. (B.12)}$$

where [P] is the optimal price given by Equation (B.6).

Appendix I. Formula Derivations

C. Profit Maximization

The well-known expression for profit is given by Equation 3.2 of Chapter 3:

$$I = R - V - F$$
$$I = (P - VC) Q - F$$

The profit before and after a price change is, respectively:

$$I_0 = (P_0 - VC_0) Q_0 - F_0$$
$$I_1 = (P_1 - VC_1) Q_1 - F_1$$

where I, P, Q, VC and F represent profit, price, quantity, unit variable cost, and total indirect fixed cost, respectively.

I. Special Case

In the special case, the unit variable cost VC and the total indirect fixed (overhead) cost F do not change as a result of an incremental percentage price change $\blacktriangle P$, i.e., $F_1 = F_0$ and $VC_1 = VC_0$. Let Δ represent an incremental dollar change and $\blacktriangle$ an incremental percentage change.

1. The Contribution (Profit) Impact Formula (PIF)

$$\Delta I = \Delta K = (P_1 - VC_0) Q_1 - (P_0 - VC_0) Q_0$$
$$\Delta K = P_1 Q_1 - VC_0 Q_1 - P_0 Q_0 + VC_0 Q_0$$

$$\text{Let} \quad VC_0 = P_0 (1 - CM_0)$$
$$P_1 = P_0 (1 + \blacktriangle P)$$
$$Q_1 = Q_0 (1 + \blacktriangle Q)$$

$$\Delta K = P_0 Q_0 \{(1 + \blacktriangle P)(1 + \blacktriangle Q) - (1 - CM_0)(1 + \blacktriangle Q) - 1 + 1 - CM_0\}$$

$$\Delta K = R_0 (\blacktriangle P \, \blacktriangle Q + \blacktriangle P + CM_0 \, \blacktriangle Q)$$

$$\text{Let} \quad \blacktriangle Q = - \mathcal{E}_0 \, \blacktriangle P$$

$$\Delta K = R_0 \{- \mathcal{E}_0 (\blacktriangle P)^2 + \blacktriangle P - \mathcal{E}_0 \, \blacktriangle P \, CM_0)$$

$$\text{Let} \quad \Delta K = K_0 \, \blacktriangle K$$
$$K_0 = R_0 \, CM_0$$

$$\blacktriangle K = \frac{1}{CM_0} \{- \mathcal{E}_0 (\blacktriangle P)^2 + (1 - \mathcal{E}_0 \, CM_0) \, \blacktriangle P\} \qquad \text{Eq. (C.1)}$$

Equation (C.1) may be called the *profit impact formula* since it gives the impact on total contribution and profit resulting from a percentage price change. If one plots the PIF with $\blacktriangle P$ on the x (horizontal) axis and $\blacktriangle K$ on the y (vertical) axis, it takes the shape of a parabola which rises from zero to a maximum at $\blacktriangle P^*$, the optimal $\blacktriangle P$, and returns to zero.

2. The Total Contribution After an Incremental Price Change

$$\text{Let} \quad K_1 = K_0 (1 + \blacktriangle K)$$

Inserting Equation (C.1):

$$K_1 = K_0 \left\{ 1 + \frac{-\epsilon_0 (\blacktriangle P)^2 + (1 - \epsilon_0 CM_0)\, \blacktriangle P}{CM_0} \right\}$$

$$\text{Let} \quad K_0 = R_0\, CM_0$$

$$K_1 = R_0 \left\{ -\epsilon_0 (\blacktriangle P)^2 + (1 - \epsilon_0 CM_0) \blacktriangle P + CM_0 \right\} \qquad \text{Eq. (C.2)}$$

3. The Optimal Percentage Price Change

Taking the first derivative of Equation (C.1) with respect to the incremental price change $\blacktriangle$ P and setting the result equal to zero results in the percentage price change for total contribution maximization:

$$\blacktriangle K' = -2\,\epsilon_0\, \blacktriangle P + 1 - \epsilon_0\, CM_0 = 0$$

$$\blacktriangle P^* = \frac{1 - \epsilon_0\, CM_0}{2\,\epsilon_0} \qquad \text{Eq. (C.3)}$$

4. The Optimal Condition

The optimal condition exists when the optimal percentage price change as given by Equation (C.3) is zero, i.e., no price change is required for profit maximization:

$$\blacktriangle P^* = \frac{1 - \epsilon_0\, CM_0}{2\,\epsilon_0} = 0$$

$$\epsilon_0 = \epsilon^* = \frac{1}{CM_0} \qquad \text{Eq. (C.4)}$$

where ϵ^* represents the optimal P.E.D. for profit maximization.

5. The Price Range for Positive Total Contribution Changes

By setting Equation (C.1) equal to 0, one obtains the two points on the x ($\blacktriangle$P) axis at which the percentage contribution change is zero:

$$\blacktriangle K = \frac{1}{CM_0} \{- \epsilon_0 (\blacktriangle P)^2 + (1 - \epsilon_0 CM_0) \blacktriangle P\} = 0$$

$$\blacktriangle P = 0; \quad \frac{1 - \epsilon_0 CM_0}{\epsilon_0} \qquad \text{Eq. (C.5)}$$

Comparing the second root of Equation (C.5) where $\blacktriangle K = 0$ with Equation (C.3), it is seen to equal twice the optimal percentage price change for contribution maximization. Hence the price range for positive contribution changes extends from $\blacktriangle P = 0$ to $\blacktriangle P = 2 \times \blacktriangle P^*$.

6. The Optimal Price

$$\text{Let} \quad P^* = P_0 (1 + \blacktriangle P^*)$$

Inserting Equation (C.3):

$$P^* = P_0 (1 + \frac{1 - \epsilon_0 CM_0}{2 \epsilon_0})$$

$$P^* = \frac{P_0}{2 \epsilon_0} \{1 + \epsilon_0 (2 - CM_0)\} \qquad \text{Eq. (C.6)}$$

7. The Total Contribution Price Range

A mathematical solution would involve finding the two roots of the total contribution curve K_1 of Equation (C.2) using one of the standard algebraic techniques. More simply, one can make this determination by locating the two points where $K_1 = 0$ on a typical total contribution curve such as shown in Figure 12-2 of Chapter 12. The first point at which this occurs is when $P_1 = VC_0$. This is the case because, by definition, no contribution dollars are earned until this value has been reached. The second price point where $K_1 = 0$ occurs when P_1 equals two times the optimal price P^* less the unit variable cost VC_0. This follows from the fact that the parabola is symmetrical. The price range for which total contribution can be earned under the given conditions is therefore:

$$VC_0 < P_1 < (2 P^* - VC_0)$$

Inserting Equation (C.6) for P*, and letting

$$VC_0 = P_0 (1 - CM_0)$$

$$VC_0 < P_1 < \frac{P_0 (\epsilon_0 + 1)}{\epsilon_0} \qquad \text{Eq. (C.7)}$$

By comparing Equations (B.7) and (C.7), it is apparent that the upper price limits for sales revenue and total contribution are equal. This makes sense since with zero sales revenue total contribution must be zero as well.

8. The Optimal Percentage Quantity Change

$$\text{Let} \qquad \blacktriangle Q = -\epsilon_0 \blacktriangle P$$
$$\blacktriangle Q^* = -\epsilon_0 \blacktriangle P^*$$

Inserting Equation (C.3):

$$\blacktriangle Q^* = \frac{\epsilon_0 CM_0 - 1}{2} \qquad \text{Eq. (C.8)}$$

9. The Optimal Quantity

$$\text{Let} \qquad Q^* = Q_0 (1 + \blacktriangle Q^*)$$

Inserting Equation (C.8):

$$Q^* = Q_0 \left(1 + \frac{\epsilon_0 CM_0 - 1}{2} \right)$$

$$Q^* = \frac{Q_0}{2} (\epsilon_0 CM_0 + 1) \qquad \text{Eq. (C.9)}$$

10. The Optimal Total Contribution Change

From Equation (C.1) with $\blacktriangle P$ replaced by $\blacktriangle P^*$:

$$\blacktriangle K^* = \frac{1}{CM_0} \{ -\epsilon_0 (\blacktriangle P^*)^2 + (1 - \epsilon_0 CM_0) \blacktriangle P^* \}$$

From Equation (C.3):

$$1 - \epsilon_0 CM_0 = 2 \epsilon_0 \blacktriangle P^*$$

$$\blacktriangle K^* = \frac{1}{CM_0} \{ - \mathcal{C}_0 (\blacktriangle P^*)^2 + 2 \mathcal{C}_0 (\blacktriangle P^*)^2 \}$$

$$\blacktriangle K^* = \frac{\mathcal{C}_0}{CM_0} (\blacktriangle P^*)^2 \qquad \text{Eq. (C.10)}$$

11. The Maximum Total Contribution

Let $\quad K^* = K_0 (1 + \blacktriangle K^*)$

Inserting Equation (C.10):

$$K^* = K_0 \left(1 + \frac{\mathcal{C}_0 (\blacktriangle P^*)^2}{CM_0}\right)$$

$$K^* = \frac{K_0}{CM_0} \left\{ CM_0 + \mathcal{C}_0 \frac{(1 - \mathcal{C}_0 CM_0)^2}{4 \mathcal{C}_0{}^2} \right\}$$

$$K^* = \frac{K_0}{4 \mathcal{C}_0 CM_0} (4 \mathcal{C}_0 CM_0 + 1 - 2 \mathcal{C}_0 CM_0 + \mathcal{C}_0{}^2 CM_0{}^2)$$

Let $\quad K_0 = R_0 CM_0$

$$K^* = \frac{R_0}{4 \mathcal{C}_0} (\mathcal{C}_0 CM_0 + 1)^2 \qquad \text{Eq. (C.11)}$$

12. The Optimal Unit Contribution Margin

From the definition for the unit contribution margin, one obtains the optimal unit contribution margin after the incremental price change:

$$CM^* = \frac{P^* - CV_0}{P^*} \qquad \text{Eq. (C.12)}$$

where P^* is the optimal price given by Equation (C.6).

13. The Optimal Sales Revenue

Of much interest is the sales revenue after an optimal price change for profit maximization. This may be computed by inserting the optimal price change $\blacktriangle P^*$ into Equation (B.2) of Appendix B:

$$R^* = R_0 \{ 1 - \mathcal{C}_0 (\blacktriangle P^*)^2 + (1 - \mathcal{C}_0) \blacktriangle P^* \}$$

$$R^* = R_0 \left\{ 1 - \frac{\epsilon_0 (1 - \epsilon_0 CM_0)^2}{4 \epsilon_0^2} + \frac{(1 - \epsilon_0)(1 - \epsilon_0 CM_0)}{2 \epsilon_0} \right\}$$

$$R^* = \frac{R_0}{4 \epsilon_0} \left\{ 4 \epsilon_0 - (1 - \epsilon_0 CM_0)^2 + 2 (1 - \epsilon_0)(1 - \epsilon_0 CM_0) \right\}$$

$$R^* = \frac{R_0}{4 \epsilon_0} \left\{ 1 + \epsilon_0^2 CM_0 (2 - CM_0) + 2 \epsilon_0 \right\} \qquad \text{Eq. (C.13)}$$

14. The Optimal Price Elasticity of Demand

At the optimal price the condition of Equation (C.4) applies:

$$\epsilon^* = \frac{1}{CM^*} = \frac{P^*}{P^* - VC_0} \qquad \text{Eq. (C.14)}$$

By inserting Equation (C.6) for P^* into Equation (C.14) one obtains an expression for the new optimal price elasticity of demand based entirely on parameter values existing prior to the optimal price change:

$$\epsilon^* = \frac{\dfrac{P_0}{2 \epsilon_0} \left\{ 1 + \epsilon_0 (2 - CM_0) \right\}}{\dfrac{P_0}{2 \epsilon_0} \left\{ 1 + \epsilon_0 (2 - CM_0) \right\} - VC_0}$$

$$\epsilon^* = \frac{P_0 + \epsilon_0 (2 P_0 - P_0 + VC_0)}{P_0 + \epsilon_0 (2 P_0 - P_0 + VC_0) - 2 \epsilon_0 VC_0}$$

$$\epsilon^* = \frac{P_0 + \epsilon_0 (P_0 + VC_0)}{P_0 + \epsilon_0 (P_0 - VC_0)} \qquad \text{Eq.(C.15)}$$

Clearly, the optimal P.E.D. for profit maximization is always $\epsilon^* \geq 1.0$.

15. A Comparison of Optimal Prices

Pricing Proposition 11 (Chapter 11), which states that for the optimal prices for sales revenue and contribution maximization to be equal requires that the product's variable cost be zero ($VC_0 = 0$), can also be proved mathematically. If one sets the optimal price for sales revenue maximization [P] given by Equation 13.6 (Chapter 13) equal to the optimal price for contribution maximization P* given by Equation (14.6) above, one obtains:

$$[P] = P*$$

$$\frac{P_0}{2 \, \mathcal{E}_0} (\mathcal{E}_0 + 1) = \frac{P_0}{2 \, \mathcal{E}_0} \{1 + \mathcal{E}_0 (2 - CM_0)\}$$

$$\mathcal{E}_0 + 1 = \mathcal{E}_0 (2 - CM_0) + 1$$

This expression requires that $CM_0 = 1$ which, in turn, means that the unit variable cost must be zero ($VC_0 = 0$). Thus, in the special case of zero unit variable cost the two optimal prices are the same.

In a practical case where the unit variable cost is not zero, the difference between the optimal prices for total contribution maximization and sales revenue maximization can be shown to be:

$$\Delta P = P* - [P]$$

$$\Delta P = \frac{P_0}{2 \, \mathcal{E}_0} \{1 + \mathcal{E}_0 (2 - CM_0)\} - \frac{P_0}{2 \, \mathcal{E}_0} (\mathcal{E}_0 + 1)$$

$$\Delta P = \frac{P_0}{2} (1 - CM_0) \qquad\qquad \text{Eq. (14.16)}$$

Clearly, where CM_0 (%) is 100% ($VC_0 = 0$) the price difference is zero.

II. General Case

In the general case, we assume that incremental price changes do result in cost changes: Specifically, let:

$$F_1 = a \, F_0$$
$$VC_1 = b \, VC_0$$

The dollar profit change as a result of an incremental price change:

$$\Delta I = I_1 - I_0 = P_1 Q_1 - b \, VC_0 \, Q_1 - a \, F_0 - P_0 Q_0 + VC_0 Q_0 + F_0$$

$$\text{Let} \quad VC_0 = P_0 (1 - CM_0)$$
$$P_1 = P_0 (1 + \blacktriangle P)$$
$$Q_1 = Q_0 (1 + \blacktriangle Q)$$

$$\blacktriangle Q = - \mathcal{E}_0 \, \blacktriangle P$$

The profit impact of an incremental price change can then be shown to be:

$$\Delta I = R_0 \{1 - \mathcal{E}_0 \, (\blacktriangle P)^2 + \{1 - \mathcal{E}_0 + b\,\mathcal{E}_0 - b\,\mathcal{E}_0\,CM_0)\,\blacktriangle P - b - CM_0\,(1-b)\} + F_0\,(1-a) \qquad \text{Eq. (C.17)}$$

This is the *profit impact formula* (PIF) for the general case. Taking the first derivative of Equation (C.17) with respect to $\blacktriangle P$ and setting the result equal to zero, one obtains the optimal percentage price and quantity changes for profit maximization:

$$\Delta I' = - \mathcal{E}_0 \, \blacktriangle P + 1 - \mathcal{E}_0 + b\,\mathcal{E}_0 - b\,\mathcal{E}_0\,CM_0 = 0$$

$$\blacktriangle P^* = \frac{1 - \mathcal{E}_0 \{1 - b\,(1 - CM_0)\}}{2\,\mathcal{E}_0} \qquad \text{Eq. (C.18)}$$

$$\text{Let} \qquad \blacktriangle Q^* = - \mathcal{E}_0 \, \blacktriangle P^*$$

$$\blacktriangle Q^* = \frac{\mathcal{E}_0 \{1 - b\,(1 - CM_0)\} - 1}{2} \qquad \text{Eq. (C.19)}$$

The maximum dollar profit change is obtained by inserting Equation (C.18) into Equation (C.17):

$$2\,\mathcal{E}_0 \, \blacktriangle P^* = 1 - \mathcal{E}_0 + b\,\mathcal{E}_0 - b\,\mathcal{E}_0\,CM_0$$

$$\Delta I^* = R_0 \{1 + \mathcal{E}_0 \, (\blacktriangle P^*)^2 - b - CM_0\,(1-b)\} + F_0\,(1-a) \qquad \text{Eq. (C.20)}$$

If one lets b = 1 in Equations (C.18) and (C.19) one obtains Equations (C.3) and (C.8), respectively, for the special case while setting a = b = 1 reduces Equation (C.20) to Equation (C.10).

Appendix II. Hypothetical Case Studies

A. Revenue Maximization: The Metropolitan Transit Authority - Midwest (MTA)

The Metropolitan Transit Authority - Midwest (MTA) provides public transportation services for a major Midwestern city and surrounding suburbs offering about 1.8 million rides a day. The MTA has over 13,000 employees while its rolling stock includes 1,200 rapid transit cars and 2,200 buses. The authority has been plagued by severe financial, service, and organizational problems for several years. A succession of public transportation professionals has been unable to turn the company around. There have been four executive directors in three years with the last one, who came from another major city with impeccable transportation credentials, serving just a year and a half before resigning. The city's leading daily, the *Herald Tribune*, has characterized the MTA as being "in shambles through years of waste, mismanagement, political intrigue, and fiscal famine."

In order to stem the tide of red ink from the MTA, the city's popular but increasingly exasperated mayor, Dick Dooly, has recently decided to make a major management change. Rather than pick another transportation expert for the vacancy, Mr. Dooly reached out to the business community and hired a retired commercial real estate mogul named Robert Belforte to lead the MTA. The mayor believes that the only way the MTA can be made profitable is to have it run like a business and that a successful businessman like Mr. Belforte would be a logical choice.

Mr. Belforte assumed his new position in February of this year and in mid-July the *Herald Tribune* introduced him to the general public in their *Herald Tribune Magazine*, a supplement to their Sunday issue. In this lengthy article with the heading "Mr. Fixit. Robert Belforte is taking a hard-nosed business approach at the MTA, but he admits he may be in for the ride of his life," Mr. Belforte frankly admitted, with no apologies given, that "I have no qualifications for this job." He does have a strong belief, he told the interviewer, that the customer is numero uno and this must be reflected in the attitude of MTA employees who previously thought their jobs consisted of driving trains and buses rather than serving the public.

Robert Belforte wasted no time in transforming this unwieldy bureaucracy into a modern business corporation. When he took over, the executive director had twenty-five individuals reporting to him including eight deputy executive directors with each deputy running his own fiefdom.

Not surprisingly, there was little coordination of activities among them to ensure an effective and efficient operation. Bolstered by a recent report from a prestigious management consulting firm commissioned by the MTA board, Mr. Belforte cut the number of deputies to three whom he renamed vice presidents while he himself took the title of president. The new titles were meant to promote a business model within the organization. To reduce costs, he closed down a number of rapid transit stations that were rarely used but were also served by bus routes. To improve service, Mr. Belforte introduced printed time schedules for all rapid transit and bus routes and installed a system of controls to maintain departure and arrival times. Other cost reduction and service improvement ideas are in the planning stage.

The major problem at the MTA now as ever are insufficient funds for daily operations and capital improvements. This year's operating expenses are expected to come to $780 million. Just over half of expenses are typically covered by fares collected from passengers while a subsidy from the Regional Transportation Authority in the form of a percentage of sales taxes plus state matching funds and some federal funds pay for most of the remaining outlays. Typically there is still a shortfall which last year amounted to $51 million. Another one is expected for this year especially since the latest recession has reduced the amount of sales taxes being collected.

On January 1 of this year, and before Mr. Belforte came on board, the MTA raised fares across the board. Prior to this date, a rush hour fare cost $1.25 while the non-rush hour (off-peak) fare was $1.00. Before the fare changes went into effect, MTA officials had presented the MTA board with five fare proposals all of which provided for fare increases. The option favored by the board was the one with the highest fare increase (20%), the largest expected increase in fare revenue ($34.5 million), and the smallest anticipated decline in ridership (4.6%). After public hearings, the MTA board approved this option and the new fare structure was implemented. Rush-hour fares are now $1.50 while off-peak fares were raised to $1.15. The cost for transfers was raised from 25 cents to 30 cents.

A few months into the new fare structure, MTA officials became alarmed when they noticed that ridership had dropped by 10% which was over twice of the 4.6% they had anticipated. By April, Mr. Belforte had become convinced that the fare increase instituted by his predecessor had been a mistake. He subsequently informed the MTA board of his opinion and proposed that an immediate fare cut of 50 cents to $1.00 be implemented. The new fare would apply to both rush-hour and off-peak hour traffic. He proposed to start with Sundays only and, if the experiment proved successful, extend it to the entire week.

Fare reduction has strong support both within MTA's new management team and outside. Mr. Belforte favors a fare reduction because in his business experience price reductions have always led to increases in both demand and sales revenue. In the July *Herald Tribune* interview he is quoted as saying "We believe service reductions and fare increases are self-defeating in that they cut ridership and lower revenues." The *Herald Tribune* supports him in this. In an April editorial headed "MTA should try fare-cutting gamble," the paper had advised that "decreasing fares would have the long-term value of increasing ridership—the MTA's best hope for the future." The MTA board is known to have strong doubts about fare reductions as a means of generating additional sales revenue and has not yet acted on Mr. Belforte's proposal.

Analysis

The information available to us is insufficient to make a complete analysis of the problems faced by the MTA. Among missing statistics are the number of fare paying customers using the MTA trains and buses on a daily basis, the proportion of full to discounted fares (available to students and seniors), the proportion of daily rush hour to off-peak passengers, the number of weekly and monthly passes sold at a discount, and the sales revenues generated by each category. Yet despite this information shortfall we can, with the help of the formulas and pricing rules of thumb given previously in *Pricing for Profit*, evaluate the pricing options available to MTA's management and board and develop some recommendations. The three main pricing options are i) keep the 20% fare increase implemented at the beginning of the year, ii) implement a fare structure using the optimal fare and maximum fare revenue change as computed by the formulas presented in Chapter 13, and iii) reduce fares to $1.00 across-the-board as proposed by the new MTA president.

i) Keep present fare schedule: The finding that the fare increase led to a 10% reduction in ridership can be used to estimate the P.E.D.s for the rush hour and off-peak segments as follows.

Ridership Segment	Fare Before	After	Change Fare	Rides	Estim. P.E.D.
Rush hour	$1.25	$1.50	20.0%	(10.0%)	0.50
Off-peak	$1.00	$1.15	15.0%	(10.0%)	0.67

By Equation (13.1) of Chapter 13, the percentage sales revenue changes will be:

For the rush hour segment:

$$\blacktriangle R = -(0.50)(0.20)^2 + (1 - 0.50)(0.20) = 0.080$$

For the off-peak segment:

$$\blacktriangle R = -(0.67)(0.15)^2 + (1 - 0.67)(0.15) = 0.035$$

Conclusion: The new fare structure will generate additional sales revenue of 8.0% and 3.5% for the rush hour and off-peak segments, respectively.

ii) *Implement optimal fare schedule*: The optimal fare, optimal ridership change, and maximum fare revenue change can be computed using Equations (13.3), (13.8), and (13.10) as follows:

For the rush hour segment:

$$[\blacktriangle P] = (1 - 0.50) / (2)(0.50) = 0.50$$

$$[P] = (\$1.25)(1 + 0.50) = \$1.87$$

$$[\blacktriangle Q] = (0.50 - 1) / 2 = (0.25)$$

$$[\blacktriangle R] = (0.50)(0.50)^2 = 0.125$$

For the off-peak segment:

$$[\blacktriangle P] = (1 - 0.67) / (2)(0.67) = 0.25$$

$$[P] = \$1.00 (1 + 0.25) = \$1.25$$

$$[\blacktriangle Q] = (0.67 - 1) / 2 = (0.17)$$

$$[\blacktriangle R] = (0.67)(0.25)^2 = 0.042$$

Conclusion: For the rush hour segment, the optimal price is $1.87 which would reduce ridership by 25% and add 12.5% to fare revenue. For the off-peak segment, the optimal price is $1.25 resulting in a ridership drop of 17% and additional fare revenue of 4.2%.

iii) *Reduce fares*: For this option, the estimated P.E.D.s are:

Ridership Segment	Fare Before	After	Change Fare	Rides	Estim. P.E.D.
Rush hour	$1.50	$1.00	(33.3%)	10.0%	0.30
Off-peak	$1.15	$1.00	(15.0%)	10.0%	0.67

For the rush hour segment:

$$\blacktriangle R = -(0.30)(-0.333)^2 + (1 - 0.30)(-0.333) = (0.266)$$

For the off-peak segment:

$$\blacktriangle R = -(0.67)(-0.150)^2 + (1 - 0.67)(-0.150) = (0.065)$$

Conclusion: A fare reduction to $1.00 for both rush hour and off-peak traffic would reduce fare revenue by 26.6% and 6.5% from present levels, respectively.

Recommendation

Remarkable about this case is the very low price elasticities of demand found for MTA's transportation services but these are likely to be typical of the public transportation sector. The reason is that individuals working in the city's offices and retail establishments have few alternatives other than drive their own vehicles to town. This is not a viable option for most because city parking tends to be restricted and expensive. Economically speaking, public transportation companies, like the MTA, are operating government-sanctioned monopolies. Their demand curves are therefore inelastic and very steep. This, in turn, has significant pricing implications. According to our pricing rule of thumb, (see, for example, Table 8-1 of Chapter 8) whenever demand is inelastic, i.e. the P.E.D. is less than 1.0, a price increase is always called for if the pricing goal is to maximize revenue.

It appears, therefore, that the decision of the MTA board and previous administration to raise fares in January of this year was absolutely correct. The calculations above show that fare revenues for rush hour and off-peak hour traffic will add additional revenues of 8.0% and 3.5%, respectively. Clearly, these fares should be kept in effect. Under no circumstances should the MTA board agree to a fare reduction as proposed by the new MTA management. Such an across-the-board reduction to $1.00 would not add to revenue but cut it substantially—by 27% and 7% for the rush hour and off-peak hour segments, respectively.

If Mr. Belmont experienced an increase in sales revenue when cutting prices in his business career, it was because the commercial real estate market is very competitive and demand curves for properties tend to be more elastic. In such circumstances, i.e., where the P.E.D. is larger than 1.0, a lowering of prices does indeed lead to higher revenues. This is not the case in public transportation. Clearly, Mayor Dooly was unaware of the differences among businesses and may have picked the wrong businessman for the job at least as far as the fare issue is concerned.

The optimum price adjustments necessary for maximum revenue improvements, namely 50% and 25% for the rush hour and of-peak hour segments, respectively, would not have been feasible as they would have caused a mass exodus from the system. As the computations above show, with fares at $1.90 and $1.25 for the two segments, the estimated ridership drops would have been 25% and 17%, respectively. Such a fare schedule would most likely have met with vociferous protests from riders who would have argued that the new fares were excessive and unfair and should be rescinded. These system users would have contended that as tax payers they were entitled to have their fares subsidized from public funds and not be made to carry the entire burden. The MTA board must have wisely decided to raise fares by only a reasonable amount with the prospect of more and smaller increases in the future. That is why the board is not likely to follow the recommendations of the new administration and the editors of the *Herald Tribune* to cut fares. It simply would not make any sense.

Appendix II. Hypothetical Case Studies

B. Profit Maximization: Fritzel's Restaurant

Fritzel's is a West Coast fast foods restaurant that, unlike other establishments of its kind, caters mostly to older adults and seniors. Its varied menu includes such old favorites as hamburger, Italian beef, and Reuben sandwiches, Chicago style hot dogs, homemade potato and lentil soups, and potato pancakes along with an assortment of desserts and gourmet coffees. The restaurant's homey décor with wood-paneled walls and sturdy wood furnishings plus the soft background music of popular hit tunes from the 1950s and 1960s is intended to appeal to an older clientele. Fritzel's is the American Dream come true of Fritz Strudel who was known as Fritzel when he grew up in his native Austria. Before his present venture, Fritz was chef for a restaurant specializing in Austro-Hungarian cuisine including goulash, schnitzel, knödel (large round dumplings), and spätzle.

One of Fritzel's most popular menu items is a gourmet hamburger sandwich Fritz created especially for mature taste buds. Unlike the typical hamburger of the big chains, which Mr. Strudel has described as a "soggy mess," his is a firmer product with a patty made of select, low-fat ground beef, chopped onion and bell peppers, bread crumbs, minced garlic, and paprika. In lieu of the standard hamburger bun the patty is served on a firm, glazed roll, known as a "Kaisersemmel" (kaiser roll) in his native Austria, which Fritz prepares according to the original recipe and steam-bakes on the premises. This hamburger had no special name until a customer once jokingly asked for a Fritzelburger. The name took hold and Fritz's gourmet hamburger is now known by that name.

A couple of days ago Fritz got into a conversation with one of his regulars named Wendy. After complementing him on the meal she had just enjoyed, Wendy casually asked Fritz how business was going. Fritz replied that despite booming sales and the ten to fifteen hours he put in each day, he was having considerable difficulty making a profit. It seems that after paying for supplies, employee wages, rent, utilities, insurance, and repairs and maintenance there was little left at the end of the month. Wendy now identified herself as Wendy Wiener, a partner in the well-known pricing consultancy of Wiener & Wurst, and offered to help him make his business profitable. She suspected that his menu was not priced correctly and offered Fritz to do a sample study for his Fritzelburger at a small introductory fee. Fritz readily agreed and the two began their collaboration.

The first thing Wendy wanted to know was how Fritz came up with the price of $3.60 for his Fritzelburger. Fritz explained that he had checked on the price of a somewhat similar product offered by Roland's, a national hamburger chain one of whose restaurants was located less than three blocks from Fritzel's. Their price was $3.30 and he had added 30 cents for the extra ingredients, he said. "That was not the wisest thing you could have done, Fritz" Wendy told him. Why, she wanted to know, was he charging just a little more than a Roland's hamburger? "You are not competing with them or their hamburgers," she told Fritz, "and it therefore makes little sense to take Roland's menu prices as a guide. The Fritzelburger is a unique product with no real competition while the eating experience Fritzel's provides too is different and unique," Wendy explained. "You are entitled to charge your customers the full value you are offering them and for which most, if not all, will undoubtedly be willing to pay." To Fritz that made sense and he nodded in agreement.

Analysis

Wendy, who had recently acquired an advance copy of *Pricing for Profit* and decided to use the price optimization methods discussed there, needed to know two essential parameters, namely, the average unit contribution margin for the Fritzelburger and its sensitivity to price changes at the present price level. Coming up with a number for the product's unit contribution margin, Wendy knew, would not be easy because that is not commonly used in the restaurant business. There another metric known as the *profit margin* is popular. It is defined as the percentage of gross sales after all operating expenses are deducted including meal ingredients, wages, rent, utilities, and depreciation. In other words, direct, incremental costs are not separated out from indirect fixed costs. In the restaurant business profit margins tend to be very slim—on the order of just 5% on average.

To get an estimate for the CM_0 Wendy needed to determine the product's unit variable cost VC_0, i.e., the incremental cost directly attributable to the Fritzelburger. The most important components of VC_0 were the ingredients that went into the product and the wages of the part-time employees. Since this was to be a preliminary analysis, Wendy accepted the numbers Fritz was able to furnish without further research. Accordingly, the unit variable cost was found to be $2.70 including $1.60 for the burger ingredients and $1.10 for wages and other incremental expenses. The unit contribution margin was therefore:

$$CM_0(\$) = P_0 - VC_0 = \$3.60 - \$2.70 = \$0.90$$

$$CM_0(\%) = CM_0(\$) / P_0 = \$0.90 / \$3.60 = 25.0\%$$

For obtaining a rough estimate of the P.E.D., Wendy proposed that this being August they run an "October Special" for the Fritzelburger in which during that month they reduce the price of this product by 10% from $3.60 to $3.25. The promotion would be advertised by large signs outside and inside Fritzel's and in some print media. Wendy would first make an accurate count of the number of Fritzelburgers sold during next month, September, and compare these to the number sold during the October promotion. Obviously, she would have to drop one day's sales for October to have the same number of days for each month. Dividing the percentage quantity change with the known percentage price change would give her an estimate of the Fritzelburger's P.E.D. at the present price-volume operating point (P_0, Q_0).

This was done and Wendy found that, on average, daily October sales of the Fritzelburger were up from September sales by 18% from 200 to 236. This meant that the product's P.E.D. was 18% / 10% or 1.80. Clearly, while demand was elastic it was not overly so. The elasticity number seemed reasonable since it represented a balance between two opposing factors. The uniqueness of the product would cause demand to be less elastic but seniors on a limited budget would make it higher. The relatively low P.E.D. also told Wendy that the Fritzelburger was under-priced. According to Equation (14.4) of Chapter 14, at a unit contribution margin of 25% the optimal P.E.D. $(\mathcal{C}^*)$ is 4.0 but since here it was only 1.8 $(\mathcal{C}_0)$, by the pricing rule of thumb of Table 8-1 (Chapter 8) a price increase was called for.

Wendy then developed more detailed results. From Table 14-2(b) of Chapter 14, she found that with a CM_0 of 25% and a P.E.D. of 1.8, the optimal percentage contribution change $\blacktriangle K^*$ achievable with an incremental price change was 16.8%. Furthermore, Table 14-1(b) told her that for the given CM_0 and $\mathcal{C}_0$ the optimal price change $\blacktriangle P^*$ was 15.3%. With this information, she was able to develop these numbers:

* Optimal price: $P^* = P_0 (1 + \blacktriangle P^*) = \$3.60 \times 1.153 = \$4.15$

* Optimal sales volume: $Q^* = Q_0 (1 + \blacktriangle Q^*) = Q_0 (1 - \mathcal{C}_0 \blacktriangle P^*)$
$$Q^* = 200 (1 - 1.80 \times 0.153) = 145$$

* Optimal revenue: $R^* = P^* Q^* = \$4.15 \times 145 = \$602$

* Optimal total contribution: $K^* = K_0 (1 + \blacktriangle K^*) = \$180 \times 1.168 = \$210$

* Optimal contrib. margin: $CM^*(\$) = (P^* - VC_0) = \$4.15 - \$2.70 = \$1.45$
$$CM^*(\%) = CM^*(\$) / P^* = \$1.45 / \$4.15 = 35\%$$

* Optimal P.E.D.: $\epsilon^* = 1 / CM^*(\%) = 1 / 0.35 = 2.9$

In summary, Wendy found these daily sales and contribution results for before and after an optimal price change:

	Before	*After*
Price (P)	$3.60	$4.15
Sales Volume (Q)	200 units	145 units
Sales Revenue (R)	$720	$602
Total Contribution (K)	$180	$210
Unit Contribution Margin ($)	$0.90	$1.45
Unit Contribution Margin (%)	25%	35%
Price Elasticity of Demand (ϵ)	1.8	2.9

To graphically show the Fritzelburger's daily sales revenue and total contribution in relation to its price, Wendy plotted the two metrics using an electronic spreadsheet with curve plotting capabilities (Microsoft's Excel). The formula for sales revenue after an incremental price change is from Equation (13.2) of Chapter 13:

$$R_1 = R_0 \{ - \epsilon_0 (\blacktriangle P)^2 + (1 - \epsilon_0) \blacktriangle P + 1 \}$$

Inserting the relevant parameter values for *before* listed above, one obtains:

$$R_1 = 720 \{ - 1.8 (\blacktriangle P)^2 - 0.8 \blacktriangle P + 1 \}$$

The total contribution after an incremental price change is given by Equation (14.2) of Chapter 14:

$$K_1 = R_0 \{ - \epsilon_0 (\blacktriangle P)^2 + (1 - \epsilon_0 CM_0) \blacktriangle P + CM_0 \}$$

which in the present case becomes:

$$K_1 = 720 \{ - 1.8 (\blacktriangle P)^2 + 0.55 \blacktriangle P + 0.25 \}$$

Wendy decided to plot daily sales revenue and total contribution against price P_1 rather than percentage price change $\blacktriangle P$ by selecting values of P_1 and using the ratio $\blacktriangle P = (P_1 - 3.60) / 3.60$ to make the conversion.

Figure B-1
Sales Revenue & Total Contribution for the

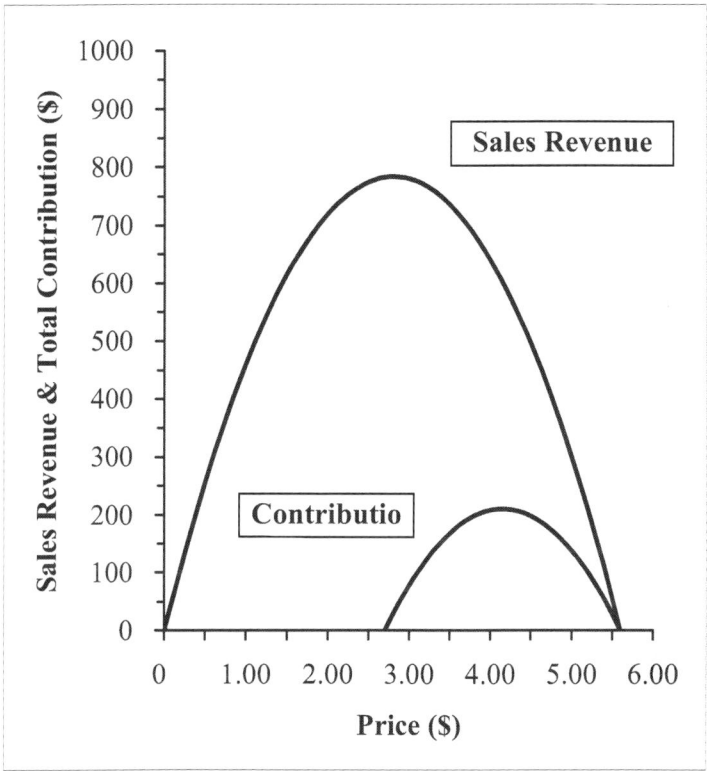

The resulting two curves for the Fritzelburger are shown in Figure B-1. Immediately apparent from this graph is the relatively small amount of daily total contribution dollars earned at all price levels in comparison to the substantial daily sales revenue for this product. The reason is, of course, the very low unit contribution margin. The highest daily total contribution achievable is seen to be about $210 at the optimal price P* of $4.15. Also observable is the fact that contribution does not begin to be generated until the Fritzelburger price is at least $2.70, i.e., the product's estimated unit variable cost (VC_0), while all sales below $2.70 are seen to produce losses. The sales revenue curve is seen to peak at about $800 reached at the optimal price for sales revenue maximization [P] of

$2.80, a reduction of 22.2% from the present price of $3.60. At that price almost no contribution dollars would be generated as the contribution curve indicates.

Recommendations

All indications are, Wendy told Fritz, that he is selling his Fritzelburger significantly below its perceived value and is losing money on the product. She recommended a price increase to $3.99 in two incremental steps rather than one in order to make the increase more palatable for her customers. The first step should be from $3.60 to $3.79 and the second three months or so later to $3.99. People just hate price increases especially in frequently purchased items, she explained, and because the price of $3.60 has been out there for a couple of years, it has become firmly established in the minds of customers. A price beyond it will signal his customers that they are getting less value causing them to reconsider their available options including changing restaurants. She also advised Fritz that along with the increase in total contribution of about 16%, he could expect substantial drops in sales volume and revenue of about 28% and 16%, respectively.

Wendy talked to Fritz about the need to get a better estimate of his direct incremental (variable) cost for all his menu items. For the Fritzelburger his estimates were accepted without further research, she said, but if these were significantly off, it would change the recommended optimum price although she felt fairly confident that he was selling an underpriced product. If, after a more detailed cost analysis of his menu items, direct variable costs are found to be high in comparison to industry standards, Fritz must try to reduce them through more cost-effective purchase practices and other means since cost seemed to be his major problem, according to Wendy. He needed to bring these incremental costs down to improve his unit contribution margins.

Wendy suggested to Fritz that he begin implementing the recommended price change and, if he found the results to be positive, consider repricing his other popular menu items such as the Reuben sandwich and the sausage and potato pancake plate. She also let Fritz know that she would be happy to sign a retainer agreement with him on behalf of Wiener & Wurst that would offer continuing assistance for profit improvements to cover cost analyses and repricing of all or part of his menu items as well as recommendations on menu changes and additions and other improvements.

Subject Index